THE
EVERYTHING®
GUIDE TO THE
INTROVERT EDGE

Dear Reader,

I am an introvert. Yet, even though I am not shy and I don't have social anxiety, I often feel like a misanthrope, like I somehow don't belong. It's a very old feeling that I wasn't able to name until I started researching introversion.

I am more content to observe than participate. After all, I'm a psychologist and people and their behavior fascinates me. There is no doubt that I fit into the core definition of an introvert, but in some ways, I am also different. I enjoy snowboarding. In fact, I love it, the thrill of flying down the mountain—*in control*. I'm not so crazy about taking air—launching off a cliff and experiencing the weightless feeling of free fall. In other words, being out of control.

What I've realized is control makes the difference. I love to ride motorcycles and don't mind going fast—very fast—as long as I maintain a sense of control. I love loud music. In fact, I am listening to loud music as I write. I can control these things. Embracing my introversion has changed my life for the better! I hope you can find useful information, inspiration, and courage in the following pages.

Arnie Kozak

Welcome to the EVERYTHING® Series!

These handy, accessible books give you all you need to tackle a difficult project, gain a new hobby, comprehend a fascinating topic, prepare for an exam, or even brush up on something you learned back in school but have since forgotten.

You can choose to read an Everything® book from cover to cover or just pick out the information you want from our four useful boxes: e-questions, e-facts, e-quotes, and e-ssentials.

We give you everything you need to know on the subject, but throw in a lot of fun stuff along the way, too.

We now have more than 400 Everything® books in print, spanning such wide-ranging categories as weddings, pregnancy, cooking, music instruction, foreign language, crafts, pets, New Age, and so much more. When you're done reading them all, you can finally say you know Everything®!

QUESTION

Answers to
common questions

FACT

Important snippets
of information

QUOTE

Words of wisdom from
experts in the field

ESSENTIAL

Quick
handy tips

PUBLISHER Karen Cooper

MANAGING EDITOR, EVERYTHING® SERIES Lisa Laing

COPY CHIEF Casey Ebert

ASSISTANT PRODUCTION EDITOR Alex Guarco

ACQUISITIONS EDITOR Pamela Wissman

DEVELOPMENT EDITOR Eileen Mullan

EVERYTHING® SERIES COVER DESIGNER Erin Alexander

THE
EVERYTHING®
GUIDE TO THE
INTROVERT EDGE

Maximize the advantages of being an introvert—
at home and at work

Arnie Kozak, PhD

Avon, Massachusetts

For the new crew: Mu, Harley, and Sumi

An Everything® Series Book.
Everything® and everything.com® are registered trademarks of F+W Media, Inc.

Published by Adams Media, a division of F+W Media, Inc.
57 Littlefield Street, Avon, MA 02322. U.S.A.
www.adamsmedia.com

ISBN 10: 1-4405-6816-2
ISBN 13: 978-1-4405-6816-9
eISBN 10: 1-4405-6817-0
eISBN 13: 978-1-4405-6817-6

Printed in the United States of America.

10 9 8 7 6 5 4 3 2 1

Library of Congress Cataloging-in-Publication Data

Kozak, Arnie.
  The everything guide to introvert edge : maximize the advantages of being an introvert at home and
at work / Arnie Kozak, PhD.
      pages cm. -- (Everything series)
  Includes bibliographical references and index.
  ISBN-13: 978-1-4405-6816-9 (pbk. : alk. paper)
  ISBN-10: 1-4405-6816-2 (pbk. : alk. paper)
  ISBN-13: 978-1-4405-6817-6 (ebook)
  ISBN-10: 1-4405-6817-0 (ebook)
1. Introverts. 2. Introversion. 3. Extraversion. 4. Interpersonal relations. I. Title.
  BF698.35.I59K69 2013
  155.2'32--dc23
                                        2013031046

Cover images © 123RF/Kheng Ho Toh

Interior illustrations by Michaela Chung (*www.introvertspring.com*); and The Contemplative Mind
in Society.

David Whyte poems, "The Sweet Darkness," and "The Opening of Eyes," reprinted with permission of
Many Rivers Press.

This book is available at quantity discounts for bulk purchases.
For information, please call 1-800-289-0963.

Contents

Acknowledgments

This book would not have happened without the efforts of my agent, Grace Freedson. Special thanks go to Erik Odin Cathcart—my friend, fellow writer, and source of encouragement.

Top Ten Things Introverts Need to Know to Thrive in an Extrovert World

1. There is nothing wrong with you! Introversion is normal and valuable—it is a connection to your interior that gives you an edge!

2. Introverts revolt! There is an Introvert Revolution underway and introverts are reclaiming their rightful place in society.

3. Don't believe the messages extroverted society has told you. You don't need to apologize for who you are and how you want to be.

4. Living in the extrovert culture, you will have to take care of yourself in special ways.

5. There are more introverts in the world than you realize. Half the population may be introverts.

6. Many famous, influential, and creative people throughout history have been introverts.

7. Being an extrovert is not ideal; it ignores the power of solitude, quiet, and contemplation.

8. Contemplative practices are the key to nurturing your introvert.

9. Introverts are subject to bias, discrimination, prejudice, and stigma especially in school and the workplace.

10. The Introvert Edge is available to extroverts, too, when they are able to tap into their interior depths.

Introduction

IMAGINE YOU ARE AT a big party. You came with a friend and she is having the time of her life. You are standing with a glass of wine in your hands wondering how much longer you will have to be there. Your energy is draining each time you have to exchange small talk with another partygoer, like air being let out of a balloon with a steady deflating hiss. You've already hid out in the bathroom twice and taken a walk outside. Your friend disappears from your side for long periods of time, flitting like a firefly and making excited chitchat with everyone she sees. You wonder, "What the hell are they talking about?" You don't feel like you have much to say other than, "Good night." When she returns, your friend says, "Isn't this the best party ever?" You suppress rolling your eyes and just nod noncommittally. "How much longer?" you sigh to yourself. Time seems to drag; you want to crawl into a corner and take a nap. You check your phone again. "Maybe I can have someone call me and fake an emergency so I can get out of this." You don't want to abandon your friend and insult the host who has gone to so much trouble to create this "terrific" party. You feel stuck, cranky, and hopeless. You silently vow to yourself that you will *never* accept another party invitation. Finally, you spot someone out of the corner of your eye who seems to be having as miserable a time as you are. You approach him and start a conversation. You agree to withdraw outside, where the stars are shining and it is quieter, to continue the conversation. Finally, you feel connected.

Perhaps you don't have to imagine this scenario. Perhaps this, or something like it, has happened to you. If so, you are likely an introvert. As an introvert, you would probably find the loud party draining. Gatherings like these are overstimulating. You don't like to spread your attention so thin; you'd prefer to sink into one substantial conversation and really get to know someone and have her know you. You are bored to tears with the "How was your summer vacation?" kind of talk. You feel uncomfortable answering the question, "How are you?" by excited acquaintances you haven't seen for a long time when you know they don't really want to know how you are; they want you to affirm that life is *great!* This is not your idea of fun.

When taken to an extreme, a dedication to positive energy, thinking, and behavior can become tyrannical. The significance placed on positive thinking in this culture can be relentless, pervasive, and oppressive. Many things are missing from the extrovert's idea of society, such as room for the interior, the value of a subjective experience, and respect for quiet, solitude, and reflection. From the standpoint of the extroverted culture, introversion is a deficit—something to overcome rather than to be esteemed, celebrated, and embraced. That is, until now.

An Introvert Revolution is underway. It is a quiet one, to be sure. There are many books, blogs, and articles that are applauding the long-neglected virtues of introversion. These authors give introverts a lexicon for understanding the mismatch between themselves and the broader culture. The Introvert Revolution wants you to embrace who and how you are and not apologize for it.

This book will explore every aspect of introverts and introversion. You can think of what's in these pages as a field guide for living a happy, productive, and creative life as an introvert, despite the loud majority of extroverts.

This book will empower you with the Introvert Edge. It will help you to claim your power as an introvert—the power that already resides within. The Introvert Edge will give this force a voice, even when that voice is soft or silent. *Sotto voce* is the authority of quiet, solitude, and stillness. It is the clout of "me" versus "we." These pages will empower you to live in an extroverted world without apology.

To be an introvert in today's world requires freedom from the noisy cult of extroversion. With this book, you'll learn practical wisdom to reclaim, redirect, and reappropriate your strength as an introvert—a composed, calm, and confident voice rising above the din of chaos, clamor, and confusion.

CHAPTER 1

Introversion Is Not Contagious

Introversion is not a disease, condition, or deficiency. It is a basic dimension of personality. There is nothing wrong with you if you are an introvert, but like a "stranger in a strange land," you may feel out of place in a culture that is dedicated to extroversion. Understanding what introversion is and what it is not is the first step in embracing the Introvert Edge.

Introversion Is a Basic Way of Being

Introversion is one of the basic dimensions of personality. In fact, it may be the most basic dimension. Introversion exists on a scale with extroversion and you are mix of both. No one is a pure introvert or a total extrovert. If you are an introvert, your center of gravity will be with introvert traits. If you are an extrovert, your center of gravity will be with extrovert traits. Not all introverts fit the stereotype and neither do extroverts. You can also be in the middle. Just as there are people who are ambidextrous, there are people who are ambiverts—having a balance of introversion and extroversion.

QUOTE

"We are a vastly diverse group of people who prefer to look at life from the inside out. We gain energy and power through inner reflection and get more excited by ideas than by external activities. When we converse, we listen well and expect others to do the same. We think first and talk later."—Laurie Helgoe, *Introvert Power*

Common Understanding of Introversion

Personality science doesn't have an ironclad definition of introversion-extroversion. The particular traits that are included or excluded vary by the theory, and research has not been able to provide a definitive resolution of these differences. The definition of introversion provided here should be viewed as a fluid, evolving concept. Here are the things that can be agreed upon:

- Introverts favor the interior to the exterior.
- Introverts lose energy in social exchanges. Introverts conserve energy because social interactions are taxing; extroverts spend energy because the same social interactions are energizing.
- Introverts need solitude to recharge energy.
- Introverts can be skilled at social interaction and often are.
- Introverts experience social interactions differently from their extroverted companions. Extroverts are assertive, dominant, gregarious,

social, and talkers versus introverts who are listeners, thoughtful, prefer small groups to large, prefer writing, and value deep discussion.

- Introverts will be more drawn to the interior, imagination, and solitude.
- Introverts and extroverts differ in how they handle stimulation. Introverts have a lower threshold for overstimulation than extroverts. They have a lot of internal stimulation; extroverts seek and need more external stimulation.
- Introverts process information differently. Introverts like depth—going deep in uninterrupted chunks of time; extroverts enjoy breadth and are more amenable to interruptions.
- Introverts approach tasks differently. Extroverts dig right in and multitask; introverts tend to be more focused and deliberate.

You may find that your way of being an introvert does not neatly fit this definition. Some introverts enjoy thrill seeking on occasion, like snowboarding or skiing. The idea that all introverts are retiring bookworms is false.

Clarifying Misconceptions

Introverts are not antisocial. Introverts can be highly sensitive to the needs of others. Introverts are not asocial either. They prefer certain kinds of social environments—more intimate, less stimulating ones than extroverts. There can be no or little difference between introverts and extroverts in sociability. They both like people, love them, and want to be with them—just in different ways.

In her book *Introvert Power*, Laurie Helgoe makes a useful observation on the *location* of social interactions. Making this distinction puts introverts "back on the map." She says, "Extroverts understandably need more face-to-face time because that's where the interaction is located. Introverts need more *between* time—between words in a conversation and between conversations—because the interaction is located within."

A lot of misconceptions surround introversion. Some of these include:

- Being quiet equals suffering; introversion is a burden.
- Use of mental health services equals problems rather than curiosity about the mind's interior.

- Happiness only comes from active positive emotions like enthusiasm, ebullience, and boisterousness, instead of quiet positive emotions like peace, calm, serenity, ease, and mindfulness.

Psychologist Marti Olsen Laney provides a good metaphor to characterize the differences between extroverts and introverts. Introverts are like a rechargeable battery. When you use the battery (that is, socializing), the power is drained and needs to be removed and recharged. Extroverts are like solar panels that need the sun (that is, socializing) to charge. More sun equals more energy. This captures a key difference between what she calls innies (introverts) and outies (extroverts). You cannot charge a rechargeable battery by placing it in the sun. It needs to be taken out of service for a period of time to restore.

A First Look at Defining Introversion

According to the American Heritage Dictionary, an introvert is "a person characterized by concern primarily with his own thoughts and feelings." The second definition is "a shy person." The dictionary's definition does not accord with the definitions provided by psychological research.

Introversion Gets a Bad Name

Some of the psychological definitions give introverts a bad reputation and are inaccurate. For example, Henry Gleitman's textbook *Psychology* states, "To be sure, both introverts and many neurotics have something in common; they are both unsociable and withdrawn. But, in psychologist Hans Eysenck's view, their lack of sociability has different roots. The healthy introverts are not afraid of social activities; they simply do not like them. In contrast, neurotically shy persons keep to themselves because of fear, they want to be with others, but are afraid of joining them." Another basic dimension of an introvert's personality is neuroticism or emotional stability. People low in emotional stability (or high in neuroticism) worry, are nervous, insecure, and can be hypochondriacs. People high in emotional stability (or low in neuroticism) are calm, relaxed, hardy, and secure. As suggested in the textbook definition, introversion and emotional stability overlap.

Eysenck's theory divides a circle with two intersecting lines creating four sections. Each of these quadrants corresponds to one of the ancient humors. If you are stable and extroverted, you will be: sociable, outgoing, talkative, responsive, easygoing, lively, and carefree. This corresponds to the sanguine (or blood) humor. If you are introverted and stable, you will be: calm, even-tempered, reliable, controlled, peaceful, thoughtful, careful, and passive. This corresponds to the phlegmatic humor. If you are extroverted and unstable, you will be: touchy, restless, aggressive, excitable, changeable, impulsive, optimistic, and active. This corresponds to the choleric humor. If you are introverted and unstable, you will be moody, anxious, rigid, sober, pessimistic, reserved, unsociable, and quiet. This corresponds to the melancholic humor. The original definition in the text seems to refer only to emotionally unstable introverts. It is not true that introverts do not like social activities; they just experience them differently.

QUOTE

"One of the things that probably made it more difficult for me growing up is that I didn't understand who I was and felt the need to strive to be an extrovert in order to be accepted. I thought there was something wrong with me and that I wasn't being what I was supposed to be: talkative and exciting."—Babette K.

Myths about Introverts

Misconceptions and mischaracterizations about introverts abound. Here is a list of common myths about introverts.

1. Introverts don't like to talk.
2. Introverts are shy.
3. Introverts are rude.
4. Introverts don't like people.
5. Introverts don't like to go out in public.
6. Introverts always want to be alone.
7. Introverts are weird.
8. Introverts are aloof nerds.

9. Introverts don't know how to relax and have fun.
10. Introverts can fix themselves and become extroverts.

Source: Carl Kingdom (*www.carlkingdom.com/10-myths-about-introverts*)

Part of the muddle surrounding introverts is confusing the melancholic and phlegmatic types, that is, happy and unhappy introverts. The melancholic introvert is shy and fearful. The phlegmatic introvert is calm and thoughtful. Extroverts can be mischaracterized, too. The happy extrovert is carefree and ebullient while the unhappy extrovert is restless and impulsive. Most descriptions of introversion and extroversion do not make these distinctions. This gives a bad rap to introverts and extroverts by lumping them all together. Each individual will be different. Any general description will not capture this individuality and is therefore limited.

The Difficulties of Being an Introvert in an Extrovert Culture

Somehow, a third to a half of the population got excluded. Introverts, unlike other marginalized groups, do not have a clearly demarcating difference. There is no one thing like gender, religious affiliation, or sexual orientation that is the basis of the stigma. As an introvert, you may not even know you are an introvert, or you know something is amiss but you may not be able to identify it. Being an introvert in a culture of extroverts is hard. You may feel that you are somehow missing out. It is easy to sense that you are somehow lacking something that everyone else seems to have.

QUOTE

"The introvert is pressured daily, almost from the moment of awakening, to respond and conform to the outer world."—Marti Olsen Laney

Disempowered, Disenfranchised, and Demoralized

Hidden discrimination against introverts is the most difficult to deal with. It is invisible and hard to identify. It may nag at you in the background of your conscious awareness, but this may be the first time you are acknowledging it. All the images that you see on television, in movies, and in advertising glorify the extrovert while ignoring the introvert. Introverts may be portrayed as shy, anxious misanthropes instead of competent, thoughtful individuals. Introversion does not fit in with the prevailing American ideal of go-getters, glad-handers, and back-slappers.

Introverts have been disempowered by a competitive, extroverted culture. They have succumbed to the lie that they are boring, antisocial, asocial misanthropes, inferior, and in the minority. Signs of a disempowered introvert:

- You think you're antisocial, because you often prefer to be alone.
- You see yourself as boring, because you don't talk as much as everyone else.
- You worry that something may be wrong with you.
- You fear missing out on what everyone else is enjoying.
- You berate yourself when you don't feel like joining in.
- You criticize yourself for not accepting every social invitation.

In the dating context, studies show that women want to be entertained, and find men who are humorous to be most attractive. This fondness for being entertained reflects a larger pressure on introverts. You may be funny, but not in the boisterous way that fits the extrovert-dominated culture. Your humor may be more subtle, witty, or dry. Your humor may come from the periphery rather than being center stage. You are likely not going to be the one dancing around the party with a lampshade on your head!

Disempowered No Longer

Like any stigmatized group, introverts have been at a disadvantage. They may be overlooked for promotions and ridiculed, or they might just feel disenfranchised, like they don't belong. You will have to learn to navigate the pitfalls of the extroverted culture to find a place that suits your particular style of being in the world. By embracing your gifts as an introvert, you can get the Introvert Edge and re-empower yourself. You don't have to make apologies, excuses, or explanations for who you are. The Introvert Edge gives you a powerful advantage to reclaim key values of quiet, solitude, and contemplation.

Just think about life today. Where are there places for silence, stillness, and contemplation? Certainly, there are no reality television shows with such themes. No introverts can survive *Survivor*. Life is fast paced and frenetic. There is no time for quiet, stillness, or contemplation. You are expected to work fast, eat fast, and sleep less. In the modern workplace, you may be required to work in teams whether you like it or not. Your children may be forced to work in groups, whether they like it or not.

Where can you find some peace, tranquility, and respite from the daily onslaught of information, people, and to-do lists? It may be a challenge to find a physical place amid the chaos of raising a family, maintaining a household, and a career. That place of quiet may have to be within your own mind.

Introverts Revolt

The Introvert Revolution is a permission slip to embrace your quiet side, to empower your interior, and to become as the great poet Rilke said, the "guardian of your solitude." Bestselling authors like Laurie Helgoe, Marti Olsen Laney, and Susan Cain have paved the way for this new conscious-ness about introversion. You no longer have to apologize for wanting to say no to most (or every) social invitation that comes your way. You no longer have to feel guilty when you'd just rather be alone. You don't have to say you are sorry for being thoughtful, pensive, or intellectual. You no longer have to feel like a misanthrope. You are an introvert and proud of it!

QUOTE

"In an extroverted society, the difference between an introvert and an extrovert is that an introvert is often unconsciously deemed guilty until proven innocent."—Criss Jami, author

For the extrovert reader, you would benefit from tapping into your introvert side. There is much strength and value there. Gregariousness can be balanced by contemplation; energy can be harmonized with silence.

Social Skills Versus Social Preferences

Introverts do not lack social skills; they just like to use them differently than extroverts. Being "on" is currency for introverts. Extroverts are rich, they can spend all the money they want and don't deplete their reserves. Extroverts are like people who can eat whatever they want and not gain weight. How annoying. Introverts spend their currency in social situations, especially ones that are hectic, chaotic, or very public. Private, quiet, one-to-one, or small group interactions are less expensive. There are plenty of extroverts who may be quite active socially, but are not very skilled at it. They can be buffoonish, insensitive, bellicose, garrulous, and even jerks (not that introverts are incapable of being jerks, they are just less public about it). Extroverts are seen as more social because the culture has set a particular kind of gregarious style as the benchmark for sociability. Extroverts like to hear themselves talk; they like to be in the thick of things. Introverts prefer to listen and observe from the periphery (again, these are generalizations).

Conservation of Resources

If social energy is currency, then extroverts are in an enviable position. Life is less expensive for them. It is as if they are subsidized by the culture. Whereas introverts must be very conscious of how they spend their energy. They must scrimp and save. Each time they spend, they must restore their bank account by retreating into solitude. Introverts, therefore, have fewer degrees of freedom in the extrovert culture. They will feel pressure to be "on," participate, and may be conspicuous when they withdraw to recharge their batteries. When they work in an open floor plan office, this private respite may be impossible to find. They may go into the bathroom just to have a little quiet.

As an introvert, you must be more frugal and forward planning with your social energy. It's like being in survival mode, needing to pay careful attention to your rations of water and food. While you lack this external freedom, you have other internal freedoms that compensate. But in the "real" world you must be careful to budget and save. The fiscal differences between introverts and extroverts, to continue the metaphor, make introverts vulnerable to negative social judgments. A lack of understanding regarding what introverts require can lead the extroverted public to see introverts as misanthropes, wallflowers, and shrinking violets.

QUOTE

"Therapy provides a forum for a curious introvert to transform internalized problems into insight and liberating change."—Laurie Helgoe

As an introvert, you will need to practice fiscal conservatism with your energy. You will have to practice replenishment after each excursion into the taxing world of social interaction. This is the bane and the benefit of being an introvert. It requires more self-care to nurture the interior. It is true that you may be less wash-and-wear than your extrovert contemporaries, but there are many benefits to being an introvert that make the challenges worthwhile.

The Introvert from the Extrovert's Perspective

Extroverts may be suspicious of introverts. "Why are they so quiet? What are they withholding?" There is a tendency for human beings to commit what is known as the "psychologist's fallacy." The fallacy happens when you project your own values, perceptions, and sensibilities onto other people. The assumption is that they experience the world in the same way you do. This mistake has led to problems in cross-cultural research, and when it comes to introverts and extroverts there is a cross-cultural divide.

What's Going On in There?

When extroverts see introverts not speaking and not showing much facial expression, they assume that the introverts are feeling what they would be feeling in that situation. Maybe it's angry, sad, or confused. For introverts, however, they may be taking time to formulate thoughts, to make the connections in their memory that will give them something to say. They are not angry, sad, nor confused. It is hard for introverts to think on their feet. They have a lot of elevator moments—where they think of the right come-back a few minutes after an encounter. Introverts need time to let informa-tion percolate. Extroverts don't get this. This time lag can also come across as passivity or cautiousness. Shy people may withhold saying something because they are afraid of being judged for saying it. Introverts will pause before talking not because of fear, but because they are processing informa-tion in a different, deeper way. It may look the same from the outside, but inside there is a world of difference.

You may have been made to feel out of place, inferior, or weird for being the way you are. You may have subjected yourself to this bias. The extrovert culture is so dominant that even introverts want to be more like extroverts. Now, there is a growing consciousness that introversion is not something to apologize for. There is no reason to be ashamed. Remember, there is noth-ing wrong with you. Even so, you may also struggle with guilt for not meeting the social expectations for others and yourself. Self-acceptance is the key to overcoming guilt, and understanding your unique introvert gifts is the key to vanquishing shame.

Benefits of Introversion

You may be wondering, "What are these introvert benefits?" Being comfort-able with solitude, your interior life, and sensitivity to the world opens you up to creativity, innovation, and inspiration. Introverts have a tendency to exam-ine each part of their lives, whether it is a project, problem, or relationship. Introverts are keen observers who look before they leap, think before they speak, and are comfortable with the silence, uncertainty, and ambiguity of the subjective experience. Many great thinkers have been introverts—think Einstein, Newton, and Darwin. Many great artists have been introverts—think T. S. Eliot, W. B. Yeats, and Marcel Proust. Many great leaders have been introverts—think Abraham Lincoln, Mahatma Gandhi, and Al Gore.

Your introversion is your strength, but also a liability if your inward focus goes unchecked. The riches of the interior are separated by a razor's edge from obsession and self-pity. The information in this book will help you to maximize your introvert benefits and to minimize your introvert disadvantages. Your introversion can be a competitive edge—your capacity to listen, absorb, and to ponder.

"There is no such thing as a pure extrovert or a pure introvert. Such a man would be in a lunatic asylum."—Carl Jung

The Introvert Revolution

Why aren't introverts more visible? Many introverts hide their introversion in an effort to fit in. They may be skilled at being pseudo-extroverts or they may not realize they are introverts. You can find out by asking your family members, friends, and coworkers about introversion. You may be surprised how many of them acknowledge introvert tendencies. You may be realizing it applies to yourself more than you thought.

Defy the Majority

Remember, you can be social and be an introvert. You can be a public figure and be an introvert. You can be affable, charming, and talkative and still be an introvert. The question is not only about skills and behaviors, but also about how that public sociability affects you. If you feel like you need to recharge your batteries after being with people, working in groups, and making small talk—this defines you as an introvert. If you prefer solitude and peace to chaotic, noisy, and free-form social gatherings, you are an introvert. Susan Cain defines the Extrovert Ideal as a preference for "action to contemplation, risk-taking to heed-taking, certainty to doubt." It could also be called the Extrovert Hegemony, the Extrovert Expectation, the Extrovert Tyranny, and the Extrovert Compulsion.

"We're told to be great is to be bold, to be happy is to be sociable. We see ourselves as a nation of extroverts—which means that we've lost sight of who we really are."—Susan Cain, author

Society lacks an emphasis on the contemplative and runs the risk of being too much on the surface. Risk taking is prized over mindful caution. This also creates global financial catastrophes. Organizations that prefer well-spoken certainty to doubt in uncertain circumstances invite disaster.

The Value of Contemplation

The Introvert Revolution brings the value of contemplation, mindfulness, and doubt to the forefront and backs away from the bravado that is so characteristic of the American way. The Introvert Revolution is a response to the extrovert society. It privileges quiet, contemplation, subjectivity, calmness, and solitude. It recognizes patience and the power of the individual mind. It eschews constant groupthink. It's hard to be a calm, circumspect, and quiet person in this impulsive world. The Introvert Edge gives you the knowledge and skills to navigate this territory.

Introverts are no longer in the shadows. They have something to offer in business, education, and society. The notion that introversion is just a lack of extroversion is changing, and an introversion that stands on its own is emerging. The quality of life is not defined by how excited, enthusiastic, and ebullient you are. Society is ready to go deeper, to the depths of the interior, to find new riches. These treasures are not as shiny as the stuff found on the surface—the magnetic, energetic, collaborative dance that extroverts have created. The way has opened for a new approach to personality—a new way to be in the world. This is an exciting time to be alive, to be fully yourself without apology. This is the time to embrace your Introvert Edge.

CHAPTER 2

Confirming Your Introversion

You may not know that you are an introvert. When you look around, all you see is a lot of extroverts, and you may be pushing yourself to be a pseudo-extrovert without realizing it. Everyone has a mix of both introvert and extrovert traits, and you may need help to find your center of gravity. This chapter will examine theories of introversion, the ways introversion is measured, and the limits of these assessments.

There Are More of You Than You Think

Look at the person on your right; look at the person on your left. At least one of you is an introvert. Introversion is much more common than you may think. It is estimated that from one-third to a half of the population is introverted. The lower estimates may be based on skewed samples. The best estimate places the number around 50 percent.

Keep in mind that not everyone will be an obvious introvert. Many have learned to be pseudo-extroverts and therefore don't stand out. Introverts may have been acting like extroverts for so long that they have forgotten they are introverts at all!

FACT

The Myers-Briggs Type Indicator (MBTI) and the NEO Personality Inventory are the most widely researched instruments to measure introversion, as well as other personality traits.

Author Laurie Helgoe laments, "Lies about introversion are so imbedded in the fabric of our culture that even the literature geared toward correcting misconceptions inadvertently promotes them." The biggest lie is that extroverts are in the majority. Myers-Briggs Type Indicator research from 1998 puts introverts at about half the population. A 2001 study puts that number at 57 percent.

Jung's Theory of Personality Types

The renowned Swiss psychiatrist and psychoanalyst, Carl Jung, was the first to use the terms introversion and extroversion. Jung was a student of Sigmund Freud, and was Freud's anointed successor, until they had a falling out over what motivated human beings. Freud wanted to limit these motives to two things: sex and aggression. Jung felt this was too narrow, and wanted to include other things, like creative and spiritual impulses.

Jung was the first to describe introverts and extroverts as enduring psychological types based on temperament. Children are born into the world with their type already decided, and it is not the result of how they are nurtured. Jung based his theory on years of clinical observation, which is the basis for the Myers-Briggs Type Indicator (MBTI), one of the most popular assessment instruments in the world, used widely in education, business, counseling, and coaching.

Basic Differences

On first reading, Jung seems to favor the extroverted attitude when he says, "Everyone knows those reserved, inscrutable, rather shy people who form the strongest possible contrast to the open, sociable, jovial, or at least friendly and approachable characters." This description seems to give introversion a bad rap. The introvert is guarded and shy, protecting the self from the outside world. Jung cites the great artist, William Blake, who referred to extroversion and introversion as "prolific" and "devouring," respectively. Which would you rather be? "Devouring" sounds selfish and negative.

Digging deeper into the types, this initial bias falls away as Jung discusses the strengths and weakness of each type. The extrovert is a multiplicity—connecting to myriad people and projects. The introvert is a monopoly preferring a smaller circle of intimate relationships and focusing on one project at a time. The extrovert is at home with consumerism and materialistic culture. Introverts are neither anticonsumerist nor antimaterialist, they just don't base their identity upon it as much as the extrovert.

Outer Versus Inner

Jung notes that extroverts have an "inexhaustible fascination" with the world and are "so outer directed that even the most obvious of all subjective facts, the condition of his own body, receives scant attention." Introverts are interested and acquainted with the interior, including the condition of their bodies. The interior of the body is a rich source of information for intuition, empathy, and emotional regulation. Mindfulness meditators, who are more inclined to be introverts, have a greater sense of their bodies. Mindfulness meditation involves focusing on something happening in the present moment such as the sensations of breathing and the body, and returning attention to these sensations each time attention wanders. In fact, studies such as one by Sarah Lazar at Harvard have found that mindfulness meditators have an increased brain structure called the insula. The insula is responsible for paying attention to the state of the body or what is known in psychology as "interoception," or what neuroscientist Dan Siegel calls the "sixth sense."

QUESTION

What is an extrovert?
"His interest and attention are directed to objective happenings, particularly those in his immediate environment. Not only people but things seize and rivet his attention."—Carl Jung

Extroverts are dedicated to a "harmonious social life" and are committed to this outer-directedness, so much so that they can neglect what is going on in their own bodies (until something goes wrong and demands their attention). In the extreme, the extrovert is an outer-directed surface, while the introvert is an inner-directed depth.

The introvert is connected to subjective reality, whereas the extrovert may be disconnected from it or may simply devalue it. The perceptual world of the extreme extrovert would be two-dimensional, whereas the introvert's world would be three-dimensional—the third dimension is depth. The introvert remembers that all perceptions are subjective, even the "objective" ones, because they are relative to the person perceiving them. The extrovert may forget this and lapse into a form of what philosophers call "objectivism." The objectivist viewpoint squeezes out the subjective and insists on only what can be measured or observed. The inner life is ignored.

▼ INTROVERT—EXTROVERT COMPARISON

Introvert Qualities	Extrovert Qualities
Subjective	Objective
Inner	Outer
Depth	Surface
Draining	Energizing*
Interior	Exterior
Solitude	Social
Reflection	Action
Individualistic	Conformist

Introvert Qualities	Extrovert Qualities
Iconoclastic	Suggestible
Shy	Bold
Slow	Fast
Thoughtful	Impulsive
Quiet	Noisy
Doubt	Certainty
Heed-taking	Risk Taking

*The two types experience social situations differently. Extroverts feed off the energy of large groups, whereas introverts are drained by such activity. Both are social, but the movement of energy is different and consistent with the outer-versus-inner distinction. You happen to live in a society that is outer oriented, so the extrovert is at home and the more valued type.

Jung observed a paradox with introverts that made them precarious. Introverts were "educators and promoters of culture," who showed the value of "the interior life, which is so painfully wanting in our civilization." However, he acknowledged that their "reserve and apparently groundless embarrassment naturally arouse all the current prejudices against this type." It seems that Jung did not differentiate between shy and non-shy introverts. When he referred to "reserve" and "embarrassment," he lumped together emotionally stable and unstable introverts (high and low in neuroticism). This is a mistake that has been perpetuated since Jung's initial writings in the 1920s.

Defining Introversion from Personality Theory

Many personality theorists have studied introversion and extroversion. Susan Cain in *Quiet* says about her seven years of research into this field, "There are almost as many definitions of *introvert* and *extrovert* as there are personality psychologists." The Big Five Theory of Personality is the most well known. It sees introversion and extroversion occurring along a continuum of "extroversion." You either have more or less of the extroverted traits. The Myers-Briggs Type Indicator has had a large influence in business, coaching, and counseling. Introversion is not a mold; it is a basic tendency. Introverts will have different personalities based on their biology, learning, and experiences.

The Myers-Briggs Type Indicator (MBTI)

The Myers-Briggs Type Indicator is a tremendously popular way to assess introversion as well as other personality predispositions. According to the Myers & Briggs Foundation website:

"The purpose of the Myers-Briggs Type Indicator® (MBTI®) personality inventory is to make the theory of psychological types described by C. G. Jung understandable and useful in people's lives. The essence of the theory is that much seemingly random variation in the behavior is actually quite orderly and consistent, being due to basic differences in the ways individuals prefer to use their perception and judgment."

QUOTE

"There are in nature two fundamentally different modes of adaptation which ensure the continued existence of the living organism."—Carl Jung

Four Dimensions: Sixteen Possibilities

The MBTI is divided into four dimensions with two possible types for each dimension. This yields sixteen different MBTI types depending on the various combinations. The first dimension is the Favorite World and asks whether you prefer the inside or the outside. Your answer will help differentiate you as an "I" (Introvert) or an "E" (Extrovert). The next dimension focuses on information processing. There are two possibilities—"S" (Sensing) and "N" (Intuitive). Sensing types prefer to focus on basic information while intuitive types like to interpret and seek deeper meanings in things.

The next dimension involves decision making. Here you can be a "T" (Thinking type) or an "F" (Feeling type). Thinking types focus on logic and consistency, while Feeling types focus on people and circumstances. The final dimension relates to structure. Here you are a "J" (Judgment type) if you like to have things decided and you are a "P" (Perceiving type) if you remain open to new information.

▼ **MYERS-BRIGGS TYPE INDICATOR MATRIX**

MBTI Personality Four Letter Types			
ISTJ	ISFJ	INFJ	INTJ
ISTP	ISFP	INFP	INTP
ESTP	ESFP	ENFP	ENTP
ESTJ	ESFJ	ENFJ	ENTJ

I=Introversion, E=Extraversion, S=Sensing, N=Intuition, T=Thinking, F=Feeling, J=Judging, P=Perceiving

All sixteen types are seen as equal. The MBTI measures preferences and not ability, character, or traits. Presumably, the MBTI is tapping into underlying traits but it focuses on the expression of personality. The instrument was first published in 1962 and has been taken by millions of people.

QUESTION

What is an INTP (Introversion-Intuition-Thinking-Perception) MBTI type?
INTP: Seek to develop logical explanations for everything that interests them. Theoretical and abstract, interested more in ideas than in social interaction. Quiet, contained, flexible, and adaptable. Have unusual ability to focus in depth to solve problems in their area of interest. Skeptical, sometimes critical, always analytical. Source: (*www.myersbriggs.org*)

The MBTI defines introversion as "interest in the clarity of concepts, ideas, and recollected experience; reliance on enduring concepts and experiences more than on transitory external events or fleeting ideas; a thoughtful, contemplative detachment; an enjoyment of solitude and privacy; and a desire to 'think things out' before talking about them." You can visit the Myers & Briggs Foundation website (*www.myersbriggs.org*) to find out more about the different types, locate a professional who can administer the test, or take it online.

The Big Five Personality Traits Theory

The most widely researched theory of the Big Five personality traits is known as the Five Factor Model and is based on the work of Costa and

McCrae (who developed an instrument to measure them, the NEO PI). It provides an academic way to examine personality, but it is not as practical for daily life as the MBTI.

Boiling Down Multiplicity to Simplicity

How many dimensions of personality are there? There are thousands of terms in the English language that represent personality traits (as many as 18,000). Personality theorists have analyzed these traits to boil them down to basic dimensions of personality. In the 1940s, Raymond Cattell thought there were twelve. Many other theorists have suggested different numbers.

More recent research has found consistently that personality can be understood through five factors. That is, thousands of personality traits can be understood within a much simpler structure. Introversion-extroversion is the most important of these personality dimensions based on the volume of research it has generated. These five factors are extraversion (in research circles *extroversion* is spelled "extraversion"), agreeableness, conscientiousness, emotional stability, and openness to experience.

▼ **BIG FIVE PERSONALITY TYPES**

Traits	Alternate Terms	Descriptions
Surgency	Extraversion	Talkative, Assertive, Energetic
Agreeableness		Good-Natured, Cooperative, Trustful
Conscientiousness	Dependability	Orderly, Responsible
Emotional Stability (vs. Neuroticism)		Calm, Not Neurotic, Not easily upset
Culture	Openness; Intellect	Imaginative, Independent-Minded

Lewis R. Goldberg, "An Alternate 'Description of Personality': The Big-Five Factor Structure," *Journal of Personality and Social Psychology* 59, no. 6 (December 1990): 1216–29.

In a highly influential article published in 1990, Lewis Goldberg presented research confirming the Five Factor Theory. The personality trait terms associated with extroversion include: *spirit, talkativeness, sociability, spontaneity, playfulness, expressiveness, unrestraint, energy level, animation, boisterousness, adventure, energy, conceit, vanity, indiscretion,* and *sensuality.* The trait terms that load in the opposite direction are: *lethargy, aloofness, silence, modesty, shyness, pessimism,* and *unfriendliness.* You can already begin to see the problem with defining introversion as having more or less extroversion. It doesn't sound fun to be an introvert. What might these trait terms sound like if the Big Five looked at introversion as the standard? They would certainly be framed in a more positive light. Perhaps these would be on the list: *quiet*, *forbearance*, *patience*, *calm*, *peaceful*, *contained*, and *equanimity*.

Pathological Introversion

Big Five studies take an extrovert's view of the world. The emphasis on extroversion puts introversion in a negative light. Laurie Helgoe points out how the opposite of extrovert terms like "talkative" and "outgoing" become, "I have little to say" and "I don't like to draw attention to myself" in the introvert version. These sound pejorative—like a deficit instead of a valid alternative way to be.

QUOTE

"Introversion—along with its cousins sensitivity, seriousness, and shyness—is now a second-class personality trait, somewhere between a disappointment and a pathology."—Susan Cain, author

A 2012 study in the journal *Emotion* by John Zelenski and colleagues has a lot of very interesting information about introverts. The study was called, "Would Introverts Be Better Off If They Acted More Like Extraverts? Exploring Emotional and Cognitive Consequences of Counterdispositional Behavior." The researchers asked people to act like introverts or extroverts. To be extroverts, participants were told to be bold, talkative, energetic, active, and assertive. To be introverts, subjects were instructed to be reserved, quiet, lethargic, passive, compliant, and unadventurous. Do these strike you as equivalent lists? It's no wonder that acting extroverted felt better for both extroverts and introverts. But this hardly seems like a fair test. The study is a clear example of the extrovert bias that permeates the culture.

Official Condemnation

A disturbing extension of this bias can be found in the debates surrounding the new fifth edition of the *Diagnostic and Statistical Manual of Psychiatry*, or the DSM-V. Laurie Helgoe, along with Nancy Ancowitz, who writes the *Psychology Today* blog, *Self-Promotion for Introverts*, together wrote an influential post called, "A Giant Step Backwards for Introverts."

The APA (American Psychiatric Association) had proposed a pathological variant of introversion to be included in the manual. It was defined as "withdrawal from other people, ranging from intimate relationships to the world at large; restricted affective experience and expression; limited hedonic capacity" (the inability to feel pleasure).

This was not the first time that the psychiatric bible had attempted to include introversion as a diagnosis. Before the release of the DSM-III in 1980, another effort was thwarted. However, introverted personality is already listed as a disorder in the ICD-9 (published by the World Health Organization). Introverted personality (ICD-9-CM 301.21) is one of the variations of schizoid personality disorder. These "individuals exhibit a pervasive pattern of indifference to social relationships and a restricted range of emotional experience and expression, beginning by early adulthood and present in a variety of contexts. Personality disorder characterized by alienation, shyness, oversensitivity, seclusiveness, egocentricity, avoidance of intimate relationships, autistic thinking, and withdrawal from and lack of response to the environment." As you can see, the pathological variant of "introversion" bears little resemblance to the preferred view of introversion.

Introverts do desire and enjoy close relationships. While introverts may spend time in solitude, they don't seek it exclusively (not all introverts are loners). Introverts do enjoy the world, although in ways that are different from extroverts. Fortunately, through the efforts of Helgoe and Ancowitz, all mention of introversion will be expunged from the forthcoming DSM-V (and also the ICD-10).

Take the Quiz

There are different ways to measure introversion, ranging from formal academic research approaches (for example, the Big Five) to practical self-awareness based approaches (for example, the MBTI) to unscientific tests available on the Internet (for example, thepowerofintroverts.com).

To assess the Big Five is a time-consuming process. Samuel Gosling and his co-researchers developed a brief Ten-Item Personality Inventory (TIPI) that can be used to get a quick and dirty approximation of personality. There are two questions for extraversion and introversion that you rate on a seven-point scale. You state the degree to which you agree with the item. You can strongly disagree (1), moderately disagree (2), disagree a little (3), neither disagree or agree (4), agree a little (5), moderately agree (6), or strongly agree (7). The first question is: "I see myself as Extraverted, enthusiastic." If you agree with that statement you get points toward extroversion. If you disagree with that statement, you get points for introversion. The next question is, "I see myself as Reserved, quiet." This item is reverse scored. You can strongly disagree (7), moderately disagree (6), disagree a little (5), neither disagree or agree (4), agree a little (3), moderately agree (2), or strongly agree (1).

▼ **MAJOR POLARITIES OF HUMAN EXISTENCE**

Introverted	Extroverted
Female	Male
Yin	Yang
East	West
Dark	Light
Contraction	Expansion

These two questions appear to get at the heart of what it means to be either an extrovert or an introvert. Of course, there are many different facets to introversion and extroversion and different ways to conceptualize the experience. Even though this instrument only has two questions for introversion-extroversion that appear quite obvious, it has acceptable properties as a psychological test. The range of scores is 2 to 14. A strong introvert would score a "2" and a strong extrovert would score a "14." Anything below an "8" puts you in the introvert zone. How did you score?

Limits of Measurement

The MBTI data suggest that about half the population are introverts. Why, then, don't you see more introverts? For one, introverts are good at blending in. For another, if you split a population into two camps as the MBTI does—introverts and extroverts—most of the people will be clustered in the middle. There will be fewer of the purer cases—people who are prototypic introverts and extroverts. When you read about introverts and extroverts, you are usually reading descriptions of these prototypes, which are going to be a smaller number of people.

The NEO PI

The NEO PI (Neuroticism-Extroversion-Openness to Experience Personality Inventory) measures the Five Factor Model of personality. The scoring manual for the NEO PI has one dimension for extroversion-introversion and calls it *extraversion*. This personality factor is concerned with the "quantity and intensity of interpersonal interaction; activity level; need for stimulation; and capacity for joy." People who score high on this measure are described as "sociable, active, talkative, person-oriented, optimistic, fun-loving, affectionate." People who score low on this measurement (presumably introverts) are described as "reserved, sober, unexuberant, aloof, task-oriented, retiring, and quiet."

There are six facets of extraversion: warmth, gregariousness, assertiveness, excitement-seeking, and positive emotions. The warmth facet is defined as "close emotional ties to others. Warm people are affectionate and friendly; they genuinely like people. Low scorers are more reserved, formal, and distant in manner." This definition perpetrates a myth about introverts. Introverts have close emotional ties with others and can be warm and affectionate with a select group of people. This theory punishes introverts for being selective with their affections.

There is no bias with the gregariousness facet. Extroverts are by definition gregarious—they enjoy a greater quantity of social interactions. The assertiveness and excitement-seeking facets also accurately describe extroverts. Another problem is revealed with the positive emotions facet. Joy, happiness, love, and excitement are identified as "positive emotions." While it is certainly the case that these are positive emotions, they are high-arousal positive emotions. Missing from this conception are low-arousal positive emotions such as tranquility, calm, and peacefulness. Low scorers are not necessarily unhappy, they are just less "exuberant" and "high spirited." Well, "duh." Of course, extroverts are more exuberant and high-spirited—that is what makes them extroverts.

The problem with this model of extroversion seems to be that the opposite of extroversion is not necessarily introversion. In other words, extrovert deficiency is not necessarily the same thing as being a healthy introvert.

QUOTE

"There's little evidence that Mr. Obama dislikes people—only that he socializes in a more intimate, less backslapping style than the typical politician."—Susan Cain, "Must Great Leaders Be Gregarious?"

When you look more carefully at the items of the NEO PI that make you a high or low extrovert, further bias is revealed. If you were an extrovert you would endorse items such as: "I really like most people I meet," "I am dominant, forceful, and assertive," and "I often crave excitement." If you were an introvert, you would endorse items like: "I shy away from crowds of people," "I'm not the kind of person who must always be busy with something," and "I have never literally jumped for joy." Introverts could very well like most people they meet. They just want shorter interactions with these people.

CHAPTER 3

The Near Enemies of Introversion

Introversion is a healthy orientation. Introverts have been lumped together with all types of people, including misanthropes, loners, and hermits. While many of these people may also be introverts, most introverts are not socially challenged. Loners and misanthropes can be extroverts. These "near enemies" of introversion share some characteristics, but introverts should not be identified exclusively with any of these particular conditions. The stereotyped image of the introvert has often portrayed them as shy, retiring wallflowers, lacking in social skills. This is not the case.

The Highly Sensitive Person (HSP)

Being told you were "sensitive" was probably meant as criticism, not as an endorsement of your qualities as a human being. Many introverts are highly sensitive. They were probably high-reactive babies (very sensitive to novelty). The psychologist Elaine Aron has given sensitivity a good name through her research on highly sensitive people or HSPs. If you are an HSP, there is a strong chance that you are an introvert (although not all introverts are HSPs).

Sensitivity is not valued in this culture; it is seen as a liability. You may have been told you were "too" sensitive; you should have a "thicker skin." HSPs feel the world more intensely. You will be more prone to empathy, compassion, and other strong emotions. People may not understand your intensity. You may not understand it either. The world may seem overwhelming. If you are an HSP and an introvert, you will need to take extra special care of yourself because you live in a world that is not sensitive to the sensitive. You will have to protect yourself from overstimulation.

ESSENTIAL

A near enemy resembles one thing on the surface, but is really something completely different. In Buddhist psychology, apathy is the near enemy of equanimity because both look calm from the outside, but apathy represents not caring at all while equanimity means tranquility in the midst of adversity.

To take the HSP self-test visit Elaine Aron's website, *www.hsperson.com*, and click on self-test. You may be an HSP if you are sensitive to what is happening in your environment, including the emotions of others. You may be sensitive to loud noises, pain, caffeine, and violence in movies and television. HSPs don't like a lot of commotion, being hungry, or having too many demands placed upon them.

On her website, Elaine Aron says, "About 15 to 20 percent of the population have this trait. It means you are aware of subtleties in your surroundings, a great advantage in many situations. It also means you are more easily overwhelmed when you have been out in a highly stimulating environment for too long, bombarded by sights and sounds until you are exhausted."

Introversion and HSPs

There is great overlap between introversion and HSPs. If you are an introverted HSP, you are likely to favor the interior with a philosophical, spiritual, or contemplative approach to life. You probably hate small talk and find it grating (and draining). You probably like to be creative and are sensitive to information inside yourself, also known as your "intuition." You may have an aesthetic way of being in the world, appreciating beauty, art, and nature. Your emotions—both positive and negative—are vivid, as may be your dreams. If you are an introverted HSP, you probably prefer discussion of "real" issues (relationships, science, philosophy, geopolitics). You especially prefer one-on-one conversation where you have the luxury of time to delve into these topics. Talking is about connection, not entertainment.

If you are an HSP, the world is no glancing surface. You will notice things that others may miss. This makes you more "sensitive"—prone to becoming over-stimulated by the things happening in your environment, but it also gives you the opportunity to draw richness from that same environment. Paying exquisite attention to what is happening is akin to mindfulness. This quality of attention can enhance your sense of presence and empathy.

Benefits of Being an HSP

If you don't withdraw to recharge you can feel frazzled or suffer compassion fatigue. Being an HSP may be a burden, yet it is also a gift—the sensitivity cuts two ways. You are less separated from the world and this helps you to be conscientious and engaged and also deeply affected by the energy of the people and situations around you. Sensitivity is an equal opportunity experience. The anxiety and guilt characteristic of being an HSP motivate conscientiousness and even altruism. The sensitivity is in your psychology as well as your physiology. Like high-reactive infants who are sensitive to novel stimuli, HSPs have more robust physiological responses to stressful situations than non-HSPs. They sweat more in challenging situations. Being thin-skinned, in this case, is no metaphor. HSPs are not "cool as a cucumber" as many extroverts would be.

In a *Huffington Post* blog on "Characteristics of Highly Sensitive People," psychologist Dr. Roya Rohani Rad said, "Overall, many of our writers, creators, inventors, imaginaries, discoverers, and people who have contributed greatly to this world may fall in the category of highly sensitive. We need more of these people and we need to encourage them to unleash their potential. For those people who want to become more sensitive, they have to learn ways to overcome society's encouragement to be overly analytical, materialistic and competitive and to encourage themselves and others to cherish this trait and make the best of it."

"All virtues have a shadow."—Elaine Aron

Shyness

Not all introverts are shy and not all shy people are introverts. There are shy extroverts like Barbra Streisand. Shyness is anxiety over connecting with people, with asserting yourself in a social situation. According to the *www .shyness.com* website, "Shyness may be defined experientially as discomfort and/or inhibition in interpersonal situations that interferes with pursuing one's interpersonal or professional goals. It is a form of excessive self-focus, a preoccupation with one's thoughts, feelings and physical reactions. It may vary from mild social awkwardness to totally inhibiting social phobia." Shyness is not a preference, a way of processing stimulation, or a need to conserve energy, as introversion is. Shyness can be "fixed," but introversion can't (because there is nothing *to* fix). Research on introverts has often confused it with shyness, complicating the picture.

According to *www.shyness.com*, 40 to 50 percent of Americans report that they have chronic shyness that interferes with work, relationships, and other aspects of life. In 1994, 13 percent of Americans were found to have social anxiety disorder, which made it the third-most-prevalent psychiatric disorder.

Shyness relates to a fear of being embarrassed, shamed, or humiliated in social situations or of being judged in a negative way. Social situations are seen as a threat. For an introvert, the party may be uncomfortable—they would rather be doing something else—but self-esteem is not on the line as it is for shy people. From the outsider's perspective, the behavior of introverts and shy people may look the same, but it is motivated by different factors. The shy person at a party says, "I'd really like to talk with that woman over there, but I am afraid she will reject me." The introvert says, "I'd really like to talk with that woman over there but just don't have the energy now. I am out of here." Shyness obscures the question of introversion. If you overcome the shyness (or social anxiety disorder), then you can have a better sense of whether you are an extrovert or an introvert. What it means to be "cured" of shyness and social anxiety may look very much like what it means to be an extrovert. This bias reflects the extrovert's dominance in the culture. Shyness.com notes, "Metaphorically, shyness is a shrinking back from life that weakens the bonds of human connection." Human connection is just as important for introverts as extroverts.

Social Anxiety Disorder

Social anxiety disorder is a clinical form of shyness. People with social anxiety have a fear of being negatively judged by others and humiliated. They may have panic attacks or severe anxiety when they are in or anticipate being in social situations. Symptoms like rapid heartbeat, chest tightness, sweating, and flushing may occur. They realize that their fears are excessive or unreasonable. The fear leads to avoidance of social situations. If they can't avoid the situation, they may endure it with severe distress and may compensate for the distress by drinking or using other drugs. Their avoidance of social situations disrupts work, daily routines, or relationships.

Socially anxious people imagine others are having critical thoughts about them, talking behind their backs, noticing blemishes, wardrobe malfunctions, and dandruff. The anxiety persists even when it is recognized that it is unreasonable.

Social anxiety disorder is a treatable clinical condition and can afflict introverts and extroverts. Effective treatments are available that teach these individuals tools they can use to overcome the anxiety. For instance, instead of avoiding dreaded situations they would approach them using relaxation techniques to manage the symptoms of anxiety. Exposure to the feared situation shows that nothing catastrophic happened, which diminishes the fear.

QUOTE

> "Shy animals forage less often and widely for food, conserving energy, sticking to the sidelines, and surviving when predators come calling. Bolder animals sally forth, swallowed regularly by those farther up the food chain but surviving when food is scarce and they need to assume more risk."—David Sloan Wilson (quoted in *Quiet*)

Asperger's and Autism Spectrum Disorder

Asperger's syndrome is on the autism spectrum and is a brain disorder that impairs social skills. People with Asperger's have difficulty reading facial expressions and responding appropriately to social cues. In one experiment, subjects watched a scene from the movie, *Who's Afraid of Virginia Woolf?*, where the characters George and Martha argue intensely. Normal subjects focus on the characters in the argument, while Asperger patients may focus on some extraneous detail in the scene, such as the furniture. They have difficulty communicating, too. There may be impoverishments in imagination. Intelligence is generally normal.

People with autism have deficiencies with their mirror neuron system. Mirror neurons fire when an action is performed and also when it is observed. They create a map of the world by replicating inside what is seen outside. This makes it difficult for them to take the perspective of another and to read other people's emotions. People with Asperger's can be introverts or extroverts. The person with Asperger's has social deficits whereas the introvert does not.

Loners

The loner is most certainly an introvert, but an introvert on steroids. Loners do not seek social connection in manageable doses. They prefer to be alone in all circumstances. They experience the world best through a singular lens and provide their own validation for their experiences. They don't need confirmation from others. In her book, *Party of One: A Loner's Manifesto*, author Anneli Rufus points out that solitude is not an exception or respite for loners, as it is for introverts. Rather it is their modus operandi. She says, "We are the ones who know how to entertain ourselves."

QUOTE

"I think it's very healthy to spend time alone. You need to know how to be alone and not defined by another person."—Olivia Wilde

Like introverts, loners are taxed by gregarious social interactions. Rufus goes on to say, "After what others would call a fun day out together, we feel as if we have been at the Red Cross, donating blood." Loners may have social skills, but they elect not to use them. Loners are an extreme form of introvert. They don't want solitude to restore themselves; they want solitude as the very foundation of their lives. Rufus provides a list of well-known loners that includes: Henry David Thoreau (American author), Emily Dickinson (American poet), Alec Guinness (English actor), Erik Satie (French composer), Anthony Hopkins (Welsh actor), Stanley Kubrick (American film director), James Michener (American author), Greta Garbo (Swedish film actress), John Lennon (English musician), Piet Mondrian (Dutch painter), Franz Kafka (German writer), and Hermann Hesse (German poet and novelist).

Hermits, Recluses, and Misanthropes

The reclusive spiritual seeker meditating on a remote Himalayan mountaintop is almost certainly an introvert, but most introverts are neither hermits, recluses, nor misanthropes. Remember that most introverts are well skilled in social situations; they just prefer to use these skills in different ways, usually taking smaller doses of social situations. If a loner is an introvert on steroids, hermits are loners on steroids. They have constructed a life separate from society. They may be living off the grid. Some infamous criminals have belonged to this group and misidentifying their misanthropy as introversion has given introverts a bad name. Think Ted Kaczynski (the Unabomber).

QUOTE

"You once said that you would like to sit beside me while I write. Listen, in that case, I could not write at all. For writing means revealing oneself to excess; that utmost of self-revelation and surrender, in which a human being, when involved with others, would feel he was losing himself, and from which, therefore, he will always shrink as long as he is in his right mind. . . . That is why one can never be alone enough when one writes, why there can never be enough silence around one when one writes, why even night is not night enough."
—Franz Kafka

Most introverts want social connection in manageable doses and in the right situations. Introverts are differently social, not deficiently social as hermits, recluses, and misanthropes are bound to be.

Schizoid Personality

Schizoid is a serious personality disturbance. The schism is a split with the outside world, especially the world of others. There is an unfortunate history of confusing introversion with schizoid personality disorder (SPD). Individuals with SPD have little interest in relationships—a characteristic that is not shared with introverts. Although the schizoid's lack of interest may be confused with what extroverts perceive as aloofness in introverts.

SPD individuals tend be loners, and not just to charge their batteries. The schizoid is emotionally cold, detached, or incapable of showing feeling. This may occur on occasion, for introverts when they are depleted or overwhelmed, but it is not part of the introvert way of being. In fact, schizoids have difficulty showing any emotion toward other people. Again, this is not the case for introverts. The schizoid shows a consistent preference for solitary activities, while this only occurs occasionally for introverts. Schizoids have few, if any, close relationships, and have no interest in them. This is definitely not the case for introverts.

Introverts love people; they are not asocial or antisocial, but social on their own terms. Schizoids are indifferent to the opinions of others, derive very little enjoyment in things, including sex, and can be indifferent to social norms. Introverts care very much about the opinions of others—sometimes too much—and have no problems enjoying life, but it might not look the way an extrovert enjoys life. Finally, schizoids have a preoccupation with fantasy and introspection. The key here is *preoccupation*. Introverts have rich and ready access to their internal world, including fantasy. However, there is nothing about introversion that makes this a preoccupation. Preoccupation is unhealthy; access is healthy. There is only the most glancing and caricaturized similarity between introverts and this personality disturbance.

FACT

According to some people who knew him, statements he made about himself, and from his writings, such as the *Metamorphosis*, the writer Franz Kafka may have had schizoid personality disorder.

Unfortunately, in the history of this condition, the term introversion has often been used to refer to the schizoid's internal focus (in this case unhealthy focus). In fact, there was the sad and misguided inclusion of "introverted personality" in the previous version of the International Classification of Diseases (ICD-9). Fortunately, it was removed from the current version of that manual (ICD-10), and will not appear in the new version the American Psychiatric Association's diagnostic manual, the DSM-V.

Depression

Both introverts and extroverts get depressed and can experience clinical depression. Others may see introverts as depressed when they have low energy and are not showing much facial expression. You may confuse your own feelings of being exhausted for depression, especially if you are also sleep deprived. Indeed, fatigue is one of the clinical criteria for major depression. So, too, is difficulty in making decisions or concentrating and this can mask as the brain fog you may sometimes feel when you have become overloaded. To be diagnosed with major depression, you need to have sadness or loss of pleasure for at least two weeks. You then need five additional symptoms that may include: fatigue (as already mentioned), changes in appetite (increased or decreased), changes in sleep (insomnia or sleeping too much), being severely slowed down or agitated, trouble concentrating or making decisions (as already mentioned), low self-esteem, or suicidal thoughts.

FACT

Dysthymia is a chronic form of depression that is usually less severe than an episode of chronic depression but persists for more than two years. If you feel good when you have had sufficient rest and have recharged your batteries, then you probably don't have depression.

Remember the last time you were tapped out from being a pseudo-extrovert. Perhaps you had a big presentation at work and you were spent afterward. You may have felt heavy, exhausted, and flat, and your mind was fried. You may have looked and felt depressed. But as soon as you replenished your energy—got some good rest, spent some time in solitude enjoying downtime—you felt better. This suggests you are not depressed.

Obsessive Compulsive Spectrum Disorders

Obsessive-compulsive disorder (OCD) is a severe mental disorder that involves obsessions that are combined with a compulsive ritual of some sort. Rituals can be behavioral, such as frequent hand washing, or mental, such as counting. The obsessional component of OCD has been described as "brain lock" and it is this state that resembles the brain fog that can afflict introverts. As an introvert, you may have a tendency to be "in your head." If these thoughts become intense, you can feel locked in—unable to make decisions, unable to move, and painfully stuck. You may feel dull, dumb, and dispirited. These thoughts are tinged with anxiety. You feel ill at ease.

Managing Brain Lock

The difference between introversion and OCD is that the "brain lock" of introverts is temporary and not as severe as patients with OCD. Dr. Jeffery Schwartz wrote the book, *Brain Lock: Free Yourself from Obsessive Compulsive Behavior*, and outlines a four-step process that can also be helpful for introverts: relabel, reattribute, refocus, and revalue. To relabel, you must pay attention to what is happening in your mind and when you notice obsessional thoughts put them in context—your introverted mind is on overdrive. To reattribute, you create a mental space around the thought: "It's just a product of my mind; my introverted mind is very active; these thoughts are not real." To refocus, you redirect your attention to something outside of your thoughts—to whatever is happening in the present moment. To revalue, you see the thoughts for what they are—just thoughts, passing events in the mind. You step back from the thoughts. While they may refer to real things, they are not the reality itself. They are just thoughts.

Burnout

Burnout is another condition that can look similar to depression. Here, too, there is exhaustion and disillusionment. Burnout is an occupational hazard, especially for introverts.

ESSENTIAL

All explanations of introversion and extroversion present averages or prototypes. They seek to generalize and summarize. You will not fit these descriptions exactly. Like the fine print on infomercials, "individual results may vary."

Defining Burnout

Burnout is a major problem in the workplace, especially for certain careers like health care. American social psychologist Christina Maslach, the leading researcher on burnout says, "Staff members in human services and educational institutions are often required to spend considerable time in intense involvement with other people. Frequently, the staff-client interaction is centered on the client's current problems (psychological, social, or physical) and is therefore charged with feelings of anger, embarrassment, fear, or despair. Because solutions for clients' problems are not always obvious and easily obtained, the situation becomes more ambiguous and frustrating. For the person who works continuously with people under such circumstances, the chronic stress can be emotionally draining and can lead to burnout." Burnout can look very much like depression or lead to depression (or be aggravated by a pre-existing depression). Burnout symptoms include:

- Feeling run down and drained of energy (physical and emotional)
- Callousness and separation from people; you find it harder to care for others
- Irritability at work (with the work or with coworkers)
- Feeling misunderstood or unappreciated at work
- Your productivity is lower
- You wonder if you are in the wrong job, career, or profession
- Frustration at work
- Volume of work feels overwhelming (can't get it all done; no time to think)

Measuring and Recovering from Burnout

Burnout is measured with the Maslach Burnout Inventory (MBI). It has three scales: emotional exhaustion, depersonalization, and personal accomplishment. According to the MBI website (published by *www.mindgarden.com*): "Emotional exhaustion measures feelings of being emotionally overextended and exhausted by one's work. Depersonalization measures an unfeeling and impersonal response toward recipients of one's service, care treatment, or instruction. Personal accomplishment measures feelings of competence and successful achievement in one's work."

To cope with burnout, you must restore your energy. It is hard to care and to do the work when you are exhausted. You may need a break from the work. From this foundation of rest, you will need to reconnect with the meaning of your work. Why did you choose to do this work in the first place?

Can you remember feeling good about your work? What has changed? Is there something you can do to help you to reconnect with the meaningful aspects of your work? When you are exhausted and disconnected, it is hard to feel successful in your work. Finding something that you can accomplish right now may be a good starting point—perhaps some small project that you can get done. It can help to revise your expectations or set them aside for the time being until you can replenish your energy.

Of course, burnout can also mean you are ready for a change in your professional life—perhaps a shift to a different job function, work with a different population, or teaching a new course. Try something that will inject new energy into your work.

CHAPTER 4

The History of Introversion

Introversion is not a modern invention. There have been many introverts throughout human history. Long before the term *introvert* was used, introverts were distinguishing themselves from extroverts. References to introverts and extroverts (although not by these modern terms) can be found in the Bible and the written records of ancient Greece and Rome. Many influential people throughout history were introverts and they continue to influence the current culture. Introverts show up in film, television, and literature.

Famous Introverts

Charles Darwin was an avowed introvert. Albert Einstein was an introvert. These men are two of the most influential scientists in history. They preferred to work alone. They spent long periods of time in silence. Mahatma Gandhi was a shy introvert. Eleanor Roosevelt was quiet and worked behind the scenes of FDR's magnanimous persona. President John Quincy Adams was one of the few introverts ever to hold the office. President Barack Obama is another.

Charles Darwin was a notorious introvert, as captured in his wonderful testament to an introverted life. "My dear Mr. Babbage," he wrote to the famous mathematician who had invited him to a dinner party, "I am very much obliged to you for sending me cards for your parties, but I am afraid of accepting them, for I should meet some people there, to whom I have sworn by all the saints in Heaven, I never go out" (cited in *Quiet*).

▼ **FAMOUS INTROVERTS**

Politicians and Public Figures	Scientists and Philosophers
President Barack Obama	Sir Isaac Newton
President John Quincy Adams	Albert Einstein
President Abraham Lincoln	Charles Darwin
Mahatma Gandhi	Albert Schweitzer
Rosa Parks	Marie Curie
Eleanor Roosevelt	Alfred North Whitehead
Al Gore	Bill Gates
Warren Buffet	Steve Wozniak
Diane Sawyer	Larry Page

Not all of the people on this list are avowed introverts. Some of these are based on presumptions, inference, and guesswork.

Famous Fictional Introverts

Jean-Luc Picard, Captain of the Starship *Enterprise* (in the *Star Trek: The Next Generation* television program), is a good example of an introverted character, especially in comparison to his extroverted predecessor, Captain James T. Kirk. Captain Kirk (in the original television series from the 1960s, and in recent movie prequel portrayals) is bold, impulsive, aggressive, and hypersexual. In nearly every episode of the original television series, he is in a fistfight or seducing a woman, and somehow managing to rip or take off his shirt in the process. He is a heroic, spontaneous character that seems to thrive on the challenge of dangerous situations.

Captain Picard, on the other hand, is quiet, laconic, and thoughtful. He is fiercely private. He spends most of his time in his "ready room" alone. His spare time is spent reading the classics, practicing amateur archeology, or fencing. His one extrovert indulgence is impersonating 1940s-style private investigator, Dixon Hill, on the ship's fictional holodeck. His sexual conquests are few. There are many occasions where he is clearly pained by the diplomatic functions of his job and he is frequently retiring to his quarters where he may listen to classical music. Where Kirk would jump right into a situation and wing it, Picard is deliberate. He consults his crew and ponders a situation far longer than Kirk would. However, when a situation needing immediate action is upon the *Enterprise*, Picard is capable of becoming action oriented. After such an incident, Kirk would be energized and smiling while Picard is ready to take a nap.

Television Portrayals of Introverts

Saturday Night Live (SNL) presented two skits called "Introverts' Night Out" that portrayed introverts in a negative, stereotyped light. The characters, Neil and Jean, are nerdy wallflowers who find themselves in a bar and let loose. The result is not so much extroversion, but bizarre humor.

Extroversion Is Cool

Contrast SNL's portrayal of these socially awkward introverts with the world's most awesome spy—Sterling Archer. *Archer* is an animated situation comedy featuring the misadventures of Sterling Archer. Imagine *South Park* meets James Bond. Archer is handsome, self-absorbed, and downright sociopathic at times. He is a combination of bumbling impulsive idiot with highly refined shooting and fighting skills. He drinks heavily and spends his spare time driving fast, having sex with gorgeous prostitutes, and quoting Burt Reynolds movies. If *South Park*'s narcissistic manipulative Eric Cartman grew up rich, and became a spy, he would be Archer. Extroverted Sterling is exciting, attractive, and thrill-seeking. There is nothing boring about Archer's glamorous life.

QUOTE

"Experience has taught me that silence is part of the spiritual discipline of a votary of truth. We find so many people impatient to talk. All this talking can hardly be said to be of any benefit to the world. It is so much waste of time."—Mahatma Gandhi

The subtext: extroversion is cool; introversion is uncool. Compare Archer to his co-worker, the bookish accountant Cyril Figgis, who is portrayed as intelligent but socially buffoonish. Sterling Archer captures a number of the traits extroverts are prone to: substance abuse, accidental injuries (he is shot or thrown through the windshield of a car on a regular basis), and promiscuity.

The Self-Destructive Introvert

Don Draper, the antihero of *Mad Men*, is one of television's avowed introverts. He is never called an introvert, but he embodies many introvert qualities. If you don't know Don, he is the creative director and later partner at a prestigious Madison Avenue advertising agency. The series starts in 1960 and continues through 1968 in season six. Don is a complex character. He smokes too much; he drinks too much. He is self-destructive in relationships, and he does not like to talk about himself—a notorious enigma. In the first episode of season one, Don sits in an important client meeting. All eyes turn to him to solve the problem at hand. He pauses . . . for a long time. His superiors begin to worry; the clients get fidgety and are on the verge of leaving when Don speaks. He comes out with a brilliant solution to the problem: pithy, eloquent, and on target. The partners sigh in relief and the clients beam. Don is not the fast talking extrovert. He processes the problem deeply and takes his time before responding. He is also not self-conscious about refusing social invitations, which he does frequently. In one episode during season four, his boss and friend Roger Sterling begs him to go out to see the Ali-Liston rematch fight. Don demurs once and then again despite Roger's pleading. Why does

Don refuse? He usually says no when he is tired, has drunk too much, or, as was the case in this episode, he is working through some emotional difficulty. He values *and* protects his solitude—a good role model for introverts on that score (the secrets, infidelity, and drinking—not so much). There are many reasons why Don is not a great role model, but his willingness to take his time and to protect his energy gives him the Introvert Edge.

Movie Introverts

According to the IMDB (Internet Movie Data Base), the top ten introvert movies are: *Amelie* (2001), *Like Stars on Earth* (2007), *Bus 174* (2002), *Tesis* (1996), *Speak* (2004), *Lars and the Real Girl* (2007), *Tea and Sympathy* (1956), *A Fine Romance* (1992), *Post Mortem* (2010), and *The Devil's Playground* (2010). It is not clear that all of the characters portrayed in these movies are introverts—some of them may be loners, shy people, or misanthropes, who get confused with introverts. In the case of *Lars and the Real Girl*, the character is mentally ill. Yes, he is probably an introvert, too, but his introversion is not what leads him to create an imaginary relationship with a blow-up doll.

QUOTE

"Most people in politics draw energy from backslapping and shaking hands and all that. I draw energy from discussing ideas."—Al Gore

A Positive Portrayal of Introverts

A good representation of an introverted child (and adult) can be found in the film, *The Switch* starring Jennifer Aniston, Jason Bateman, and Thomas Robinson as the introverted Sebastian. When you meet Sebastian, you see a shy-looking boy. But when you look closer, you see that he is not shy. He is just slow to warm up. He is circumspect. He is highly intelligent and verbal, and demonstrates compassion and empathy.

Sebastian: "I don't want to climb the wall" (as Roland fits him into a harness).
Roland: "What? No. But I promise you it's gonna be fun!"
Sebastian: "I don't think so."

Roland (with a stern tone): "Sebastian, the whole reason we're having this party here is to climb the wall. We don't want the wall to go to waste now, do we? You feelin' it!?"

▼ **FAMOUS INTROVERTS**

Artists and Writers	Hollywood Actors
Frederic Chopin	Clint Eastwood
Marcel Proust	Ellen Burstyn
George Orwell	Steven Spielberg
Theodor Geisel (Dr. Seuss)	Julia Roberts
J. K. Rowling	Gwyneth Paltrow
T. S. Eliot	Alfred Hitchcock
Charles Schulz	Candice Bergen
W. B. Yeats	Steve Martin
Henry David Thoreau	Harrison Ford
Salvador Dali	Michelle Pfeiffer

Not all of the people on this list are avowed introverts. Some of these are based on presumptions, inference, and guesswork.

His mom is complicit: "This is good for him; it gets him active and athletic." Of course, his attempt at climbing and the party are disasters. The kid hates the activity and wants out. As he is stuck on the wall wanting to get down, another adult tells him, "The most important thing is to have fun." And so the extrovert conspiracy continues. When Sebastian descends the wall he chides Roland, "I hate that stupid wall and this was the worst birthday party ever." He runs to his mother and says, "Mommy, I don't want to be here."

It is also likely that Sebastian is a high-reactive child. In one scene, he and his father cover their ears when a loud motorcycle goes by, suggesting that they are sensitive to that stimulation. In another scene, Wally demonstrates his introversion. In a highly charged emotional situation, he is put on the spot. He has something important to say but he can't just spit it out. He hesitates and the moment is lost.

Wally and Roland have a heart-to-heart conversation where Wally helps to normalize introversion. Roland the extrovert says, "I can't relate to neurotic" (referring to Sebastian who has rough edges—"worries a lot, questions everything"). Wally replies, "Neurotic is simply an intense form of introspection. Okay? You're basically calling him introspective and being introspective is good. You walk around with an opinion, with point of view, and some sort of nice kind of direction." This movie portrays introversion in a positive and accurate light. The child has a rich inner world. He thinks deeply about issues that matter, he has a vivid imagination. He's not a high-energy, adventurous kid. He has other qualities. The classic extrovert doesn't understand and just looks at the world from his "let's have fun" perspective. "Doesn't everyone just want to have fun?"

Extroversion Is Downright American

Extroversion is downright American. It's fast, friendly, and efficient. It's a can-do attitude that doesn't waste its time contemplating, reflecting, or brooding. It fits with the image of America as the land of opportunity, "from sea to shining sea." Is introversion un-American? Intellect, interior, and intuition are suspect. If you can't move at the speed of business, then you are not part of the conversation, and that conversation is not about deeper meanings, but connections and opportunities. "What next?" "What can be conquered now?" "The rolling stone gathers no moss."

If you are an introvert, you are getting green with moss unless you have forced yourself to roll along with everyone else. Moving at a different speed can feel alienating—cut off from the world, marginalized, ridiculed. From the extrovert norm, introversion is seen as deficient, defective, or derelict. Your gifts may not fit with the extrovert norm. If you value ideas over parties, you may feel out of place. Your introvert gifts may be obscured by the dizzying frenzy of the extroverted world.

The Extrovert Ideal and the Cult of Personality

America was not always the extroverted nation is it today. In *Quiet*, Susan Cain documents the history of how the Extrovert Ideal came to hold sway over American culture. Several factors contributed to the transition from the Culture of Character to the Culture of Personality (or, in some cases, the cult of personality). Before the 1920s, it was a person's actions, convictions, and integrity that mattered. But then growing industries required a sales force. The Culture of Personality was about making good impressions, influencing people, and entertaining. In other words—performing. It was the era of sales and people like Dale Carnegie in his influential book, *How to Win Friends and Influence People*, became the reference standard.

"Respect for individual human personality has with us reached its lowest point and it is delightfully ironical that no nation is so constantly talking about personality as we are. We actually have schools for 'self-expression' and 'self-development,' although we seem usually to mean the expression and development of the personality of a successful real estate agent."—1921 intellectual cited in *Quiet*

Industrialization, urbanization, and immigration were largely responsible for this shift from character to personality. This shift made the fabric of social life more anonymous and suited the surface presentation of people rather than getting to know them deeply. The move away from character to personality planted the seeds of narcissism in American soil. Integrity was traded for charisma. Being liked was more important than being respected. How you came across was more important than what you actually did. Cultural historian Warren Susman provides a list of character qualities from earlier self-help manuals that included: "citizenship, duty, work, golden deeds, honor, reputation, morals, manners, and integrity." Later manuals that reflected the Extrovert Ideal cited these qualities, "magnetic, fascinating, stunning, attractive, glowing, dominant, forceful, and energetic" (cited in *Quiet*). This was the dawn of a self-conscious era that has become the cultural standard. This self-conscious era has become a full-blown Age of Self-Importance according to psychologist, Polly Young-Eisendrath.

Depth was traded for surface and deliberate for quick. Now the cult of personality and its Extroverted Ideal holds sway over American culture. It is the religion of Harvard Business School and evangelical churches and corporate America. It elects presidents (most of them) and elevates movie actors to cultural icons. The paradigm has shifted from substance to style.

Introversion Lost

In the shift from character to charisma, introverted qualities became seen as deficient, undesirable, and inferior to the Extrovert Ideal of bold loudness. The quiet stillness of introverts was overrun by the enthusiasm of extroversion. Circumspection became a liability and perhaps a sign of mental instability. And, indeed, the quiet person would find it hard to keep up in the outgoing world that had taken over. If your child was a strong introvert, he may have been seen as having a problem ("Does not play well with others"). Quiet was no longer acceptable. Even at the college level, elite schools like Harvard University and Yale University were biased against introverts. Extroverts were healthy. Introverts were "Who knows what?" Deep thinking was suspect, and apparently no longer necessary in the fast-paced exchanges of American commerce.

ESSENTIAL

Places where you're likely to find other introverts include laboratories, meditation studios, art studios, sanctuaries, monasteries, arboretums, botanical gardens, museums, libraries, meditation retreats, art galleries, coffee shops (working on a laptop), and consulting rooms.

Toastmasters International is an organization for people with fear of public speaking. It is a nonprofit that helps people to practice public speaking in a safe yet challenging environment. The skills you learn at Toastmasters can help you to sell yourself in such a way that people won't know whether you are telling the truth or not. What matters most is not content but how that content is presented. Susan Cain wonders, "Should we become so proficient at self-presentation that we can dissemble without anyone suspecting? Must we learn to stage-manage our voices, gestures, and body language until we can tell—sell—any story we want?"

Susan Cain provides compelling examples of contemporary bastions of extroversion. She attends a Tony Robbins seminar, where being energized, enthusiastic, and ebullient is the only way to be. She explores Harvard Business School, where introverts seem to be an endangered species. The one introvert she talks with feels woefully out of place and stressed by the outgoing performance demands of the classroom and the relentless team-work that is required.

QUOTE

"Introverted seekers need introverted evangelists. It's not that extro-verts can't communicate the gospel, either verbally or nonverbally, in ways that introverts find appealing, it's that introverted seekers need to know and see that it's possible to lead the Christian life as them-selves. It's imperative for them to understand that becoming a Chris-tian is not tantamount with becoming an extrovert."—Adam S. McHugh

She visits an evangelical ministry where being an introvert may be seen as an insult to God. She finds an advertisement that says, "the priest must be . . . an extrovert who enthusiastically engages members and newcomers, a team player." One pastor says, "I'm sure our Lord was [an extrovert]." How can introverts compete with that? Evangelical churches are social at their core. The mission is to convert and to convert one must recruit. To be effec-tive at recruiting, you have to be energetic, enthusiastic, and excited. People are saved more from an emotional appeal than an exchange of ideas. The social fabric of doing things together binds the community together. If you are an introvert in this setting you will feel conflict, a sense of not fitting in, and a sense of letting other people and God down.

CHAPTER 5

The Science of Introversion

The discussion of introversion has to address the question of nature versus nurture, as do all the important discussions of human development. In some ways, the nature-versus-nurture argument is a false one. Nothing is purely nature, and nothing is purely nurture. It is always a dynamic combination of both. In this chapter, you will find out what nature contributes to introversion and how introversion can arise from nurture. It's the combination of the two that makes you who you are.

The Reactive Child

Humans come into the world with certain tendencies, preferences, and pre-dilections. These are the result of genetics and early experiences in utero. As the young child develops, the environment will further shape inborn tendencies. Developmental psychologist Jerome Kagan, famous for his research on temperament, has conducted long-term longitudinal studies, starting with infants as young as four months. He has found that about 20 percent of the infants studied are what he characterizes as "high-reactive." These infants react more to sudden surprises, loud noises, and other new things. He also found that 40 percent of the infants studied are low-reactive, while the remaining 40 percent are in between. The high-reactive infants cried and squirmed in reaction to the various novel stimuli.

Which of these babies grow up to be introverts—high or low reactives? It turns out the loud babies instead of the quiet ones became introverts. This finding provides an important clue to what makes introverts introverts—how they handle stimulation. The high- and low-reactive infants grow up to be introvert and extrovert kids, respectively, when assessed at two, seven, and eleven years of age. Temperament reflects biological, hardwired tendencies in the child. Children at four months have not had time to be influenced by cultural and other experiences that will later form their personality on the foundation of temperament. Whatever introversion is, it starts at the beginning of life.

The Physiology of Reaction

High-reactive children respond to threats differently. Their bodies mount a pronounced fight-or-flight response, with changes in their physiology including increased heart rate, blood pressure, and body temperature. Stress hormones are elevated. These children's bodies are mobilized for action—a response to a potential threat. The world feels more threatening to them than to the low-reactive infants.

These basic response tendencies will show up later in life. If you were a high-reactive infant, you still have that physiological legacy inside of you. While not every high-reactive infant becomes an introvert, most do. Introverts pay closer attention to the world because, in their mind, this is the only way they will know whether there are potential threats.

Along with this vigilance comes a sensitivity that increases concentration and empathy. These tendencies may pay dividends later on in life—giving you the Introvert Edge—but they are not the skills most valued in the fast-paced and impulsive, extroverted world. When high-reactive infants grow up, they may choose solitary occupations such as writing or truck driving, where the likelihood of unexpected things is lower and the amount of quiet time is higher.

The Role for Experience

High reactivity is not the only route to becoming an introvert. Life experiences can contribute to this. While only 20 percent of young children are high-reactive, up to 50 percent of the adult population are introverts. For example, a mentor may turn a kid on to intellectual pursuit, an illness may turn a child inward toward introspection, or a loss may give an adolescent a more serious view of the world.

QUOTE

"I'm prone to wild flights of self-doubt, but I also have a deep well of courage in my own convictions. I feel horribly uncomfortable on my first day in a foreign city, but I love to travel. I was shy as a child, but have outgrown the worst of it."—Susan Cain

Sensitivity may persist into adulthood. If you were a high-reactive infant, you can learn to cope with these tendencies as an adult. Jerome Kagan has conducted studies on high-reactive kids as they reached adulthood. Kagan found that their brains were more reactive to novelty than low-reactive comparison subjects. You may become adept at public speaking, but you will retain reactivity—nervousness, sweating, and butterflies in the stomach. The great actor Laurence Olivier threw up every night before he went on stage, even though he was considered the greatest actor of his generation. It's not known whether he was a high-reactive child, but he did not allow his reactivity to inhibit his acting.

Name It to Tame It

Olivier likely used the strategy of *name it to tame it*. This cognitive technique allows you to get a better handle on emotions by naming them and putting them in context. For instance, if you get nervous before public speaking, you can remind yourself of your reactivity and that the nervousness is a result of that sensitivity. This helps to keep your more primitive brain away from thoughts that something may be wrong. You can recall memories of successful public presentations and that will calm you down further. You may never be able to get rid of this underlying tendency no matter how much therapy you do or how many self-help books you read. It will persist no matter how much yoga, meditation, or Qigong you do. It will even persist if you take medications. All of these things can help you to cope with this sensitivity, but they will never eliminate it. Naming it helps the rational brain to convince the emotional brain that the current situation is not an actual hazard. You can learn to recalibrate the threat reaction threshold. You can make it a habit to be less reactive, even though the underlying physiology will always be there.

It's in Your Genes: The DNA of Introversion

To find out if a personality trait has a genetic component, scientists often turn to twins. If identical twins (who share all of their genes) have more of a certain trait than fraternal twins (who share only half of their genes), then they can say there is a genetic component. In regard to introversion and extroversion, it appears there is approximately a 40–50 percent contribution from genes. The rest comes from environment (nurture). But keep in mind, your genes and your environment interact in complex ways. There is not just one gene for introversion or extroversion.

Genes and Behavior

One way this interaction expresses itself is through predispositions. Predisposing factors make something more likely to occur, but do not cause them directly. If you were a low-reactive child, you will be more comfortable taking risks—that is, you will be predisposed to taking risks. The more risks you take, the more comfortable you will be taking risks. A positive feedback loop emerges. The genes predispose the behavior that creates the personality. It is always a combination of genes and experiences that makes people who they are. If you were a high-reactive infant, you were predisposed to avoiding excessive stimulation, making a quiet life more appealing. The world of books may have become a welcome place (it is no surprise that universities have more than their fair share of introverted faculty).

Europeans and Americans are more extroverted than Asians and Africans. This makes sense when you consider that European explorers and travelers—likely to be more extroverted—colonized America.

QUOTE

"It's not that I'm so smart, it's that I stay with problems longer."
—Albert Einstein

The D4DR gene seems to be associated with introversion and extroversion. It has been called the novelty-seeking gene and is linked to the important neurotransmitter dopamine. Dopamine is involved with the experience of pleasure and seeking rewards. If you seek a lot of novelty (that is, you get easily bored, don't like to do the same thing over and over again), you probably have the long version of this gene. If you are not easily bored and don't seek novelty, you probably have the shorter version of this gene. Both introverts and extroverts seek to feel good and they get there in different ways. Skydiving will be exhilarating for an extrovert and that same stimulation will feel overwhelming for the introvert. With stimulation, it is the Goldilocks phenomenon—you want the porridge that tastes just right. For introverts, the cold porridge (soothing experiences) may feel just right and extroverts like the hot porridge (excitement).

The Orchid Hypothesis

In an *Atlantic* article titled "The Science of Success," David Dobbs discusses how genes interact with environment to influence child development. According to well-known primate researcher Stephen Suomi, some monkeys are born with a shortened version of the serotonin transporter gene (allele). When these monkeys are raised by neglectful parents, they are prone to behavioral problems later in life. If these sensitive youths have nurturing parents, they grow up as well or *better* than their peers. A similar pattern is evident in humans.

Children are like orchids. This gene makes children vulnerable in the hands of a poor environment and can make children bloom like beautiful flowers with the right situation. For humans, children with more of this allele will be especially sensitive to traumas such as parental conflict, death, neglect, or abuse. These adverse conditions will make them more prone to developing mental disorders like depression and anxiety in adolescence and adulthood.

There is an upside to this same vulnerability. When these children are not exposed to difficulty, they tend to thrive. The allele is a blessing or a curse depending on circumstances. Like an orchid they need the right conditions to flourish, and when they do it can be spectacular.

QUOTE

"Most of us have genes that make us as hardy as dandelions: able to take root and survive almost anywhere. A few of us, however, are more like the orchid: fragile and fickle, but capable of blooming spectacularly if given greenhouse care."—David Dobbs

The Introvert Edge cuts both ways. If you have this sensitivity, the challenge is to make it work for you. Your vulnerability can be your strength, once you understand what is possible. Susan Cain highlights the advantages of being an orchid. "Often they're exceedingly empathic, caring, and cooperative. They work well with others. They are kind, conscientious, and easily disturbed by cruelty, injustice, and irresponsibility."

Evolutionary Advantages and Disadvantages

Wouldn't it better to be energetic, fearless, and gregarious? What evolutionary advantage would introversion have? A successful group of animals needs a combination of both—actors (extroverts) and thinkers (introverts). Introverts are keen observers of the environment and can spot danger, problem solve, and understand patterns of behavior. If extroverts jump in, introverts stand on the edge and watch. When introverts don't appreciate the usefulness of reactivity, they see it as a nuisance. When extroverts don't understand the value of reactivity, they see introverts in a negative light.

Consider blushing. This physiological reaction indicates a concern for morality and is part of the social conscience that allows groups of people to live together cooperatively. Sociopaths cannot feel embarrassment. It is an authentic emotion because it is not under voluntary control and is therefore an important social signal of concern for the feelings of others. It is a pro-social emotion that seeks harmony.

Survival and Adaptation

How does the trait of sensitivity or reactivity provide some advantage for evolution? Evolution is often thought of as survival of the fittest, and from this vantage point, energetic, exuberant, and exploratory extroverts would seem to have the advantage. But evolution is really survival of the ones who can adapt to their environment. The sensitive type is paying closer attention to the environment and this may be a more efficient strategy for adaptation under many circumstances.

Being impulsive can be expensive. Being vigilant is a more conservative strategy—it safeguards energy and calories (which might have been hard to come by when human ancestors were evolving hundreds of thousands of years ago). Research psychologist and voice for highly sensitive people (HSP) Elaine Aron, says that HSPs are good at "avoiding dangers, failures, and wasted energy, which would require a nervous system specially designed to observe and detect subtle differences." Susan Cain further notes this remarkable finding: "From fruit flies to house cats to mountain goats, from sunfish to bushbaby primates to Eurasian tit birds, scientists have discovered that approximately 20 percent of the members of many species are 'slow to warm up.'" The fact that 20 percent of animals within certain species and humans exhibit sensitivity points to the biological value of this orientation.

What percentage of highly sensitive people are introverts?
70 percent are introverts, the remaining 30 percent are extroverts. Diversity of extroverts and introverts within a group helps the group to survive the challenges of their environment. Introverts have an important place at the table. Context is everything. Vigilance will be rewarded in a dangerous environment. Estimates of the percentage of introverts in society vary from 25–50 percent. On the low side, you can assume that a culture needs fewer introverts than extroverts (that is, observers versus doers). The other way to look at this is that the introverts are so accustomed to adapting to the extrovert culture that they have become effective pseudo-extroverts.

Stimulation

One of the important names in introvert research is Hans Eysenck. He believed that introverts and extroverts differ in the level of stimulation they desire. Extroverts need a lot. Introverts not so much. Introverts can get easily overloaded with too much commotion. Extroverts crave it.

There is a discrepancy between the optimal environments for introverts and extroverts. What the introvert finds comforting—a quiet repose—the extrovert finds boring. There are different kinds of stimulation—some that are pleasant, some that are unpleasant, and you may feel overloaded by one kind but not another. You may, for instance, enjoy loud music or snowboarding, but you find the social demands of a party taxing. The brain mechanisms for arousal preference point are not fully understood, but science does know there are important differences in how introverts and extroverts process stimulation. Knowing this, you will need to seek your optimal levels of stimulation and not feel bad when you are overwhelmed in a situation that goes outside of your comfort zone.

"Extroverts exercise more, but introverts suffer fewer accidents and traumatic injuries. Extroverts enjoy wider networks of social support, but commit more crimes."—Susan Cain

One of Eysenck's studies exposed subjects to drops of lemon juice on the tongue—a very stimulating experience if you have ever tried that (you can even do this in your imagination!). Sure enough, introverts salivated more than extroverts because of their sensitivity to sensory stimulation. Another experiment had extroverts and introverts play a difficult word game while listening to headphones that produced random noise. The participants got to adjust the volume of these noises and, not surprisingly, the introverts preferred a lower volume (55 versus 72 decibels). Both groups performed equally well on the task. When the volumes were switched, performance decreased for both groups dramatically. The overstimulation of the loud noise led to poorer performance by the introverts, presumably because they were overwhelmed. The extroverts, too, had difficulty performing, presumably because they were understimulated and bored.

The Neuroscience of Introversion

Introverts and extroverts process information differently. Marti Olsen Laney, author of *The Introvert Advantage,* cites neuroscience research that has revealed different patterns of brain blood flow. Extroverts tend to be oriented to their senses and utilize a "short" circuit in their brains. Introverts tend to go deeper with processing information, taking it in, comparing it to other experiences, and thinking through the implications. Introverts have a "long" circuit.

FACT

The autonomic nervous system has two branches—the sympathetic and parasympathetic. The sympathetic is the fight-or-flight system and readies you for action with huge increases in energy. The parasympathetic is calming and turns off the sympathetic. Once a crisis has passed, the body and mind relax and restore.

Dopamine and Feeling Good

Neurotransmitters communicate information in the brain and turn different brain functions on and off. Dopamine is one of these major neurotransmitters and is associated with pleasure and reward. Cocaine stimulates dopamine release, as does getting something you want. Extroverts have a low sensitivity to dopamine and therefore need to generate more of it to feel just right. Extroverts power up their bodies with adrenaline to augment stimulation. Introverts are more sensitive to dopamine and therefore need less stimulation. Their autonomic nervous systems tend to be in a more restful state and brain metabolism is associated with the neurotransmitter acetylcholine (integral for the functioning of memory and other cognitive processes).

If extroverts had an ad campaign, it would read, "Extroversion, brought to you by adrenaline!" The introvert campaign would say, "Introversion, brought to you by acetylcholine." There are two pathways that have been identified. The extrovert pathway is excitatory and involves dopamine, adrenaline, and the activation of the fight-or-flight system. Think: "Turn it on." The introvert pathway involves acetylcholine, the turning off of the fight-or-flight system, and conservation of energy. Think: "Turn it off." You have a set point that will be your optimal comfort place. This set point is a function of your temperament (how you were born) and how this temperament developed over the course of your life. Where your "just right" Goldilocks point of stimulation lies will tell you whether you are an introvert or an extrovert.

The Stress Response

The autonomic nervous system is involved with the stress response. This system works best when it turns on and off in short bursts to deal with an intermittent crisis or opportunity. If you are constantly involved in extrovert activities like skydiving, the system will be turned on, and perhaps more often than it should. The system also turns on with strong negative emotions like anger.

The system can also be activated by imagination. Introverts are at risk for chronic stress from rumination when they get lost in their thoughts and those stories turn to anxious themes. Being in your head may be second nature to you, so much so that you don't realize that you can turn it off. This is where contemplative practices become key, balancing the potential downside to introversion—thinking too much.

Cross-Cultural Perspectives

Not every culture has the same values, customs, and philosophies as those of the United States and other developed countries of the West. Not all cultures are as individualistic as those in the West. Personal identity in America is considered what researcher Ed Sampson called Self-Contained Individualism. It is as if you are a container separated from but interacting with other containers. In the East, personal identity is more distributed across groups of people (called by Sampson: Ensembled Individualism). Not surprisingly, extroversion seems to go along with Self-Contained Individualism, while introversion corresponds more with the Ensembled approach to identity—the assertive individual versus the harmonious cohesion of the group. The qualities of the introvert are valued in a place like China, where being studious, diligent, and soft-spoken are linked with respect and success.

East and West

One place you can see these cultural differences is in athletics. There is no substitute for hard work. Elite athletes must be dedicated and have dedicated parents that motivate and support their children. Former professional soccer player, motivational speaker, and author Rasmus Ankersen points out that 35 percent of the top 100 female professional golfers are from Korea. That culture supports the self-sacrifice needed for elite status.

While it may be a generalization, Asia is more introverted than Europe or the United States. There is an inversion of values between China and the United States. A shy, sensitive child would be valued in China, and sought as a leader, while the same child might be ignored in the United States.

ESSENTIAL

Dreaded or difficult situations for introverts include brainstorming sessions, mandatory teamwork, open-office plans, parties, formal occasions, the first day of school, public speaking, business networking events, job interviews, conversations around the water cooler, and the meet-and-greet at church.

Older Chinese children prefer friends who are humble, hardworking, and honest, while their American counterparts go for cheerful, enthusiastic, and sociable. Susan Cain quotes writer, Michael Harris Bond, a cross-cultural psychologist who focuses on China: "The Americans emphasize sociability and prize those attributes that make for easy, cheerful association. The Chinese emphasize deeper attributes, focusing on moral virtues and achievement."

The Buddha encouraged his followers to say not only what was true, but also what was beneficial. Speech had to be relevant, and he discouraged gossip, idle chitchat, and speaking for the sake of speaking. Perhaps this influence can be seen in the cultural differences that prevail today between East and West. Today in America, the emphasis is on how something is said and not on the content of that message. Without charisma, it may be difficult to get your message heard, no matter how valuable it is. It is hard to be promoted in the business world unless you can self-promote and exude confidence. If you are a culturally quiet Asian, for instance, you may find it hard to ascend the corporate ladder.

CHAPTER 6

The Introvert Mind

Introverts think differently. Their brains process information in distinctive ways. When compared to extroverts, introverts are not smarter in the conventional way that intelligence is defined. However, they can thrive in situations that suit their predilections, and they can suffer in circumstances that don't. Introverts are more concerned with mind. They have been and continue to be philosophers, scientists, and thinkers. They are at home in their minds and also run the risk of being "in their heads" too much—prone to worry, obsession, and rumination.

Cognitive Styles

Introverts are not smarter than extroverts. They have the same range of IQs, but they perform better in academic settings once past elementary school. Introverts process information differently. You may find that it takes time to respond to something. You absorb it and think about it before you respond. Extroverts can speak more rapidly because they are processing information quickly—it's all right there for them, while you may have to reach. You may need to be prompted (you are better at recognition than recall memory), and because of this it takes you more time to come up with something to say. You don't just blurt out what comes to mind because there may be nothing there (yet)! It takes time for words to emerge.

Introverts are careful thinkers. They also receive a majority of advanced degrees and academic awards such as Phi Beta Kappa. They are better at critical thinking and solving problems that require insight. Extroverts tend to prefer speed to accuracy and are more likely to give up when a problem becomes difficult. Introverts look before they leap, consider the problem at hand more thoroughly, and persist longer. Experiments show their work to be more accurate. Introverts may have more persistence at difficult tasks and are more likely to inspect a problem carefully before acting on it, leading to higher success in solving problems.

QUOTE

"My anxiety was not about the pressure to socialize. I became anxious because I couldn't *think*, and, without my own mind, I felt like I was disintegrating."—Laurie Helgoe

Go Deep or Go Home

The Myers-Briggs Manual from 2003 says, "Introverts appear to do their best thinking in anticipation rather than on the spot. It *now seems clear* that this is because their minds are so naturally abuzz with activity that they need to shut out external distractions in order to prepare their ideas." Introverts like to incubate ideas rather than to process and express them quickly. They are more like curators—collecting, organizing, and appreciating ideas. Extroverts are more like publicists—expressing in colorful, energetic tones.

Image credit: Michaela Chung, Introvert Spring (*www.introvertspring.com*)

As an introvert, you probably prefer to focus on one or two things at a time and really delve in. Your power is concentration and persistence. You'd rather go deep than broad. You run counter to the multitasking craze, which is really not more efficient for anyone, whether they are introverts or extroverts (although extroverts may enjoy it more). Slow, diligent, and attentive effort is not as glamorous as the buzz of the extrovert, but it gets things done. The culture tends to ignore the toil in the background. You may overlook the value of this effort, too. "No big deal," you may think. Most of what you get done, however, happens in this deliberate fashion.

Rumination

The human mind has two modes of operation—the default mode network (DMN) and an experiential mode. As the name suggests, you are most often in the default mode. DMN thoughts are self-referential. You are the star of stories that anticipate the future, remember the past, and generate opinions about what is happening in the present. The alternative to the DMN is paying attention to your senses and what is happening in the present moment without commentary (that is, self-talk). A painful version of the DMN is rumination. Here the stories are tinged with anxiety. They repeat, reproach, and recriminate. They generate stress.

QUOTE

"Stress is basically a disconnection from the earth, a forgetting of the breath. Stress is an ignorant state. It believes that everything is an emergency. Nothing is that important. Just lie down."—Natalie Goldberg

As an introvert, you have ready access to the interior of your mind. This can lead to contemplation and creativity or self-criticism and doubt. Being oriented toward the interior is a double-edged sword. If you are not careful, you may cut yourself on rumination. If you find your thoughts running to this negative place, you can use your enhanced introspection to redirect attention to a more neutral place. One rubric is to shift from the painful story to the sensations in the body. You can also monitor what you say to yourself. Instead of saying, "This is awful, why is this happening to me?" you can say, "This is happening." This latter statement is factual and neutral and devoid of that sense of "me" that becomes the core of the painful story.

Social Cognition

A 2011 study conducted by Inna Fishman, Rowena Ng, and Ursula Bellugi of the Salk Institute-Laboratory for Cognitive Neuroscience examined the question: "Do Extraverts Process Social Stimuli Differently from Introverts?" To define introversion, they cite old sources and perpetuate the biased (and inaccurate) view of introversion: "Extraversion, a fundamental personality dimension, captures the social aspect of personality. Extraverts have a preference for seeking, engaging in, and enjoying social interactions, whereas introverts prefer to avoid social situations and tend to be reserved, withdrawn, or shy in social settings."

Faces and Flowers

Other neuroscience studies have shown differences in the ways that introvert and extrovert brains process information, especially in their sensitivity to the neurotransmitter dopamine. This study showed that the most extroverted of the twenty-eight adult subjects allocated more attention to faces in a perception task. They assumed that faces are more important and motivating for people who score higher in extroversion. This study, as well as every study that relies on the NEO PI (Neuroticism-Extraversion-Openness to Experience Personality Inventory; a popular assessment of extroversion and other basic personality traits), is biased against introversion. It defines introversion in the negative—as an absence of extroversion that does not measure or capture the more socially *selective* nature of introverts. In this study, people who scored high in extroversion reacted more quickly to faces. These reactions are measured in milliseconds and are therefore unconscious. The researchers concluded, "Overall, these results suggest that the sociability characterizing extraverts, including enjoyment of social activities and preference for social interactions over being alone, might be associated with enhanced processing of social stimuli, likely due to a heightened intrinsic psychological significance that such stimuli carry for extraverts." Introverts just don't seem to care (as much).

This conclusion seems like a stretch. Again, the differences are measured in milliseconds so the extroverts' "superior" response is only a fraction of a fraction of a second. The other key finding is that the introverts did not make a distinction between a picture of a human face and a picture of a flower, that is, they were not surprised by the sudden appearance of a human face. Extroverts did make this distinction between the flower and the human face. Does this mean that introverts (or, again, people who measure low in extroversion) are unconcerned with social phenomena?

In an interview with *LiveScience* (*www.livescience.com*) the lead investigator of the study, Fishman, said, "[This] supports the claim that introverts, or their brains, might be indifferent to people—they can take them or leave them, so to speak. The introvert's brain treats interactions with people the same way it treats encounters with other, nonhuman information, such as inanimate objects for example."

FACT

A 2000 study by Richard Lucas and Ed Diener published in the *Journal of Personality and Social Psychology* found that extroverts were not more sociable than introverts (both spent the same amount of time in social situations). However, extroverts were more "reward-seeking" in those social situations. This finding is consistent with other studies that show extroverts are more reward-seeking.

Perhaps the introvert brain (or the brain lacking in extroversion) sees the flower and the human face as equally valuable. Is this a bad thing? The "indifference" indictment supports the erroneous notion that introverts are misanthropic loners. Introverts care about people (and flowers) and express this differently than their extroverted counterparts. It is unfortunate when the science misses this important distinction. Different is not deficient.

Doing Versus Being

The extroverted world emphasizes doing rather than being. Action is what is most valued. There is a cartoon from the *New Yorker* magazine that portrays a man in an old-fashioned elevator. In response to the operator's standard question, the man says, "Neither up nor down, I'm good here." The cartoon is funny because that response is so unexpected. He must want to *go* somewhere. He must have *something* to do. Yet, he is saying that he is content to be where he is. This could be a definition of happiness—not wanting things to be different than they are in this moment. If you don't want to add or subtract anything from what you are experiencing, then you are naturally in a place of contentment.

The Eight Senses of Now

The alternative to incessant doing is to pay attention to your senses. Neuroscientist Dan Siegel identifies eight senses. The first five are the standard senses: seeing, hearing, touching, smelling, and tasting. He then identifies "interoception" as the sixth sense. Interoception is attention to the internal processes of the body—feeling all the sensations that are present. The seventh sense focuses on the internal subjective mental processes of thinking, images, and emotions. The seventh sense notices process not content.

Here, you become aware that thoughts, memories, and fantasies are present without getting caught up in their particular storylines. The eighth sense connects you to people and the environment around you. It is the sense of you in relationship to the rest of the world. When you shift your attention from the task at hand to the world around, you are embracing the Beginner's Mind—being open to what is happening without preconception. When you let go of the storytelling, you can come in contact with what is actually happening in this moment.

QUOTE

"Tocqueville saw that the life of constant action and decision which was entailed by the democratic and businesslike character of American life put a premium upon rough and ready habits of mind, quick decision, and the prompt seizure of opportunity—and that all this activity was not propitious for deliberation, elaboration, or precision in thought."—Richard Hofstadter

The introvert's comfort with the interior is a natural fit for tapping into being versus doing. You are probably already inclined toward less doing and more observation. Paying attention to your eight senses brings you into mindful awareness of the world—inside and out.

Energy Patterns

Do you have the time? The time to think; the time to be? If you have the time, do you have the energy to make the most of it? The hectic pace of life can squeeze time and energy. If you don't have time to reflect, your energy will be drained. If your energy is drained, it is hard to hold the space of quiet you need for the Introvert Edge. America is chronically sleep deprived and it is clear that good energy is not a top priority. If you don't value energy, everything else will deteriorate. If you are constantly doing things in the desperate pursuit to cross things off your to-do list, there may be no time and no energy to just *be*. This is a fast-food culture. Time is money. Much of life is geared toward maximizing efficiency. Contemplation is not valued. Creativity is not valued (unless that is your job). The quest to do it and to do it fast is how the extroverted world works.

Creating Time with Energy

If introverts ran the country, you would see a lot of differences. Life would be deliberate instead of pressured. You would have the time to think, pause, and reflect. You would see less fast food. You would see value placed on the interior, sanctuary, and retreat. You would see more containment than spontaneous expression. You would see more attunement with nature rather than domination over it. When things get quiet, you can access your mind and connect to creative energies. When you take care of yourself and nurture your solitude, you will have the energy to make the most of time. It is hard to find the solace of silence. The daily melee of the extrovert circus makes it hard to stop and think—to just be without doing—something (of course, you are always doing something even it is just paying attention to the process of being alive).

ESSENTIAL

If you are an introvert driving in loud, chaotic, overstimulating traffic, pay extra close attention, because these conditions can impair your thinking and performance. If you are an extrovert or an introvert driving with sleep deprivation, be sure to increase your level of stimulation by listening to loud music, opening the window, or drinking coffee.

When your energy is depleted it will be hard to think. It is possible that you have spent much of your life in an overloaded state, not functioning with optimum energy. Your thinking may be fuzzy, vague, and blank. You may underestimate your intelligence. It may be hard for you to have perspective on your intellectual gifts because your brain is overstimulated much of the time. You need time to think and good energy to support that thinking.

The Importance of Retreat

For those who call New York City home, Vermont is a popular retreat spot. There are only 600,000 people in the entire state—about the number you would find in a medium-size city, such as Boston. There are many spiritual and secular places you can go. One retreat spot is Claudia's Cabins near Stowe, Vermont. Here you can rent a log cabin, set back in the woods. You can enjoy the silence of the days undisturbed by traffic, human noise, and commotion. You can enjoy the swaying pines, the brilliant stars, and the cool nights. You can pick vegetables out of the garden and wild flowers from the vast meadow that looks out over the mountains.

Meditation Retreats

Introverts need retreat. The Kripalu Center for Yoga and Health (*www .Kripalu.org*) has a program called Retreat and Renewal. You can go anytime to its beautiful Berkshire Mountain campus and meditate, practice yoga, take walks in the labyrinth, swim in the lake, eat wholesome food in silence or in conversation, dance, or just sit on the patio and take in the view of the mountains. As the name suggests, retreat leads to renewal. This is especially important for introverts. As you move through your days, your energy is tapped by being a pseudo-extrovert at work or at home. Energy is going out and needs to come back in.

Another form of refuge is the formal meditation retreat. You can go, for example, to the Insight Meditation Society (IMS), in Barre, Massachusetts (*www.Dharma.org*). Here you can explore your experience in noble silence—no talking, reading, or writing for the duration of the retreat. A common interval is ten days of doing sitting and walking meditation—in silence. For a respite that combines thinking and silence, you can visit the Barre Center for Buddhist Studies in Barre, Massachusetts (*www.bcbsdharma .org*). Here you can take three- and five-day workshops on the teachings of the Buddha, in a beautiful rustic farmhouse that sits on peaceful, secluded grounds. A directory of retreat centers can be found at retreatfinder.com and findthedivine.com. An international listing of Buddhist-style retreat centers can be found at Inquiring Mind (*www.inquiringmind.com*).

You are probably overdue for a retreat right now. It is common practice to have a daily meditation or yoga practice that is punctuated with regular retreats. Some people go away on ten-day retreats each calendar year. This can be a formal retreat like the ones at IMS, or a self-directed retreat at a place like Claudia's Cabins. Retreats are valuable as routine maintenance, and anytime you need a "tune-up." The retreat environment is way to reconnect with your introvert power. It is the ideal place to sharpen your Introvert Edge. You come back to your daily life sharp, crisp, and, clear.

Finding the Time: Micro-Retreats

You may protest, "This all sounds great, but I don't have the time to go away on retreat." You may have to examine your priorities. Can you elevate self-care to the top of the to-do list? To take care of yourself, you may need to re-engineer your daily life. You may need to recruit support from loved ones for child care and so forth. Some places like IMS have family retreats. Can this be your next vacation? If a retreat is impractical at this time, you can consider a home-based micro-retreat.

In the classic *Miracle of Mindfulness*, venerable mindfulness teacher Thich Nhat Hanh recommends taking time each week to be silent and mindful. You can do this at home, preferably when the house is empty and you are less likely to get disturbed. For a designated period of time, go on a media fast. Turn off your television, phone, and iPod. Slow things down and give your full attention to each task that you do, from taking a shower to washing the dishes to eating your meals. You can also engage in formal sitting and walking meditation. Even if you can only carve out an hour per week, you can restore some energy.

Another example of micro-retreat is what Julia Cameron, author of *The Artist's Way*, calls the "Artist Date." Here you take yourself out at least once per week to do something that fills your creative well. You do this activity alone, and it could be anything from a walk in the woods to an art gallery visit.

Retreat in This Very Moment

The present moment is another place you can retreat. There is a meditation practice called The Three-Minute Breathing Space that can be found in the book, *The Mindful Way Through Depression*. With this meditation, the first minute you observe what is happening in mind and body and the environment around you. The second minute you bring your attention to the process of your breathing. The third minute you open that attention to include your entire body. Can you find three minutes to do this practice? Attention to breathing is beneficial for three reasons. The first is that it is portable and you can't forget to bring it with you. You can have a micro-retreat in any moment. Second, breathing is happening right now in the body. The present moment is a place to take respite from thinking, stress, and other pressures. Third, each breath you take is colored by your current emotional state. By connecting with your breathing for these three-minute intervals, you can acquaint yourself with your emotional life and keep your finger on the pulse of your feelings. This can lead to greater emotional intelligence.

While it is easier to enjoy a retreat in a protected environment, you can have a retreat right in the middle of a noisy city. The principles are the same as the secluded retreat—give your full attention to the tasks at hand and set aside your technology (even a book is technology). Unplug and just be in the world. Whether it is quiet and filled with the sounds of nature or is bustling with people, vehicles, and noise, give it your full attention. The more crowded the city, the more anonymous you can be. Take the time to make the time.

CHAPTER 7

Emotional Intelligence

Long neglected as trivial, inferior, or superfluous, emotions are now once again the subject of serious research. There is a growing recognition that children need to be taught emotional skills early in life to be fully functioning human beings in adulthood. Adults need emotional intelligence to navigate the challenges of work, relationships, and life. Introverts have a natural connection to emotional intelligence because they are more focused on the interior where emotions reside.

Understanding Emotional Intelligence

Emotional intelligence (EI) has become a cultural buzzword since the release of Daniel Goleman's bestselling book, *Emotional Intelligence*. This book helped to put emotions back on the map and to make them a legitimate subject matter for research. EI overlaps with the Big Five personality traits, in particular neuroticism and extroversion, but can also refer to concepts such as zeal, self-esteem, and self-control. Researchers John D. Mayer and Peter Salovey developed the original theory of emotional intelligence. According to them, EI was defined as the "ability to engage in sophisticated information processing about one's own and others' emotions and the ability to use this information as a guide to thinking and behavior. That is, individuals high in EI pay attention to, use, understand, and manage emotions, and these skills serve adaptive functions that potentially benefit themselves and others."

FACT

The Four-Branch Model of Emotional Intelligence (EI) by Mayer, Salovey, and Caruso includes: (1) perceiving emotions accurately in oneself and others; (2) using emotions to facilitate thinking; (3) understanding emotions, emotional language, and the signals conveyed by emotions; (4) managing emotions so as to attain specific goals.

As you can see from this definition, EI is the capacity to reason about, and with, your emotions. The neuroscientist Antonio Damasio, in books such as *The Feeling of What Happens* and *Descartes' Error: Emotion, Reason, and the Human Brain*, makes it clear that reason *requires* emotion. This runs counter to centuries of thinking that saw reason and emotion as separate processes. Reason was valued because it was essentially human. Emotions were devalued because they were essentially animalistic. What Descartes and others missed until recently is how reason depends on the proper functioning of emotional systems in the brain. The more connected with and informed by your emotions you are, the more intelligent you will be.

Introversion and Multiple Intelligences

Howard Gardner popularized the theory of multiple intelligences in the 1980s. He encouraged the educational world to think of intelligence more broadly, beyond the verbal and math skills that comprise the standard IQ test. The full range of intelligences includes: musical, body-kinesthetic, logical-mathematical, linguistic, spatial, interpersonal, and intrapersonal. Intrapersonal intelligence is closest to emotional intelligence. According to Gardner in his groundbreaking book, *Multiple Intelligences: New Horizons in Theory and Practice*, intrapersonal intelligence is "knowledge of internal aspects of a person: access to one's feeling life, one's range of emotions, the capacity to make discriminations among these emotions and eventually to label them and to draw on them as a means of understanding and guiding one's behavior."

QUOTE

"Because I rant not, neither rave of what I feel, can you be so shallow as to dream that I feel nothing?"—R. D. Blackmore

Do introverts have the edge with emotional intelligence? One of the features of emotional intelligence is skill with the information coming from feelings. Introverts are more familiar with the interior because they spend more time there. They are oriented to the inner world. Introverts heed Socrates's admonition: *know thyself.* Introverts are less "busy" doing things and have more time, inclination, and skill to focus on this internal information. Extroverts may just be too busy to bother looking inside.

Listening: The Foundation of Presence

A popular adage advises that you have two ears and one mouth and you should use them in that ratio. The extroverted society is devoted to talking. You don't see many reality TV programs where the participants meditate and talk quietly—how boring! One exception is the HBO series *Enlightened*, starring Laura Dern, who portrays a corporate type named Amy Jellicoe. She has a nervous breakdown, goes to rehab, and discovers yoga and meditation. She attempts to bring these practices back to the office with humorous results.

When was the last time you felt someone really listened to you? Not just heard you but also actually listened? Listening requires interest and interest requires presence. In the moment, you have to relinquish your own agenda so that you can attend to the person you are talking with. Introverts are well suited to this task because they are great observers. You'd rather listen than talk in most instances. You are more likely to let the words sink in rather than blurt out a reply.

QUOTE

"Fish held the silence for so long that I had to restrain myself from prodding her. That's never a good idea. Sometimes people hesitate because they don't have the courage to come out with whatever needs to be said; other times they desperately want to speak but can't find the words. Jabbing them prematurely tends to shut them up. Outwaiting them gives them the time to say more than they intend."
—Adam-Troy Castro

Sophia Dembling, author of *The Introvert's Way: Living a Quiet Life in a Noisy World*, speaks to the perils of being a good listener. "Something about me attracts people with a lot to say. Introverts tend to be excellent listeners. I'm certainly better at listening to chatter than producing it and I'm bumfuzzled by people I see in cars, on streets, at the supermarket, nattering away on their cell phones. What do they find to talk about so long and enthusiastically? I say what needs saying—usually a sentence or two—and then stop. Sometimes I lose interest in what I'm saying midway through a sentence and stop there (to my husband's irritation). Introverts' listening skills can serve us well, and I am proud of mine. But one reason listening can be exhausting for us is that we pay attention. We listen hard."

Being Loud Is Not Necessarily Being Smart

Extroverts are perceived as being more intelligent because they are more forceful, confident, and articulate when it comes to expressing their opinions. Being loud is not the same as being smart or being right. A loud voice can promote groupthink more than considered critical analysis. Loud is valued in this culture. Participation is expected in school and the quiet voices may get overlooked.

Patience is your edge as an introvert. You can absorb information, process it, and formulate an articulate response. Your extroverted counterparts may dominate airspace, but in situations where everyone has a chance to be heard—loudest will not necessarily be best. Your intelligence resides in your thoughtfulness, your deep consideration of issues, and your ability to work an issue through. Concentration and the presence of mind to persist and process is your Introvert Edge.

Listening Within: The Key to Wanting

Listening to yourself is the key to happiness. The purpose for animals', including human animals', feelings is to guide them in making important decisions. They approach things that feel good (like food and sex, which help organisms to survive and reproduce). They avoid things that feel bad (potential threats). They ignore things that are neutral (after all, they've got better things to do with their energy than waste it on irrelevant details).

These three comprise the basic feeling matrix: pleasant, unpleasant, and neutral. In any given moment, your body is registering a feeling tone, one that will probably be more nuanced than the basic three. This feeling is information on how you might proceed in the moment. For example, you are out to dinner and reviewing the menu. How do you choose what to eat? You can think about it: "I had chicken for lunch so I shouldn't order chicken for dinner." But what if you really *want* chicken? If you can pay attention to your body, you will get a *feeling* for some of the items on the menu. Feelings reveal your wanting in that moment better than shoulds.

To benefit from this information, you have to turn attention within—a tendency you already have as an introvert. You have to trust your instincts. There are many situations far weightier than what to order for dinner and for which you will have incomplete information. "Should I marry Sally?" "Which job should I take?" "Where should I go to school?" "Whom should I vote for?" Your feelings are a rich treasure trove of information. Listening to your body is the gateway to this bounty. Dr. Brown clarifies, "Real people have to decide quickly and without much knowledge whether to do things such as sell their stocks, buy earthquake insurance, divorce their spouse, proceed with a dangerous cancer treatment, punish or praise their children, lie to the IRS, or vote for Pat Buchanan. Even if it were possible in principle to make such decisions with absolute certainty, which it is not, real people could not wait around for certainty to be attained. They have to act, and they do so on the basis of their feelings."

Gut Feelings

Bestselling author Malcolm Gladwell documents many such instances of responding to feelings in his book *Blink*. One example he provides is the detection of a well-executed sculpture forgery. When the experts saw the statue, they knew there was something "off" about it, although they could not say what. Their bodies *told* them, via unconscious hunches, the information they needed to detect the fraud.

To get the most access to your inner feeling life, you need to disable your internal critic, or the censor that seeks to curtail, suppress, and inject doubt into thoughts, feelings, and actions. There are many ways to nurture access to feelings and to circumnavigate the censor. Meditation and journaling are two important ones. By meditating, you pay explicit attention to the energy of feelings that are present in the body and notice how they change moment by moment. Journaling is the practice of private writing that is not edited or censored. By journaling, you practice hearing yourself think on paper and this allows you to access your internal treasures from a narrative perspective

Compassion and Empathy

The ability to sit still can nurture compassion and empathy. In fact, sitting still and listening is a prerequisite. As an introvert, you already have these skills. You may find the extrovert's tendency to dominate conversations to be the opposite of empathic. Your Introvert Edge can be seen in how attuned you are to the person you are with. Attunement requires receptiveness to what is happening in the moment. Many introverts go into fields where empathy skills are required—like counseling. It's a natural fit.

QUOTE

"How intense can be the longing to escape from the emptiness and dullness of human verbosity, to take refuge in nature, apparently so inarticulate, or in the wordlessness of long, grinding labor, of sound sleep, of true music, or of a human understanding rendered speechless by emotion!"—Boris Pasternak

Listening to others is the gateway to compassionate communication. Listening fosters presence and to be present with another person is a powerful experience. Meditation teacher and author Sharon Salzberg said: "The simple act of being completely present to another person is truly an act of love."

As an introvert, you are more inclined to listen than your extroverted counterparts. The challenge for you is the noise that may come from your own mind. Your storytelling mind can run interference and cut you off from being present with another (and even yourself). Quieting your internal dialogue can open you to the moment where you can receive what is being said and demonstrate that you are right there with that person. They *will* notice your presence, even if they are doing all the talking.

Overcoming Fear: Lessons from *The Fear Project*

Surfer and journalist Jaimal Yogis has explored different dimensions of fear in his book, *The Fear Project*. This book combines memoir, interviews, and scientific review to provide a liberating outlook on fear. Extroverts are naturally wired to be less fearful. They seek out thrills and stimulation while introverts are naturally wired to be more cautious.

ESSENTIAL

Jaimal Yogis is the author of *Saltwater Buddha: A Surfer's Quest to Find Zen on the Sea*, and he's featured in the documentary film, *Saltwater Buddha*. Jaimal says, "I really didn't find some ultimate truth, I did find something, I think, in the water. It's the water we all came from. The water that binds us. The water that gives us life."

Jaimal reminds us that "much as we like to make it into the villain, fear isn't bad. In fact, it's often our fear of fear—our aversion to accepting and understanding this very natural emotion—that can cause fear to spin into unhelpful panic and anxiety disorders." How can you befriend fear? An important dimension of having a better relationship with fear, stress, and anxiety is to understand how they manifest. You can notice fear as a sensation in your body—a changing set of physical energies. In a sense, that is all they are—just electrochemical reactions in the body. Of course, these sensations are linked to a story—a reason why you are afraid, even if that reason is not having a clue. The story holds the "fear of fear" dimension. For example, you have had an argument with your spouse. The storyline is a fear that this disagreement is going to escalate into something worse. The mind runs wild with catastrophic scenes, all of which are highly unlikely. Your job is to redirect your attention away from the story to what is happening in your body. There is just that energy in your body and it will eventually dissipate when you are not proliferating that unrealistic story.

Mindfulness and Fear

Mindfulness can help you to attend to the sensations in your body. You can seek to identify where in the body they are occurring, what pattern of movement you can detect, and anything else related to their physicality. When you are paying attention to your body, you are not paying attention to the story. This migration of attention helps you to get out of the painful emotions the story brings.

Extroverts thrive on the energy of fear, anxiety, and stress—the very same emotions that feel overwhelming to you. If you tend to avoid activities that stimulate anxiety, then your reactivity may only get worse in the future. Physical activity like exercise can make your body more comfortable with the sensations that might arise with fear, like rapid heartbeat and sweating. The combination of mindfulness and exercise can be a potent antidote to fear.

Jaimal laments, "We now live longer and more pain free than at any other time in history. According to the World Bank's most recent data, even in the developing world, humans are healthier than ever before. We are also richer than ever before and, according to *Foreign Policy* magazine, the world is more peaceful right now than at any time in the last century. But if you look at the statistics on anxiety disorders, watch the news, or check in with your stress thermostat on any given day, it seems that we're more scared than ever." Anxiety disorders affect introverts and extroverts alike. The fearlessness of the extrovert and the thoughtfulness of the introvert can be a potent combination for managing fear. When you can develop your inner extrovert's boldness and keep your introvert's introspectiveness away from rumination, you can reclaim your life from stress, anxiety, and fear.

The Introvert Advantage: Handling Reward

Extroverts are more likely to be reward-seeking—driven by the pleasure center of the brain. Introverts are more likely to be circumspect, disciplined, and plan driven. In other words, extroverts need to seek excitement to feel good, while introverts can feel good with lower levels of stimulation. Extroverts seek that high, because their brains are less stimulated than introvert brains. Extroverts are driven by the pursuit of this high—making them more successful, and more vulnerable to risks gone bad. They like to do things that have a big thrill payoff—adventures that involve risk, such as gambling, gravity sports, and sexual conquests.

Dopamine is the neurotransmitter associated with reward, and extroverts are less sensitive to it—meaning they need more of it (along with adrenaline too for an added boost). Introverts need less external stimulation than extroverts because the internal milieu of the brain is already very stimulated. It will be the extrovert that seeks that dopamine rush that comes from thrill-seeking, risky behaviors. Evolutionary psychologists such as Daniel Nettle have documented the risks of extraversion and sensation-seeking. These include being hospitalized due to accident or illness, traumatic injury, criminal and antisocial behavior, and being arrested. They are also more likely to have affairs and remarry. For introverts, life may seem, from the outside, to be less exciting, but it is safe from most of the pitfalls of impulsiveness. Think about it this way, an introvert may be happily stimulated gazing at the moon while the extrovert wants to get in a rocket ship and fly to the moon to get that same level of happy stimulation. Humanity needs a combination of both circumspection and reaching beyond the familiar.

QUESTION

What are the parts of the brain that are innervated with dopamine and responsible for response to rewards?
Ventral striatum, amygdala, and the medial prefrontal cortex.

Introverts are less likely to take financial risks and more likely to perform better at gambling games that involve complex decision making. One study found that top-performing investment bankers were emotionally stable introverts. The key may be delay of gratification. Delay of gratification, patience, and foresight are all qualities of emotional intelligence.

Risk: Reward and Disaster

The intoxicating promise of risk taking and reward seems to be responsible for the great financial collapse of 2008. Extroverts dominate the culture of Wall Street, and introvert opinions may not have been heeded in the reckless exuberance of risk-taking leading up to the financial meltdown and the global financial catastrophe that followed. Charisma, influence, and risk taking combined to create a perfect storm with explosive consequences. Now, perhaps, you are not feeling so bad about being an introvert?

Reward seeking is not only an interesting feature of extroversion; it may be what makes an extrovert an extrovert. Extroverts, in other words, are characterized by their tendency to seek rewards, from top dog status to sexual highs to cold cash. They've been found to have greater economic, political, and hedonistic ambitions than introverts; even their sociability is a function of reward seeking, according to this view—extroverts socialize because brief hits of human connection are inherently gratifying.

Chris Cooper (cited in *Quiet*) has done studies on introverts and extroverts. He has found that introverts are "geared to inspect" and therefore make fewer errors in experimental tasks than impulsive extroverts who are "geared to respond." When introverts make a mistake, they slow down, when extroverts make a mistake they speed up—making them more prone to further mistakes, but also further opportunities.

Introverts are more circumspect, controlled, and thoughtful. Excitement means different things for the introvert and extrovert. For the extrovert, excitement means: "More of that!" For the introvert, excitement means: "Whoa Nellie. What is actually going on here?" It's the difference between being propelled forward and being sparked into vigilance. It's a different take on opportunity. Extroverts seek the reward. Introverts inquire for potential danger. Extroverts floor it, and introverts hit the brakes.

The Introvert Disadvantage

As an introvert, you may take things to heart and feel them more intensely. You may take things more personally, which can lead to brooding, self-reproach, and rumination—all of which can lead to a sense of being overwhelmed. Becoming intimate with how your mind works is an important first step. You don't try to change its sensitivity but bring awareness to it. You don't apologize for it; you embrace it—the source of your strength—but it has a downside. You can get engulfed in thoughts. Mindfulness helps to bring awareness to your internal mental processes with an open, curious attention.

When you notice you are beating yourself up—STOP. This is a popular mindfulness technique presented by Bob Stahl and Elisha Goldstein in their practical *Mindfulness-Based Stress Reduction Workbook*. *S* stands for "stop." Stop what you are doing, most likely an internal conversation. *T* stands for "take a breath." Pause and bring your attention to breath—one cycle of the in breath and out breath. *O* stands for "observe" what is happening in the body and the mind. Occupy your body. Feel the sensations within. *P* stands for "proceed" with whatever is the best way to take care of yourself in the moment. The STOP technique is a balm for rumination.

Talking Back to Fear

Mindfulness practice can be helpful in conjunction with journaling or writing practice. Taking your thoughts from the deep interior of your mind and externalizing them on paper helps to create a safe distance to view them. When your internal dialogue is going rogue, you can make an executive decision to address the fears. Most of what comprises rumination is based on protectiveness. Ask yourself, "What am I trying to defend myself against?" Chances are the perceived threat is just that—perceived. It may be based on biased or distorted information. It may be exaggerated. Try to put it in context. Try to let it go.

Your primitive emotional brain may be trying to hijack you into fear. You can talk back to the fear—to the part of your brain responsible for registering that fear (a tiny structure called the amygdala). If you personalize the threat, it will loom larger. If you say, "Why is the happening to me?" the emphasis on "me" will exaggerate the emotion. If, instead, you say, "This is happening," the statement is neutral, descriptive, and matter of fact. No cause for alarm. Just something happening in this moment. Can you embrace it?

Don't Beat Yourself Up

If you have a habit of treating yourself harshly, you may want to consider kindness. Think of the loving attention you give your pets, your friends, and random anguished strangers. Why not give this same loving attention to yourself? In the Buddhist traditions, this attention is known as loving-kindness. It is a forgiving and compassionate intention. Don't own everything. You are not responsible for the well-being of the entire world. Of course, you may be concerned for the whole world and that is part of your strength. Care for others rests on the foundation of care for self. It's like the safety drill on an airplane—put your oxygen mask on first before you assist others.

QUOTE

"Sometimes the most important thing in a whole day is the rest we take between two deep breaths."—Etty Hillesum

As an introvert, you may also be too self-reliant at times. Pay attention to this tendency and recognize when it might be time to reach out to a trusted, safe, and available friend. It's easy to get caught up in a web of stories and swept away by the emotions of these imagined scenarios. Not every thought is a veridical account of reality. Even though you are more accustomed to the interior, it can be helpful to get an outside perspective. Let that perspective in when it is right.

You may need a change of scenery—get out and move. Do some yoga or qigong or take a brisk walk around the block. Unplug from your technology and your internal dialogue. Move from thinking mode to experiencing mode and engage with something that involves movement, playfulness, or pleasurable sensing like listening to music, looking at art, getting a massage, or eating a special treat.

CHAPTER 8

Happiness

Happiness is an elusive obsession. Everyone wants to be happy. It is often considered the goal of life. For humans, the pursuit of happiness is a complicated affair. Other animals seem to be happy with the basic necessities. Dogs are happy with food and a master. Add a little play and they will be *very* happy. Many humans are unhappy in the midst of astounding abundance—the downside of having such big brains. Do introverts have an edge with happiness?

What Is Happiness?

For most of its first century, the field of psychology focused on problems—the disorders of the mind. It wasn't until recently that the field of positive psychology was founded. Positive psychology focuses on what's right about people instead of what's wrong. It investigates topics like resilience, motivation, and, yes, happiness.

One of the founders of positive psychology is Martin Seligman. Years ago, Dr. Seligman did important experiments on learned helplessness and developed a model of human depression. In these experiments, animals were subjected to an unpleasant situation from which they could not escape. Later, when they were able to escape (the physical obstacle was removed), they did not take advantage of their newfound freedom. They stayed and continued to experience the unpleasant sensations. Humans can get stuck in the same mode of helplessness. Seligman thought if he could figure out how depressed people behaved, he could figure out how happy people behaved, too.

The Five Pillars of Well-Being

Seligman's latest book, *Flourishing: A Visionary New Understanding of Happiness and Well-Being*, outlines the five pillars of positive psychology. These are arranged with the acronym PERMA: positive emotions, engagement, relationships, meaning, and accomplishment.

ESSENTIAL

According to the Positive Psychology Center at the University of Pennsylvania, positive psychology is: "The scientific study of the strengths and virtues that enable individuals and communities to thrive. The field is founded on the belief that people want to lead meaningful and fulfilling lives, to cultivate what is best within themselves, and to enhance their experiences of love, work, and play."

This model does not focus exclusively on being positive and avoids the trap of the "cult of optimism." Seligman cautions, "I detest the word *happiness*, which is so overused it has become almost meaningless."

There is no one solution for happiness. There is no quick fix, either. To be happy you need to experience positive emotions (at least some of the time but without trying so hard to have them). The first pillar of PERMA is positive emotions, and these positive emotions can be the high-intensity kind—joy, enthusiasm, ecstasy—or the low-intensity type—tranquility, peace, calm. It would be difficult to have a definition of thriving that did not include the low-arousal emotions, but many researchers seem to leave these out. A more inclusive definition of positive emotions doesn't mean everything has to go well. It doesn't mean you have to court unbridled optimism. Stoicism was an ancient Greek philosophy that emphasized the perception of situations rather than the situations themselves. If you can, as the Stoics taught, embrace your circumstances with wisdom, detachment, and resolve, you can find contentment in the midst of any situation (the Buddha, by the way, taught a very similar thing).

Engagement is the next pillar of PERMA and is very similar to the concept of mindfulness. To be engaged is to be fully present with the activity at hand. When you are engaged, you are giving your full attention to whatever you are doing. Your self-conscious internal dialogue drops away and you are just with the experience of the moment. It is important to spend time out of your head and in the body—the senses, movement, and being. Engagement naturally gives rise to the low-arousal positive emotions, perhaps even some high-arousal ones like joy. Indeed, it is self-consciousness that often stands between you and delight.

Meaning is the third pillar. Here, Seligman rotates the lens to focus on others. To live a meaningful life is to expand your scope of concern beyond yourself to something larger. This inevitably takes the form of serving others in some way through your work, volunteerism, or caring. Seligman's earlier efforts articulating the vision of positive psychology stopped with these three: positivity, engagement, and meaning (as developed in his book *Authentic Happiness*). However, something was missing from that vision, and thus, another two pillars were included. His emphasis has shifted from happiness to well-being—a slightly different concept. To strive for happiness can be a trap. If the focus is on well-being, instead, there is more latitude.

You don't have to be relentlessly happy in the way that the extrovert society says you should be happy. It is similar to the difference between curing and healing. People want to be cured of diseases and in some cases this is possible. Some cancers are curable. Once you are diagnosed, you undergo surgery, chemotherapy, and radiation. After a period of remission, you may be declared, "cured." Chronic diseases such as rheumatoid arthritis cannot be cured. What now? Your best bet is to heal—to become whole by accepting your illness, adapting to it, and not defining your happiness as the absence of it. In other words, you can have the disease and still have well-being when you can bring an accepting attitude to it.

Relationships that are healthy, nurturing, and positive are another pillar of PERMA. Quality connections to others count most here. The final pillar is accomplishment. A theory of well-being cannot be complete without a place for achievement. Human beings enjoy doing things for their own sake—solving problems, building stuff, and doing things that have never been done before. Achievement can take many forms and does not have to coincide with some preconceived societal norm. If you are that person with rheumatoid arthritis, getting up and making a cup of tea will be an accomplishment. Some activities can hit two or more, even all, of these pillars.

For example, you volunteer for Habit for Humanity. You spend a Saturday building a house. You are engaged in this activity—time flies, you are in flow. You feel good while you are doing it. It's hands-on and you can see what you've accomplished by day's end. You are with other people, helping them, working together. You feel good about contributing and about belonging to this organization whose mission accords with your values. This kind of day fosters durable well-being for introverts and extroverts alike. Turning away from the culture's idea of a meaningful life—buy lots of stuff and have lots of fun—probably gives you a better chance of being happy in the long run.

Whose Happiness?

If happiness is defined narrowly as access to high-arousal positive emotions like enthusiasm, elation, and excitement, then extroverts have the clear advantage. If happiness is broadened to include low-arousal positive emotions like peacefulness, calm, and tranquility, then introverts have the edge. Context is important and culture provides context. Studies show that if you are out of sync with your cultural context—extroverted in the introverted cultures of Asia or introverted in the extroverted culture of America—you may be more prone to depression.

The extroverts' version of happiness is the one that has dominated in this culture. Introverts are just as likely to be happy if low-arousal emotions are included. Extroverts are happier when they are pursuing rewards. Extroverts are more concerned with outcomes and introverts are more focused on process—the destination versus the journey.

FACT

The top ten happiest nations according to the 2013 Better Life Index Survey (which measures all facets of life including "income, education, health, work-life balance and life satisfaction") are: Switzerland, Norway, Iceland, Sweden, Denmark, Netherlands, Austria, Canada, Finland, and Mexico. The United States did not make the top ten.

Being happy all the time is a difficult expectation—and one bound to make you less happy. The extrovert circus can make introverts feel bad for not enjoying the party more. Calm is not deficient in the face of ebullient joy. These are different emotions and different ways of being. It is good to experience both.

Introverts are more open to what Dr. Jon Kabat-Zinn, PhD, called the "full catastrophe" in his bestselling book, *Full Catastrophe Living*. Unrelenting happiness is an ideal—an image created by Hollywood and portrayed in early TV shows like *Father Knows Best* and *Leave It to Beaver*. The reality, though, is that people struggle with the stress of everyday life. They also struggle to find meaning. Coping with stress and the quest to make life meaningful requires access to the entire range of human experience. It invites an open curiosity and even attention to *whatever* is happening now.

The Happiness Industry

Go to your local independent bookstore and look at the psychology/self-help section of books. Whatever the problem, there are books offering *the* solution. The major problem besetting Americans seems to be a lack of self-esteem. This culture is obsessed with happiness yet seems incapable of finding it.

FACT

The self-help industry is estimated to be worth over $10 billion. Books, audio, and video, seminars, motivational speakers, personal coaching, weight-loss, and stress-reduction programs generate this revenue. This does not include self-help work that occurs in the context of psychotherapy and counseling (add tens of billions more).

Oliver Burkeman says in his book *The Antidote: Happiness for People Who Can't Stand Positive Thinking*: "For a civilization so fixated on achieving happiness, we seem remarkably incompetent at the task. Self-help books don't seem to work. Few of the many advantages of modern life seem capable of lifting our collective mood." There are entire industries devoted to the pursuit of happiness. Self-help books sell by the millions and are notorious for not being effective. People keep buying them to find the next great secret to their happiness only to be disappointed.

The Religion of Healthy Mindedness

About a century ago in the classic book *The Varieties of Religious Experience*, William James discussed what is known today as the power of positive thinking and the law of attraction. James talks about people who are likely extroverts, "In many persons, happiness is congenital and irreclaimable. When unhappiness is offered or proposed to them, [they] positively refuse to feel it, as if it were something mean and wrong." Introverts are less likely to perpetrate this self-deception.

The religion of healthy mindedness is an obsession with positivity. Anything negative is seen as self-sabotage and to be avoided at all costs. One must focus only on the positive in order to secure what one wants. Any mishaps that occur are the result of previous poor mental hygiene—negative thinking. This approach is very consistent with the extrovert cultural ideal and perhaps this explains its huge popularity. It is not natural to avoid the negative. Humans are creatures of rhythm. You will naturally have fluctuations in mood, and not all negative feelings are useless. In fact, they can be quite valuable. Beware any New Age philosophy that preaches this extreme. Embrace the middle way between the extremes of militant happiness and lugubrious self-preoccupation.

Embrace the Negative

These so-called mind cures require practitioners to enforce a thought-police state to keep out negative thoughts. James cites the claims made by mind cure theologians: "If your thoughts are of health, youth, vigor, and success, before you know it these things will also be your outward portion. No one can fail of the regenerative influence of optimistic thinking pertinaciously pursued." Such a claim makes the introvert feel alienated—"How come I'm not getting all that good stuff? What's wrong with me?" Nothing is wrong with you! You are not built to eschew the dark. The shadows are a rich source of knowledge, soulfulness, and potential for growth.

FACT

William James is one of the founders of American psychology and he was also a philosopher. He wrote the first textbook of psychology in America: *The Principles of Psychology* in 1890. He taught the first psychology course on American soil. William James Hall now houses the psychology department at Harvard.

There is an alternative to the cult of positive thinking. It's called reality. Happiness can be found in the calm moments of life. There doesn't need to be excitement, you don't have to be out having a great time *all the time*. You can be here now and find solace. The inner world is just as valid as the outer world. As Oliver Burkeman details, the path to happiness is "negative." To be happy it is best not to try so hard, and it is also important to embrace negative emotions. Pessimism has its place, inasmuch as all alternatives have a place. To court the possible and not just the desired helps to ground you. It puts life in context and absolves you from the cult of positive thinking. There is nothing wrong with optimism, but an obsessional preoccupation with optimism is counterproductive. Pretending that every moment of life is fabulous, mind blowing, and the best fun you have ever had ("That was so amazing!") is not the introvert way.

To tolerate the negative—uncertainty, doubt, and pain—is to be free in the world. To put your energy into avoiding, denying, or glossing over these things is to be bound, limited, and anxious. To commit yourself to positivity at all costs puts you in a precarious position. At any moment, you can fall from grace. Something shifts in your mind and energy contracts. Anxiety spikes as you try to "correct" your mood. After all, you *should* be happy at all times. If you can increase your tolerance and not be spooked by every dip in your liveliness, you are less encumbered by the vicissitudes of fate. Feelings come and go; fortunes rise and fall. Life is lived instead of managed.

The Role of Adversity in Happiness

Is there room for the darker emotions? American culture seems to be obsessed with being happy, and to be happy means to banish sadness, grief, and anxiety. These normal states are often made into disorders and treated with medication. There are many who have clinical conditions and need these treatments, but it is well known that antidepressant medications (which treat depression and anxiety) are overprescribed for the afflictions of daily living.

Happiness has gone from a right to pursue to an entitlement. If you are not happy, then you are being left behind or there may be something terribly wrong. The darker emotions get devalued. The poet Rainer Maria Rilke bemoaned this fact in "The Tenth Elegy" of his *Duino Elegies*. "Why didn't I kneel more deeply," he inquires, to accept the anguish that beset him. He views this as a "squandered" opportunity for self-awareness.

FACT

Rainer Maria Rilke was one of the most influential poets of the twentieth century. He was born in Prague to German-speaking parents and lived from 1875 to 1926. Eleven collections of poetry were published before his death (and many posthumously). He was also a prolific letter writer. According to Ulrich Baer, who edited and translated *Letters on Life*, Rilke wrote thousands of letters.

Miriam Greenspan speaks to the value of grief, fear, and despair in her book *Healing Through the Dark Emotions*. She points out there is a lack of emotional intelligence among humans. She says, "Our emotional illiteracy as a species has less to do with our inability to subdue negative emotions than it does with our inability to authentically and mindfully *feel* them. What looks like a problem with emotional control actually has its source in a widespread ignorance about how to tolerate painful emotional energies and use these energies for emotional, spiritual, and social transformation." The quest to banish negativity only gives it more ground. The way beyond is through. You cannot be a whole human being without a place for the light *and* dark emotions.

Forget about Being Happy

Ironically, the best way to become happy is to forget about happiness. The explicit pursuit of happiness is futile, as Oliver Burkeman has pointed out in summarizing the research literature, the Stoics, and Buddhism. If you are trying to have positive thoughts, how do you know if you are being successful? Your brain has to check for the presence of negative thoughts—thus bringing the very thing into mind that you are trying to avoid. This is called "ironic process" and it explains the parlor game, "Don't think of a pink elephant." Of course, you just thought of a pink elephant. Your brain is the most complex thing in the known universe but it cannot execute the simple instruction of "don't think of a pink elephant." You have to bring the elephant to mind to know you are successful. Ironic.

The limbic system (also called the emotional brain) has the job of figuring out what is relevant. It scans the environment looking for threat and opportunity and motivates you to pursue or avoid accordingly. It also tells you to ignore something that is neutral (you've got better things to do with your attention). When you force yourself to be "happy" like the extroverts around you, all the things that are a threat to that happiness all of a sudden become relevant, your emotional brain zeros in on them to make sure they are not getting in the way of your happiness. The very pursuit of happiness becomes the obstacle to achieving it.

If you are a golfer, you may be more aware of this phenomenon. You are standing on the tee and there is a pond on your right. You tell yourself, "Don't slice it into the water." The next thing you know, your ball is sinking to the bottom of the pond. Your brain seemed to only hear the last part of the instruction—"slice it into the water" and it commanded your body to execute that instruction faithfully. The brain does not seem to be able to figure out the "don't" part. To avoid slicing it into the water, you have to create a clear image of the result that you want and to make sure the last instructions your brain has are consistent with what you want instead of what you don't want.

FACT

The human brain weighs approximately three pounds and uses 25 percent of the body's glucose. It contains 100 billion nerve cells (neurons) and each of these neurons makes up to 100,000 connections with other neurons. Each one of these connections has multiple electrical states. The number of connections and combinations in the brain is staggeringly large.

Burkeman says, "The effort to try to feel happy is often precisely the thing that makes us miserable. And that is our constant efforts to eliminate the negative—insecurity, uncertainty, failure or sadness—that is what causes us to feel so insecure, anxious, uncertain, or unhappy." The key is to embrace the very things that you would otherwise try to eliminate—uncertainty, failure, and sadness. These are inescapable experiences of any human life. You cannot eliminate uncertainty. You cannot avoid all failures. You cannot avoid sadness (unless you don't care about anything or anyone). If you can accept these feelings as normal, then you won't feel so bad when they are present. The consumer culture promulgated by Madison Avenue suggests that you should never have any of these things and if you do there is something wrong with your life. No worry, just buy this product and everything will be okay! Life should not include any inconvenience, discomfort, or illness. There is a product for that. "Ask your doctor if [insert medication here] is right for you."

Trying Without Trying

Modern day incarnations of the cult of positive thinking include bestselling books like *The Secret*. It adheres to what Burkeman calls "unfalsifiable ideology of positivity." According to systems that promote the "law of attraction," when you focus obsessively on the positive things you want, the universe *must* give them to you. If you fail to get what you want, you simply didn't try hard enough. The theory can never be falsified, that is, proven wrong. These "manifesting" ideologies defy logic, reason, and common sense. They are appealing because they exploit the brain's vulnerability to coincidence— "I prayed for what I wanted and I got it, therefore my thoughts *caused* it to happen."

Trying to be happy may be futile, especially if you are trying to emulate the extroverts around you. Ruminating doesn't work either. Anything that engages the default mode network of the brain—whether going high or low—will not bring you to happiness. Happiness is not found in stories (unless they are memories). Happiness is an experience where the story and the sense of self-telling the story is absent.

The effort to exclude negative things from your experience creates a boundary line of tension that needs to be defended. It is like erecting a fence. It takes energy to do so and then you have to post guards on the fence to make sure that unpleasantness is not trying to sneak over the wall and ruin your day. As Robert Frost said, "Before I built a wall, I'd ask to know, what was I walling in or out." If, instead of the wall, you are more inclusive—allowing all experiences, pleasant and unpleasant—then that energy is freed to actually experience well-being. Acceptance is the key to happiness. Resistance creates misery. Don't buy into the tyranny of optimism. Life is always a mix. If you can "kneel more deeply to accept" the negative experiences of your life, a wonderful freedom opens up. If you don't try to be happy, you just might find yourself enjoying the moment. If you stop putting pressure on yourself to be like the happy people you see on television, then you can relax into the moment. If you stop comparing yourself to your extrovert colleagues, you won't feel so bad about being different. Your introversion is strength. You are closer to the heart of all feelings. It is a paradox of psychology that by trying to be happy you will not become so. You have a better chance by not trying so hard.

CHAPTER 9

Creativity and Introversion

There is a natural fit between the creative process and introversion. Creativity often stems from the interior, a place where introverts are at home. Many of the most influential creative people in history were introverts. You may find that including creative activities in your life is a way to nurture your introvert. Most creation is done alone in quiet without the distractions of the exterior world and also done best without the intrusions of the doubting, criticizing, and plaintive thoughts.

Fostering Creativity

It is hard to create something if you can't sit still. Tolerance of and preference for solitude may be a prerequisite for the creative process. Groups did not create the great art classics of humanity. While Leonardo da Vinci had assistants, a committee did not design the Mona Lisa. Artists most often work alone and they are more likely to be introverts (although, as with any rule, there are exceptions). Engineers, while often part of a team, do much of their creative work alone. Today, however, the image of the reclusive inventor is giving way to collaborative work. To be creative, you may have to resist this groupthink at the office. You may need to carve out pieces of solitude so you can get your best thinking done. You may have to recover from the outgoing demands of the social workplace to nurture your energy and creativity.

QUOTE

"Introversion, for me, is a gift that provides me both the freedom to let my mind wander into creative spaces and the intensity of focus necessary to relentlessly pursue creative ideas no matter their apparent value to others. As an artist, I have come to see introversion as a gift that has enriched my life far beyond my childhood aspirations."
—Erik Odin Cathcart

The artist Marcel Duchamp, now considered the grandfather of today's postmodern art movement, spent years sitting, playing chess, and essentially just thinking. In 1946, Duchamp was living in a tiny one-room apartment in New York City. The apartment had one chair and a basic metal bed. An iconic photograph of the time shows him sitting at his window, pondering the world and staring out from his self-imposed isolation. Duchamp had no formal studio at the time, or so it was thought. In reality, Duchamp was using this period of time to create what many consider his masterpiece, *Étant donnés*, a sculptural installation that now lives on permanent collection at the Philadelphia Art Museum. The work could not have the gravitas it possesses today if it were not for Duchamp's self-imposed exile from creative interactions.

Creative expression takes undistracted time. Can you imagine sitting in quiet for so long, letting the creative process percolate? You don't have to be an artist to appreciate the personal growth you will obtain and the creative inspiration from simply withdrawing slightly and sitting with yourself and your own thoughts.

Accessing the Unconscious

Your conscious mind is preoccupied with to-do lists, self-consciousness, and meeting the expectations of others and society. Creativity does not come strictly from the conscious mind, but must be fed from the clear, cold, deep waters of the unconscious. There are two major sources of interference that keep you from harvesting this creative flow—being too busy out in the world and being too busy in your storytelling mind. Extroverts may get too caught up in day-to-day activities, and this whirl of action keeps the interior riches at bay. This is a risk for introverts too.

The demands of contemporary life are unrelenting: two working spouses, jobs that exceed forty hours a week, raising children (and the incessant activities that require driving them across suburbia), maintaining a home, exercise, and so on, until you drop from exhaustion. Down time has been squeezed out. Weekends are for catching up on all the things you couldn't get to during the week—food shopping, laundry, and trips to Home Depot. This busyness afflicts introverts too. What unconscious? As an introvert caught up in this whirlwind, you will be more taxed than your extrovert counterparts. Life may feel *more* stressful for you. If you don't slow down and reclaim some time for yourself, the creative process may be lost.

QUOTE

"Art is not a making-oneself-understood but an urgent understanding-of-oneself. The closer you get in your most intimate and solitary contemplation or imagination, the more has been achieved, even if no one else were to understand it."—Rainer Maria Rilke

Your interior commotion can be just as tense as the relentless activities of daily living. You pore over your to-do list, rehearse meetings in your mind, review, analyze, and scrutinize every interaction you have had. Your mind never stops. It is always leaning into the future, commenting upon the present, or dragging along the past. Life can be the dangerous combination of ceaseless doing—both inner and outer. This leads to chronic stress, to say nothing of squashing creative impulses. You are so exhausted that you just plop yourself in front of the television each evening to unwind. To access the unconscious you must slow things down. You must create time and space where you can rest into the present without the pressure of "getting something done." Then, you might be able to hear what your unconscious wants to tell you.

Slowing Down

Where can you find some time in your day and in your week to let your unconscious speak to you? You can get up earlier in the morning before the kids are awake to journal, meditate, or just sit and sip your coffee in quiet. You can carve time out of your workday to take a five-minute creativity break by doing nothing for those minutes. You can take some time before you go home—even sitting in your car in the parking lot at work or before you enter the house to have a quiet buffer before the commotion of the family evening. Regular sips of stillness can help to restore your energy and to nurture the conditions for the creative process.

QUOTE

"For fast-acting relief try slowing down."—Lily Tomlin

Notice all the places in your day where you are feeling pressure to "get it all done" and "get it done now!" Are you frustrated driving to work because the traffic is too slow? Are you speeding to get there? What would happen if you slowed down, and drove the speed limit? Are you feeling stressed at work with all the tasks you have to do? Can you do them one at a time, giving them your full attention? Each time you feel the pinch of stress, pause, and look for an opportunity to slow down. Bringing attention to the pressures can help to relieve them. This is your life in the moment—give it your full, deliberate, alert, *and* relaxed attention.

Solitary Expression

You are more likely to find introverts working in scientific, academic, and artistic fields. For example, Charles Darwin was notorious for not socializing. Observing finches was a solitary activity. Writing is a solitary activity. Extroverts vary in their preferred solitude. You can be an extroverted writer, but it suits the introvert temperament better. Time alone is a way to restore energy. The extroverted writer will find that time alone more taxing. Many of the great thinkers of the world have spent time in solitude.

Expert Solitude

To get good at something you must practice, and practice often happens in solitude. For instance, becoming an expert musician depends on how many hours you practice and how many of those hours are solitary practice. According to the often-cited study by Dr. Anders Ericsson, it might take up to 10,000 hours of practice to be an expert at something. It is only when you are alone that you can engage in what Ericsson calls "deliberate" practice. Deliberate practice involves stretching yourself by identifying what you need to work on and pushing yourself to work on it in concentrated ways—best done in the quiet of solitude. A group has its own set of motivations and you can't set the agenda all the time. Therefore, the group is not the ideal place to do deliberate practice, because you need to be pursuing what is important to you, not the group.

QUOTE

"Writing is something you do alone. It's a profession for introverts who want to tell you a story but don't want to make eye contact while doing it."—John Green, author

To become an expert, you must have patience. It also helps to have a process rather than an outcome mindset. This emphasis on attending to the here and now of the process is key in almost any endeavor, including athletics, music, engineering, and meditation. It is easier to attend to the process of the task at hand without the distracting influence of other people. In other words, solitary practice or work facilitates process and process facilitates success.

Of course, there is such a thing as group process, and this can be very valuable in its own right, but if the individual process is neglected, something may be lost. Group process is valuable for realizing how you are coming across in a social context and how people perceive you. Group process is about social awareness and it may not be ideally suited to intellectual and creative endeavors.

Creativity requires solitude and suits introverts who are comfortable in this quiet space. Extroverts may not be so comfortable alone and are more prone to becoming leaders, politicians, and other social occupations that don't require intense solitary practice. Perhaps this is why the list of introverts who have made significant scientific and creative contributions is so long.

Writing Practice

Writing is a solitary activity and can be used to nurture your inner introvert. The writing teacher, poet, and Zen meditation practitioner Natalie Goldberg recommends "Writing Practice" in her bestselling book, *Writing Down the Bones.* She sets out six guidelines:

1. Keep your hand (or hands if you are using a computer) moving at all times. Don't pause or read what you have written.
2. Don't cross out—this is not edited writing.
3. Don't worry about spelling, punctuation, and grammar.
4. Lose control.
5. Don't think; don't get logical.
6. Go for the jugular (If something comes up in your writing that is scary or naked, dive right into it. It probably has lots of energy.)

You keep your hand moving to avoid the influence of the internal critic or censor that wants the writing to be perfect (because society says things should be perfect). When you don't pause, you can get access to your unconscious and discover what you are really thinking about and not just what you think you should be thinking about. You can hear yourself thinking "out loud," as it were, through the process of writing.

Letting Go

Writing practice, which you can do for a predetermined length of time, is not public writing. You don't even have to read it yourself. You can even consider destroying what you've written so you feel comfortable saying whatever comes out of the connection between mind and pen. Because this is not public writing, punctuation doesn't matter, penmanship doesn't matter, and coherence doesn't matter. You have permission to not make sense, to contradict yourself, to say whatever comes through the mind. When you can let go of the need to make sense in the way that writing is when it is public, and when you can ignore the demands of the internal censor to be perfect, you have the opportunity to lose control. By losing control, you can find out what is really important to you. The internal censor is dedicated to what "should" be and is beholden to other people's expectations or those of society. Many of those expectations may want you to be more extroverted or to feel bad about your introversion. Journaling practice is a great way to see the influence of these expectations and let go of them on the page.

QUOTE

"The best thing about the bedroom was the bed. I liked to stay in bed for hours, even during the day with covers pulled up to my chin. It was good in there, nothing ever occurred in there, no people, nothing."
—Charles Bukowski, author

This is not a logical process; it is more connected to the romantic soul that values freedom of expression. As Natalie Goldberg points out, important issues may come up in the writing—things that are scary or raw. She advocates diving into them rather than distracting yourself or avoiding them. This is where you can learn the most about yourself.

This writing is a process of meditation. In meditation practice, you will also confront the "places that scare you," as meditation writer and teacher Pema Chodron points out. Writing practice can be an integral part of your day and an important way to keep balance when the exterior demands of work and family keep you away from your interior. By confronting what is most important and by recharging your batteries, you can bring a new energy into your day. The writing space can be a place of solace, sanctuary, and safety.

The Artist's Way

Julia Cameron is the author of the bestselling book, *The Artist's Way*. She teaches people how to access their creativity and believes that everyone (introvert and extrovert alike) has creative potential. The two key practices presented in *The Artist's Way* are solitary. The first practice is called Morning Pages. She presents a video and instructions on her website (*www.juliacameronlive.com*): "Morning Pages are three pages of longhand, stream of consciousness writing, done first thing in the morning. There is no wrong way to do Morning Pages—they are not high art. They are not even 'writing.' They are about anything and everything that crosses your mind—and they are for your eyes only. Morning Pages provoke, clarify, comfort, cajole, prioritize, and synchronize the day at hand. Do not over-think Morning Pages: just put three pages of anything on the page . . . and then do three more pages tomorrow."

The practice of Morning Pages can help you to overcome the limiting influence of the internal censor. This censor is hypercritical and stifles creativity. The censor has been very deeply conditioned by a society that places high value on perfectionism, or at least appearing so. To get around the censor, you must get to know the censor. The get to know the censor, you must spend time in silence with yourself. Morning Pages can be essential tools for introverts. They can nourish your solitude while helping you to overcome the limiting effects of the censor. Morning Pages can also be restorative and don't necessarily have to be practiced in the morning. They can help you to recharge your introvert batteries after spending time in extroverted situations. Journaling nurtures the interior and can also be a valuable practice for extroverts to discover their hidden introvert.

The second key practice in *The Artist's Way* is called the Artist Date. This is a date with yourself to do something that puts water into your creative well. Julia Cameron is explicit about the instructions: the Artist Date is to be conducted *alone*. She recognizes the value of solitude. To access the interior, you must go alone out into the world to find that nourishment. Artist Dates can be anything—walks in the woods, a visit to an art gallery, sitting by the ocean.

Whether or not you consider yourself an artist or aspire to become one, Morning Pages and Artist Dates can be useful practices for introverts. The demands of living in an extroverted world drain the water from your energy well. This well serves creativity and whatever else you have to do in the world. You must replenish that water whenever it is drained and the solitary practices of journaling and venturing out into the world alone can accomplish this.

The poet Rainer Maria Rilke said in his letters (quoted from *Letters on Life* edited and translated by Ulrich Baer): "The thoughts that enter, even the most fleeting ones, must find me all alone; then they will decide to trust me again." If you don't allow silence and solitude into your life, your creative thoughts may become shy, recondite, and avoidant. To build that sense of trust, you can invite silence through writing, creating, and holding a space of solitude where you can think, write, and create.

Thinking Outside the Box

Your Introvert Edge makes it more likely that you will think "outside the box." Your thoughts may take time to gestate, and you need to give them the time to emerge. The INTP (introversion-intuition-thinking-perceiving) Myers-Briggs type is good at thinking outside the box. INTPs may comprise 1–5 percent of the population. If you are an INTP, you like solitude, and have an analytical curiosity about things. You like to find solutions to problems.

A blog entry on the website *onlinemba.com* speaks to the introvert's curiosity: "It's these areas—strategic and deep, critical thinking, creativity and innovation, thinking outside the box—where introverts shine. In fact, these are exactly the kinds of qualities that drive successful businesses. It's no wonder then that some of the most celebrated businesspeople of recent times—Warren Buffet, Bill Gates, Charles Schwab—have been introverts. They are perhaps the best proof that nothing business school requires can trump a determined introvert."

Nine-Dot

The Nine-Dot problem provides an interesting challenge. You are presented with nine dots arranged in a three-by-three configuration (you can take a piece of paper and draw three rows of three dots). The instructions are "draw lines through each one of the dots without lifting your hand. You only get four lines." Give this a try now (spoiler ahead). Most people do not get the solution to this problem. If you don't go outside the boundaries created by the dots, you cannot solve the problem. You have to "think outside the box." One study, conducted by Richard Chi and Allan Snyder, stimulated the right brain hemispheres of subjects during the Nine-Dot problem, and this increased their likelihood of solving the puzzle (the right hemisphere likes spatial relationships). Another study by Joseph Alba and Robert Weisberg challenges the "think outside the box" assumption. Here, subjects were told to go outside the box to solve the problem. Still, most of them could not solve it even with this enhanced clue.

Cognitive Mindfulness

Harvard psychologist Ellen Langer has done research on what she calls "mindfulness." Her mindfulness is distinct from the mindfulness associated with meditation and Buddhism. Her mindfulness is a cognitive flexibility. It's an ability to not get trapped by categories, preconceived ideas, and expectations. Mindfulness redirects attention away from categories, preconceptions, and expectations to what is actually happening now. It is a skill that can be cultivated. It requires paying attention in ways that go beyond words to perceiving the problem at hand with a fresh perspective, unencumbered by prior expectations

Introverts can be "right brained" or "left brained." Your introversion can give you access to a fresh way of approaching problems when you can set aside your expectations. "Thinking outside the box" may be more myth than reality, but your curiosity will be an asset in creative situations.

Flow

Introverts may be more prone to flow because they are giving more of their attention to the present moment (link to mindfulness). Flow is about process, not outcome. Mihaly Csikszentmihalyi (pronounced Mee-high Chicksent-me-high) coined this concept and did the seminal research. He is the author of *Finding Flow: The Psychology of Engagement with Everyday Life*. Flow occurs when the challenges of what you are doing in the moment are met by sufficient skill. Too much challenge without enough skill and the task becomes overwhelming. Too little challenge and it becomes boring. Flow can happen in sports, art, writing, and almost any activity where the right combination of challenge and skill occurs.

QUOTE

"If you are interested in something, you will focus on it, and if you focus attention on anything, it is likely that you will become interested in it. Many of the things we find interesting are not so by nature, but because we took the trouble of paying attention to them."—Mihaly Csikszentmihalyi

If you're an introvert, you can seek flow by using your gifts. You have the power of persistence, the tenacity to solve complex problems, and the clear-sightedness to avoid pitfalls that trip others up. You enjoy relative freedom from the temptations of superficial prizes like money and status. Indeed, your biggest challenge may be to fully harness your strengths. You may be so busy trying to appear like a zestful, reward-seeking extrovert that you undervalue your own talents, or feel underestimated by those around you. But when you're focused on a project that you care about, you probably find that your energy is boundless. Stay true to your own nature. If you like to do things in a slow and steady way, don't let others make you feel as if you have to race. If you enjoy depth, don't force yourself to seek breadth. If you prefer single tasking to multitasking, stick to your guns. Being relatively unmoved by the rewards offered by the extrovert society gives you the incalculable power to go your own way. It's up to you to use that independence to good effect.

CHAPTER 10

Private Predilections at Work

If you are able to choose your work to suit your introvert tendencies, you may become a librarian, psychotherapist, writer, or artist. You may also work from home. Not all introverts are so fortunate, though. They find themselves working in extroverted fields, such as teaching or sales, having to work in teams, without privacy, in offices with open floor plans. Extroversion dominates corporate culture. Yet, many of the assumptions about teams, brainstorming, and open floor plans in offices may not hold up under scrutiny.

Private Made Visible: The Open Workplace

How do you cope with the expectations in your workplace? Are you expected to be a team player, to multitask, to think on your feet, to socialize with your coworkers? If so, you may find work extra stressful. These expectations are forged in the birthplace of corporate culture—business schools. Students work in teams. Projects are relentless. It's high intensity and highly competitive. It's not a place for introverts. Networking requires industrial-strength socializing. It's an overwhelming environment for introverts. Many of the leaders in politics, finance, and business are graduates from extrovert factories such as Harvard Business School. The quiet, thoughtful, individualistic approach to work has given way to an over-the-top, stylish, collective approach.

T Is for Teamwork

The workplace of today is bound to involve teams—a trend that has been growing. The belief is that teams are the key ingredients to successful outcomes in the workplace. To support teamwork, offices are increasingly going to open floor plans with movable workspaces. According to sources, as many as 70 percent of workplaces have adopted this format. You may be hard pressed to find a private space in some offices. The office has transformed from a place focused on the individual, "I," to a place focused on the team, group, or "we." Privacy is at a premium, or nonexistent. How can you cope, if you are an introvert working in such an environment? It will be difficult, but there are things that you can do to offset some of these sources of stimulation. Here are some aspects of the open workplace that drive introverts crazy:

- Meetings, meetings, and meetings
- No privacy (no door to close, shared online calendars)
- Team-building exercises
- Corporate retreats with little time for solitude
- No boundaries

The fabulous collaborative successes made possible by the Internet were emulated by businesses. Does the virtual model translate into the brick-and-mortar world of actual workplaces? Internet collaboration can take place asynchronously—meaning that contributions don't have to occur in real-time exchanges. One person can do something and then at another time another person can respond to that contribution. Examples of online and decentralized organizational successes include Wikipedia, Linux, and Craigslist. According to Ori Brafman and Rod Beckstrom, authors of *The Starfish and the Spider*, these are examples of starfish (decentralized) organizations as opposed to spider (hierarchical) organizations. "When you give people freedom, you get chaos, but you also get incredible creativity." While starfish organizations can be more nimble, adaptive, and flexible, they may or may not be commodious to introverts, depending on the availability of privacy and the demands of participation—asynchronous is good; synchronous is stressful. The Internet provides a space to hide out because most interactions do not need to be face-to-face in real time. The introvert may be caught in the middle between traditional centralized organizations that are adopting the team approach. Introverts can be at home on the Internet. It is ironic that the Internet—a place where introverts thrive—inspired the new open-office trend—where introverts struggle with its relentless collaboration.

Does Brainstorming Work?

Alex Osborn of the advertising firm BBDO invented brainstorming. His intention was to create a safe group environment for the generation of ideas. That process has taken firm root in corporate America. But does it work? Here are four principles of brainstorming:

1. Don't judge or criticize ideas.
2. Be freewheeling. The wilder the idea, the better.
3. Go for quantity. The more ideas you have, the better.
4. Build on the ideas of fellow group members.

While Osborn was an enthusiastic proponent of brainstorming and provided anecdotal evidence to support its effectiveness, research from as early as 1963 suggests that it doesn't actually work. Brainstorming continues to be popular because it appears to work, not because it actually works. It suits the extrovert's appetite for interaction and thus persists. The exception to this finding is when groups work asynchronously through electronic media. When you work in an online "brainstorming" session, you are really working in solitude. That solitude is lost when you enter an actual group in a physical location. The value of brainstorming may lie in the way it makes groups feel about themselves. A brainstorming session may enhance group cohesion but not creativity.

The Introvert's Contribution to Brainstorming

You may be out of sync with the extroverts at work when you (1) don't speak up as much as they do, (2) don't self-promote and get yourself noticed, and (3) work at a slower, more deliberate pace, thinking things through and being careful.

QUOTE

"I am a horse for a single harness, not cut out for tandem or teamwork . . . for well I know that in order to attain any definite goal, it is imperative that one person do the thinking and the commanding."—Albert Einstein

If brainstorming doesn't work to produce more ideas, then the introvert way may have something to offer the workplace. Solitude is a necessary ingredient for the creative process, and solitude helps to avoid the biasing effects of groupthink. Introverts don't necessarily want to be isolated. Humans are social creatures, introverts and extroverts alike. The goal is not to have people work in a cave. The goal is not to force people to work together in stilted, rigid ways. Sometimes, it is important to close the door and have quiet. Other times it is important to have a conversation at the water fountain, or to join an impromptu group. If these situations are prearranged, they may be less fruitful.

The best work environments contain mixtures of introverts and extroverts working in a balance of solitude and community. An environment that is all one or the other is likely to be less productive.

The Dangers of Groupthink

Groupthink can be a biasing and even dangerous phenomenon. A classic study in social psychology showed that groups can influence not only what you say, but also what you perceive. Solomon Asch devised a series of experiments where subjects were asked to match the length of a line to three choices of different lengths. For example, the length of the test line obviously matches with option B, but confederates in the study who go before the test subject all choose option C. Most subjects go along with the groupthink. Subjects are not consciously changing their answer to fit in with the group; the data suggest that their perceptions actually change. These findings suggest that groups can have a large influence on what group members think and do. If the groupthink heads in a dangerous direction, the entire group can go off the cliff together.

In the definitive dystopian novel, *1984*, it is not enough that the protagonist, Winston, says he sees five fingers (when there are actually four), he must actually *see* them. An updated version of this story was presented in *Star Trek: The Next Generation*. Captain Picard is captured by the Cardassians and a sadistic commander attempts to break Picard's spirit with torture and the perception task from *1984*. Captain Picard is rescued before he capitulates, but after the ordeal he confides to the counselor that he was on the verge of seeing five lights when there were only four.

QUOTE

"We failed to realize that what makes sense for the asynchronous, relatively anonymous interactions of the Internet might not work as well inside the face-to-face, politically charged, acoustically noisy confines of an open-plan office."—Susan Cain

Updated versions of the classic Asch studies looked into the brains of people subjected to groupthink. Participants who avoided the effects of groupthink showed increased activation in their amygdala. The amygdala is a brain structure that is associated with primitive negative emotions such as fear of rejection. But the amygdala is really an organ of salience. Its job is to scan the environment to focus the brain on what is the most important element in that environment, be it threat or opportunity (in that order). Perhaps the subjects capable of bucking groupthink were able to keep their attention on what they thought was most important—the perceptual task at hand—versus others whose brains decided the most important task at hand was fitting in and avoiding social rejection. Avoiding social rejection is a powerful motivator. Exile probably meant death for human ancestors.

Evolution has shaped you to be a social creature. However, as Jaimal Yogis points out in his book *The Fear Project*, "Experts these days have often been swayed by enormously powerful groups, and decades of research have shown that when people get together in a group, the group tends to reflect *not* the average opinion of the individuals that make it up, but the *more extreme* view." In other words—the vocal extroverts.

Coping with Conflict

Extroverts may thrive on the dynamics of confrontation. You may want to shrink and hide. Conflict can be seen through different martial arts metaphors. The typical model is the karate model where force meets force and the better argument wins.

Bob Stahl and Elisha Goldstein in their *Mindfulness-Based Stress Reduction Workbook* present another less combative metaphor. It draws on the martial art Aikido where the goal is to use the energy that is already present in the interaction to your advantage. This practice involves throws and tumbling. You take the energy of the attacker and take him in the direction he is already going. There are four steps in Aikido communication: align, agree, redirect, resolve. To align, you engage in mindful listening. Really listen to what the other person is saying. Put yourself in his shoes. What is he feeling? Try to understand where he is coming from. Ask questions to show you are interested. Recognize that he wants something—the specific thing he is arguing for in the conflict. You can also assume that everyone wants to be heard no matter what the issue is.

In the next step, find something that you can agree with. Be authentic and locate something meaningful to agree on. Use "I" statements and avoid saying "you," which can put the other person on the defensive. Now that you have made contact with him, you can start to use his energy to your advantage. Try to move the conversation in a more positive direction. Propose that you work together to find a solution. In the final step, you try to reach some resolution, even if it is not final. Here you may strike a compromise or agree to revisit the conflict again at another time. This style of communication is more suited to the introvert. You don't have to engage in verbal sparring, something that you may be uncomfortable with and even unskilled at. Your natural listening skills pay dividends. Your deliberate approach can offset defensiveness.

Gregarious seems to be the language of business, but glad-handing is probably not your style. To get the Introvert Edge, you don't have to become more extroverted (although there are occasions when being a pseudo-extrovert is the best strategy). To get the Edge, you need to do what you do best—think, listen, and form deep relationships with a select few. Engagement that goes beyond the surface is your introvert strength. Making connections and feeling connected as you work is the introvert way of working. Engagement relies on the skill of mindfulness to bring your full attention to whatever you are doing in the moment. There is a natural fit between mindfulness and introversion, and also a natural miss. The fit is that introverts are more likely to value the contemplative aspects of life. The miss is that introverts are also more likely to be in their heads, and rumination is the shadow aspect of being thoughtful. Mindfulness helps to equalize these tendencies. When you are mindful, you catch yourself ruminating and redirect yourself from the story you are thinking about to what is actually happening now.

Does the Extroverted Workplace Work?

In *Quiet,* Susan Cain cites the Coding War Games study conducted by Tom DeMarco and Timothy Lister. This large study looked at the quality of work from over 600 computer programmers at almost 100 different companies. The results were surprising.

The study found that experience and level of pay did not predict success. What did predict success was the culture at the company the programmers worked at. Privacy seemed to be the key element (62 percent of top performers had privacy versus 19 percent of the lowest). Privacy allowed people to work without interruptions in their work process.

Being interrupted by others is a big drain on productivity. Even when those interruptions are self-imposed as they are with multitasking, there is a hit to productivity. Remember that introverts tend to prefer working on one task at a time in a concentrated fashion. As an introvert, you will find the noisy bustle of the open workplace difficult to concentrate in. This hectic free-for-all, with not just noise but interruptions, is stressful. This strain may afflict extroverts too. A quiet walk in the woods facilitates learning over a noisy walk in a city. Multitasking and open offices and the teamwork they demand are myths of productivity.

QUOTE

"Open-plan offices have been found to reduce productivity and impair memory. They're associated with high staff turnover. They make people sick, hostile, unmotivated, and insecure. Open-plan workers are more likely to suffer from high blood pressure and elevated stress levels and to get the flu; they argue more with their colleagues; they worry about coworkers eavesdropping on their phone calls and spying on their computer screens. They have fewer personal and confidential conversations with colleagues. They're often subject to loud and uncontrollable noise, which raises heart rates; releases cortisol, the body's fight-or-flight 'stress' hormone; and makes people socially distant, quick to anger, aggressive, and slow to help others."
—Susan Cain

Myth of Multitasking

Multitasking drains productivity because your attention can only focus on one thing at a time, and where it seems to be doing multiple things it is actually switching between one thing and the other. This switching takes time. And while it may only take a fraction of a second, these fractions add up over the course of a workday. Not only does switching tasks take time, but also it takes time to find your place again with the task you just abandoned for another.

These disruptions are especially vexing for introverts, who like unbroken concentration. As an alternative, you can try to do one thing at a time. If you are lucky enough to have a private office it may be easier to control the tasks that you do. Everyone is fair game in a space without privacy and this is compounded by the culture of immediate communication. The effects of instant messaging, text messaging, e-mail, and all the other innovations of technology have changed the sense of what it means to be available. Twenty years ago, people somehow managed to make and enjoy social plans and conduct business without smartphones. Now, nothing gets done without them. If you don't respond to a text or an e-mail within a nanosecond of receiving it, your friends may think something terrible has happened. Being plugged in at *all* times is the expectation. Perhaps this contributes to the sense of stressfulness in the workplace. Not only is there an infinite amount of information, it is available instantaneously.

Introverted Leaders

The vocal wheel gets greased. Good ideas are often subordinated to forcefully expressed ideas, regardless of the quality of those ideas. This is the danger of unbridled extroversion. Introverts may have good ideas but the more vocal extrovert may overshadow them. Just because you are loud doesn't mean you are right. People who talk a lot, fast, or forcefully are perceived as being smarter than they are. Leaders are expected to be adept at presenting themselves, but this may not be the most important feature of leaders. It may take more than charisma to make a good leader. Introspection is an asset. In his book, *Good to Great*, Jim Collins analyzed eleven standout companies and found they all had a quiet leadership style in common described by the following adjectives: "quiet, humble, modest, reserved, shy, gracious, mild-mannered, self-effacing, understated."

QUOTE

"At IBM, [being an introvert] had its advantages and disadvantages. It allowed me to spend long periods of time getting lost in the solitude of doing design work. However, I don't think I was taken seriously at times because of my introversion—especially early in my career, before gaining a reputation. Not being assertive hurt my credibility. The moments before a meeting starts—making small talk with management—matters. You don't gain points in a meeting being a good listener."—Charles M., Engineer

Perhaps great leaders are more interested in listening than imposing their verbal will on others. Great leaders can exude a quiet confidence and are more interested in results than recognition. Studies find there is only a modest correlation between extroversion and leadership, and many of these studies don't look at actual results of leadership—only how people perceive the leaders. Perhaps this has given a misleading, exaggerated notion of the benefits of being an extroverted leader. Studies by Adam Grant, a professor of management at the Wharton School (cited in Susan Cain's work) found that extroverts are good leaders in situations where the people they are leading are passive. Introverts make good leaders when the people they are leading are proactive and contribute their own ideas. Grant says, "Introverted leaders create a virtuous circle of proactivity." Extroverts inspire; introverts empower (by listening and being open to input). Susan Cain points out how Moses is portrayed in the Old Testament as a meek stutterer charged with a great mission. "People followed Moses because his words were thoughtful, not because he spoke them well."

Networking for the Privacy Inclined

Since 2008 when Guy Kawasaki came out of the closet as an introvert, he has championed the introvert cause. Kawasaki has over 1.3 million followers on Twitter and often tweets about introverts. According to Guy, he is an "APE": Author, Publisher, Entrepreneur. He has also written *Enchantment: The Art of Changing Hearts, Minds, and Actions* and *Reality Check: The Irreverent Guide to Outsmarting, Outmanaging, and Outmarketing Your Competition*.

The Internet is an ideal place for introverts. They can interact without engaging their voice and yet be heard. They can engage from a place of quiet. They can be in or out as they please. The asynchronous world of social media lets introverts pick and choose their spots for participation. It's a much less pressured place than a face-to-face meeting. Guy Kawasaki is a great example of a pseudo-extrovert. The online world presents an intriguing paradox. An introvert may hesitate before speaking up in a classroom situation, but be quite willing to share intimate details of his life on a blog, Twitter post, or Facebook status update.

Networking can seem overwhelming but social media works much like a traditional networking cocktail party. You would not go into an event with a megaphone and broadcast your message. Instead, you would have conversations with people. Instead of freaking out that you have 1,200 "friends" on Facebook, do what you do best—have meaningful conversation with a select group of people with whom you feel a connection.

An Introvert's Work Survival Guide

In an ideal world, introversion would be accepted, valued, and nurtured in the workplace. Unless you are lucky, this is probably not the case where you work. You will have to educate your peers and superiors about the Introvert Edge and what you can bring to the table when your introvert needs are taken care of. You are thorough, thoughtful, loyal, persistent, creative, and knowledgeable. Here is a survival guide for navigating the extrovert expanses of the workplace.

The major challenges for introverts in the office can be difficulty speaking up in meetings dominated by extroverts, not being comfortable with self-promotion, and working at a slow deliberate pace. As an introvert you will need periods of undisturbed time to maximize your concentration and productivity. You resent intrusions and hate multitasking. In addition to being an introvert, you may also be a highly sensitive or reactive person. The office environment will be extra stimulating to you—a bombardment of social and perceptual energies. Knowing yourself and your limitations is a good place to start. Expanding your comfort zone through acceptance and energy management techniques will also help you to cope in this environment.

Find and Create Space

If you have a private office, close the door. If you don't have a private office, is there a quiet common area you can retreat to? Is there someone else's private office that may be available at certain times? Can you take refuge outside with a mindful walk? There is always a bathroom or bathroom stall to find temporary respite.

Request work at home (WAH or WFH, work from home) privileges. You will be more productive and more valuable as an employee if you can concentrate and avoid being interrupted as you are in the office. If working from home is not a viable option, can you stagger your work hours to enjoy solitude in the early morning or evening? If your hours aren't flexible, can you take your working assets mobile? Go to a coffee shop or some other venue. There may be people around, but they are less likely to be people who are going to ask you questions and request things from you every five minutes!

Image credit: Michaela Chung, Introvert Spring (*www.introvertspring.com*)

Communicate Your Needs

When you embrace your introversion, you can tell your coworkers what you need. Perhaps you need to be left alone for a few minutes at the beginning of the workday. You can suggest starting a meeting with a moment of silence. These moments of quiet reflection or mindfulness aren't just for memorializing the dead; silence can be a useful tool to bring a thoughtful, deliberate energy to the meeting at hand. While managing the tendency of your coworkers to interrupt you may be like herding cats, you can try to consolidate your time. Let people know when you are available for questions and input and when you are not. Just as towns have signs for "Drug-Free School Zones" you can request an "Interruption-Free Time Zone." You may envy the university professors who can post office hours and have private offices with doors they can close. Faculty members (who are mostly introverts) recognize that constant interruptions are counterproductive. The contemporary workplace (dominated by extroverts) has lost touch with this wisdom, and you may need to reclaim it.

While the Homeland Security color scheme has been abandoned, you could create your own color scheme to let people know your availability. Create a series of colored placards that you can post on your desk or office door (if you are lucky enough to have one) that indicate your level of "threat." Green is "low" risk of your being annoyed by other peoples' intrusions. You are in a good mood and office hours are open. You give everyone a green light to interrupt you. Blue is "guarded"—there is a general risk. You can be interrupted if there is something important, not just social chitchat. Yellow is "elevated." You are busy and don't want to be interrupted unless it is something really important. Orange is "high" risk. "It better be a crisis if you interrupt me!" Red is "severe." Your office is closed and you are not available. Don't even think about it unless the building is on fire. Whether you communicate this system to others or not, it is a good idea to know that you have different levels of availability, mood, and energy. You can feel less stressed at work if you make yourself available to others only at times when it is okay for you to be interrupted. You can also control these interruptions. For instance, if you are at "blue," people can talk to you but only for a minute or two.

Stay Engaged

Don't beat yourself up: If you can't come up with a response right away in a meeting, don't criticize yourself. It takes you time to formulate a response. Once you take in information, it can be like paint drying—it takes time before it is ready to touch. Being in the social environment of a meeting can be very stimulating and this excitement eats up attention bandwidth. Don't put unrealistic pressures on yourself to perform. Remind yourself of your strengths. Performing in meetings is probably not one of them.

Stay engaged even when you are feeling overwhelmed: You can take notes to keep yourself grounded or you can pay attention to your breathing. Don't be a stone. Make eye contact even when you remain silent. Show that you agree and disagree with what is happening through body language. Check your facial expressions.

Be open to positive feedback from colleagues: You have a rich interior life and if you assume everyone else does too, you may downplay your strengths and take them for granted. You have a lot to offer even though you may offer it in your own introverted ways.

Suggest periods of silence: If your company is very forward thinking, they might even consider an entire day where talking is kept to an absolute minimum—maybe even silence.

ESSENTIAL

Michaela Chung is a blogger and artist. She describes herself as a "bold introvert, copywriter, world traveler and lover of all things creative." She founded Introvert Spring. where she posts blog entries, and original cartoons on introversion. These cartoons are funny, poignant, and artful. (*www.introvertspring.com*)

Take as much time as you need to solve the problem: The medical informatics revolutionary Dr. Lawrence Weed taught that the ideal medical practice would set quality as the constant and time as the variable. In reality, medicine doesn't work that way. In many situations, time is the constant and quality is the variable. The same principles apply to many business settings. As an introvert, you may be dedicated to the "quality is the constant" approach, but your work environment is demanding that things be done on the fly. It makes you anxious to sacrifice quality for speed. Can you communicate your commitment to quality and ask for more time where it can be given? Let your team and supervisors know that you are not slow, disinterested, or incompetent when you take more time on a problem than they do Your slower approach may inject some much needed doubt, caution, and circumspection into a project. This can be a downer for unbridled extrovert enthusiasm. Introversion can provide helpful checks against unmitigated optimism (like the kind of unrealistic, risky, and destructive confidence that caused the financial crisis of 2008).

Be mindful of your presentation in the group: If your voice is low and soft, you may not be taken seriously. It is easy to ignore you when you are blending into the woodwork. Be mindful of your energy and try to put it into your voice.

Provide Your Own Safety

If your work environment does not feel safe to you (for example, it is rife with conflict) you will not feel comfortable speaking up. This is understandable for an introvert. When the group does not provide this security, you will have to provide it to yourself with mindfulness—awareness of breathing and bodily sensations. Imagine an energy field that surrounds you. It is clear and permeable but you can control what gets in. When the environment is toxic, close the membrane to protect yourself. Don't let it in; don't take on everyone else's negativity. Stay focused on your own experience. Stay connected to breath and body: While you may not be able to escape, you can drop into the energy of your body and this can provide some refuge amid the chaos. Breathe full, deep, and slow.

Practice remembering: Do you have trouble remembering names? If this is a problem for you, there are a few simple things you can do to help you remember. First, repeat the name aloud as you greet them. Next, immediately repeat the name silently to yourself after you hear it. Use mnemonics to help you connect them (for example, "Vivacious Vivian").

Recharge and Renew

Here are a few ways to recharge your energy:

- Take breaks: If your work demands an extroverted presence, can you excuse yourself for a few minutes per hour or insert spaces between meetings so you don't get so tapped out? Self-promotion requires truckloads of energy that you may feel you don't have. You are more comfortable in energy conservation mode.

- Recharge your batteries: If your work drains you, you will have to set aside time to restore your energy. Not only time, but activities that will help you to recharge.
- Find a new job, career, or calling: If you've tried all the steps above and you still find work is making you feel drained, burned out, and depleted, you may need to consider a change. It takes courage to entertain this possibility, but your happiness may be at stake.

CHAPTER 11

The Introvert in the Classroom

Your school days may be long behind you, but perhaps you have school-age children or nieces and nephews. Perhaps you are an educator. Like the business world, the educational landscape has embraced cooperative learning approaches. The physical layout of classrooms has changed, and teaching has moved from individual to group-centered. Introverted children can feel lost in the chaotic, high-impact, and noisy extroverted classroom. If you have a school-age introvert in your life, you need to help him or her cope, and thrive, in this new educational world.

Coloring Outside the Lines

The educator Mark Phillips writing for Edutopia.org, said, "I tend to shy away from books that focus on helping a child to 'overcome' being an introvert. Although I think it's important to help introverted children learn to effectively navigate our extrovert-dominated world, I don't see introversion as a characteristic that needs to be 'overcome,' and neither do psychologists." Introversion is normal and more present than you might think in the classroom. If each student were assessed with the MBTI, you'd find that perhaps half were introverts. Yet many of these kids have already learned to be effective pseudo-extroverts. They pass for extrovert, but pay a penalty.

Introverted gifted children are particularly prone to bias in the classroom. An article by the educators Jill Burruss and Lisa Kaenzig titled "Introversion: The Often Forgotten Factor Impacting the Gifted" says, "It is not surprising that school is not a positive experience for many gifted introverts. It can be loud, crowded, superficial, boring, overstimulating, and focused on action, not reflection."

Introverted kids in an extroverted classroom can feel overwhelmed. Once overstimulated they will have a hard time concentrating. Feeling pressured to talk may inhibit them from sharing. They may isolate themselves because being in the center of the group is too stimulating.

Cooperative Learning

The present-day classroom is now geared toward teams, groups, and interaction. Perhaps schools have changed their approach in order to prepare kids to work in the modern workplace without walls. This is called cooperative learning.

According to a 2002 nationwide survey, *What Do Teachers Teach? A Survey of America's Fourth and Eighth Grade Teachers* conducted by The Center for Survey Research & Analysis at the University of Connecticut, 55 percent of fourth-grade teachers prefer cooperative learning, compared to only 26 percent who favor teacher-directed formats. Only 35 percent of fourth-grade and 29 percent of eighth-grade teachers spend more than half their classroom time on traditional instruction, while 42 percent of fourth-grade and 41 percent of eighth-grade teachers spend at least a quarter of class time on group work. Among younger teachers, small-group learning is even more popular, suggesting that the trend will continue for some time to come.

QUOTE

"Every child should be graded on class participation—and parents don't help their children when they argue otherwise."—Jessica Lahey, Educator

Look at the classroom from the introverted child's perspective. It is loud, chaotic, and interactive. Where can she find solace, respite, and quiet? School can be a nonstop assault for highly sensitive, introverted kids. The day starts with getting woken up at an obscenely early hour. Young children and teens have a greater need for sleep that is offset from adult hours, that is, they need to sleep in later. School starts too early and kids are likely sleep deprived. Being tired will magnify all other challenges for the introvert. After being roused from blissful sleep, the child may have to prepare for school in the stressful morning household rush, competing for attention with other siblings and dealing with the parents' haste to get everyone out the door. After this relaxing start, it's on to the school bus—a noisy, chaotic, melee. In school they navigate crowded hallways and arrive at a classroom arranged in pods. Respite from this classroom is a rushed lunch and a free-form recess. The introverted child may feel out of her element for the entire day, not having a quiet moment at all. She may feel drained by the time she has to get back on the school bus for one final assault on her senses.

The extroverted kid jumps out of bed and feeds off the energy of the early morning commotion. He's stoked to see his friends on the bus and engages them in animated discussion. The party continues at school—nonstop talk, interaction, and play. Energy builds throughout the day as one stimulating activity follows another. By the time he gets home, he's ready for more. Most schools are designed for these gregarious extroverted kids. The quiet kids may get lost in the shuffle. They are much more likely to feel stressed by the school environment. Many of these kids have learned to fake it—to be effective pseudo-extroverts, but their energy pays the price.

To Participate or Not to Participate

Should introverts be forced to participate in the classroom setting even if it is uncomfortable for them? After all, they will need pseudo-extrovert skills to function in the corporate world. Educator Jessica Lahey argues this case in her *Atlantic* article, "Introverted Kids Need to Learn to Speak Up at School." Her insistence on participation is unpopular, "The parents of introverts complain that I am not meeting their child's unspoken educational needs, or that I am causing serious emotional trauma by requiring their child to speak up in school." To assume that all introverts or even strong introverts have social anxiety is false. Introverts can participate, but they may need some protection in order to do so. It may take them a bit more time to formulate a response, and they should be given the opportunity to do so. Teachers can do this by giving everyone a turn to contribute in a classroom discussion or assign kids to contribute in a particular class. This gives the introvert time to prepare and a chance to hold the floor. Lahey makes the important point that classroom participation is an analogue for the world outside of school: "A student who is unwilling to stand up for herself and tell me that she does not understand the difference between an adverb and a verb is also less likely to stand up for herself if she is being harassed or pressured in other areas of her life."

Katherine Schultz, cited in a *Washington Post* article, "Why Introverts Shouldn't Be Forced to Talk in Class" argues against Lahey's position: "I would argue that Lahey's advocacy for grading or counting classroom participation ignores the value and uses of silence in the classrooms, overlooking the myriad of other ways students participate." She points out that silence is not just a function of temperament but may reflect the culture of the classroom. The other ways students may participate other than by speaking is body language, attentiveness, and note taking. Introverts may be better at participation if they have had some downtime prior to the dialogue. Teachers could provide a period of quiet, such as a meditation, and this may prime the introverts to participate.

An Introvert Guide for Teachers and Parents

Educator Mark Phillips cautions, "Having grown up as an introverted kid myself, I've always been aware that rewards for classroom engagement should not be measured only by oral contributions. Many of my best students were ones who rarely spoke in the large group, were active in smaller groups (and the smaller the better) and had a great deal to share with me privately in papers."

Another educator, Tony Baldasaro, writing for *Edutopia* (*www.Edutopia .org*), the website of the George Lucas Educational Foundation, echoes Phillips's observation, "I don't see introversion as anything different than being left- or right-handed, boy or girl, naturally athletic or not. It's a part of who we are, and just like those other qualities, introversion is not something to be 'overcome.' In fact, I would argue that as educators it is our job to harness the sometimes hidden gems hiding within our introverted students."

He advises three domains that are critical for introvert learners: time, space, and asynchronous learning opportunities. It may take your introverted students longer to do things in the classroom because they are processing more deeply. It takes them time to assimilate information, organize it, and then express it. Time is in short supply in schools, but time pressures will work against introverted students. A space is needed where an introverted kid can go to have peace and quiet to work alone on an assignment. It is a place he can go when he is at his limit and feeling overwhelmed. If a dedicated space is not possible, introverts may be more comfortable on the periphery of the classroom rather than in the middle of the action.

QUESTION

Is your child an introvert?
Your child has strong introvert tendencies when they enjoy a lot of time alone, take time to warm up, and think things through before speaking. Introvert kids have more needs for privacy, quiet, and time to rest and restore. They can be highly concentrated and good observers.

Baldasaro also suggests headphones as a way to give an introvert some portable privacy. These can insulate them from the commotion of the classroom and also make them more impervious to interruptions. Baldasaro talks about the advantages of online learning environments for introverted kids: "The asynchronous environments found on the Internet can provide introverted students with the ideal space needed for them to learn. The freedom to explore their passions, the ability to connect with similar learners, and the time to participate at their personal pace and depth, all with the solitude needed by the introvert, can make these communities the ideal space for learning and creativity to blossom in the introvert."

Here are some recommendations for teachers to help their introvert students:

- Introversion is not pathology. Celebrate introspection. Understand that kids have different styles. Treat social skills deficits separately.
- Realize that many of the kids in your classroom are already accomplished pseudo-extroverts. Balance teaching methods to serve all the kids in your class. Susan Cain urges, "Extroverts tend to like movement, stimulation, collaborative work. Introverts prefer lectures, downtime, and independent projects. Mix it up fairly."
- Recognize that introverts may have intensity for particular subjects that separate them from their extroverted peers. Nurture these interests.
- Be careful not to overwhelm an introverted child with unwieldy group work. Smaller groups are likely to be more beneficial.
- Make sure all kids know how to work independently.
- Be sensitive to where introverted kids sit in the classroom. Avoid high-traffic, high-commotion areas.
- Don't force kids to speak publically if they are not comfortable.
- Introverted children may not perform well in group play situations. This could be a problematic standard for a competitive admission process.
- You wouldn't force your left-handed students to become right-handed, so you shouldn't force your introverted students into exclusively extrovert environments.

Parents' Guide for Choosing Schools

If you are the parent of an introverted child and you are wondering where to educate your child, you should check out any school you consider in order it see if it will be a fruitful environment. You want to make sure that the classroom will not be an extrovert circus. Look for schools that value autonomy. Make sure that group activities are not the only activities of the classroom. Moderation is key.

The size of groups matters, too. Large groups can be overwhelming for quiet kids and they can get lost. Does the teacher supervise the groups? How are the virtuous behaviors of caring, kindness, compassion, empathy, and responsibility fostered? What is the general feel of the school? Is it chaotic? Are there pockets of peacefulness? Does the faculty understand the needs of introvert kids? Are they sensitive to their special requirements? Will your child have an opportunity to delve into what interests him? What's the policy on bullies? Will your child find like-minded introverts? School will be the proving ground for a child's introversion. She will learn to value it or she will come to see it as a liability—something she must hide in order to get by. A well-chosen school will ennoble your child's introversion. It will help her to become a good introvert citizen of the world.

Introverts in Higher Education

Writing for the *Chronicle of Higher Education* (*www.chronicle.com*), professor William Pannapacker talks about giving his class the assignment of completing the MBTI (Myers-Briggs Type Indicator). During his experiment, none of the students came out as an "I"—introvert. He was puzzled: "I knew my students well enough to suspect that I was not the only one with that tendency. A third of them barely spoke in class unless called upon. A few hardly spoke to anyone. Perhaps the introverted choices on the test were too stigmatizing to consider (e.g., 'Would you rather go to a party or stay home reading a book?'). The students had used the test to confirm that they had the right, 'healthy' qualities."

It was uncool to be introverted. His students thought that introversion was aberrant—a form of mental illness or "spiritual brokenness," as one student argued. The students tried to persuade Pannapacker that he was not an introvert because he was up in front of the class acting extroverted. The students did not understand what introversion is and had been deeply biased by the extroverted culture.

Students in higher education are pressured by extrovert norms for participation in the classroom. Seminars are by definition interactive and might be an intimidating environment for introverts. Faculty members may be unaware of how their introverted students are experiencing the interactive environment and mistake their silence for disengagement. The value of participation is so deeply woven into the fabric of academic life that it goes unnoticed, and introverts become the collateral damage. If you grade on participation, you may be penalizing the most introverted of your students.

"As an introvert, I notice that every classroom at school has a few introverts. They are quiet and avoid answering questions but often have the best things to say. Introverts don't find their silence to be a bad thing. They have extreme focus on small details. In discussions they prove to have good insight, understanding, and opinions. If introverts ruled the world, life would be calmer and maybe more productive but less shared and expressive."—Ethan J., tenth-grader

While the academy is currently full of introverts, this landscape may be changing. Pannapacker describes how the process for applying for faculty positions has become rigged against introverts (or at least introverts who are not skilled pseudo-extroverts). He says, "When there are so many job candidates with excellent written credentials, 'fit' and personality take on a magnified importance. One could hardly devise a more brutal process for disadvantaging introverts than the two-day, on-campus interview—involving multiple high-stakes meetings with important strangers, a public lecture, and a teaching demonstration, all in an unfamiliar location with little or no time to recharge between events." At best, this scenario will be exhausting for introverts. At worst, it will inhibit their performance and they won't have a fair shot of getting the job.

Future Directions

Well-adjusted kids don't need to be popular, but they do need to have some quality relationships. If an introverted child is stressed to the point of being overwhelmed during the course of the school day, they are less likely to be effective learners. Bringing consciousness to the challenge of being an introvert can help kids to prepare for life beyond school. They may want to think of careers that suit their introvert temperament.

According to Amy Chang writing for Yahoo! Education, six careers for introverts are: accountant, graphic designer, medical records and health information technician, financial analyst, computer programmer, and technical writer. All professions, even solitary ones, may require meetings or presentations on occasion, but these careers will involve much less of that and can be a comfortable place to be an introvert. More energy can go into the work rather than trying to fit into the extrovert culture. Any activity that produces a sense of *flow* will be a haven for the introvert. When introvert kids can work uninterruptedly on something they enjoy, they lose their sense of time. Self-consciousness drops away and there is just the activity. A sense of well-being accompanies this type of engagement.

Mark Phillip, again writing for Edutopia.org, warns that, "Our classrooms contain too many forgotten introverted students who may need help, but are not getting it and/or have gifts that aren't being either elicited or supported." If you are a teacher, you will need to make an extra effort to reach out to the introverts in your classroom. It's easy to get wowed by the verbal extroverts, but the introverts have much to offer. If you are a parent of an introvert, you may need to talk to your child's teacher and develop a plan for drawing her out.

CHAPTER 12

Raising Resilient Introverts

Your child will show his or her introvert or extrovert tendencies early in life. If you have an introverted child, wonderful! Introvert kids have strengths that will blossom with the right encouragement. With the right guidance, they will learn to be at home with their introversion. When they learn introvert self-care skills, they will become resilient and enjoy the Introvert Edge.

Extrovert Parent with an Introvert Child and Vice Versa

Families come in all combinations of introverts and extroverts. If you have a mixed family, you face particular challenges. One particular challenge is extroverted parents who have an introverted child. Without sufficient understanding, this can be a disconcerting situation. Some of the behavior you are concerned with may be due to your child's introversion. Can you find the value in what your child has to offer? There is strength in quiet. It may be imagination, empathy, or compassion.

QUOTE

"As a psychologist, I have yet to see a child brought to therapy because he is too social and his parents are concerned that he seems to have little access to his inner life."—Laurie Helgoe

As a parent, you of course want the best for your child. You will probably conform to the extrovert culture's expectation of what children should be like. They should be verbal, active, and happy. Introvert kids may be seen as passive or even having something wrong with them. They may appear depressed, especially if their special introvert needs are not being attended to. Some parents may even take their kids to specialists to "fix" them. A good psychologist will not treat your child's introversion, but will help him to recognize his own strengths and to validate his experiences. The specialist can help your child learn to cope with the demands of the extroverted world. Your child is not at a disadvantage. Once he learns to care for his introvert needs (energy maintenance, privacy, et cetera), he can become thoughtful, intelligent, creative, and articulate. Introverts can thrive in the world just as extrovert kids can, although they will need some extra help with coping. Introversion is temperament, and while kids can learn to become skillful pseudo-extroverts (just as you probably have), you cannot change their basic temperament.

A seven year old is quoted in *Quiet* as saying, "School is hard because a lot of people are in the room, so you get tired. I freak out if my mom plans a play date without telling me, because I don't want to hurt my friends' feelings. But

I'd rather stay home. At a friend's house you have to do the things other people want to do. I like hanging out with my mom after school because I can learn from her. She's been alive longer than me. We have thoughtful conversations. I like having thoughtful conversations because they make people happy."

Introvert Parent with an Extrovert Child

If you are an introverted parent raising an extroverted child, another set of challenges emerges. How can you keep up with her and her relentless need for stimulation, activities, and social opportunities? This combination burdens the introvert parents. If your spouse is an extrovert, he can help to pick up some of the slack. As the introvert, you are at risk for exhaustion meeting all the needs of your child. Society "tells" you that all these needs are requirements: soccer, scouting, and countless other extracurricular activities. If you don't provide these activities for your children you are selling them short. Never mind the fact that you become an amateur chauffeur. Your introversion can be an asset for your child. You can help him to access his introvert qualities and learn self-care strategies from a young age. You can nurture your child's sensitivity, internal curiosity, and empathy skills.

Mixed Siblings

If you have more than one child, chances are they will be a mix of introverts and extroverts. Even if you and your partner are extroverts, you can have an introverted child (because genes don't explain all of introversion). Having a mixed group will present some interesting challenges. Your introvert child will need breaks from the extroverted, sometimes raucous play of his brothers and sisters. He may need his own room or certainly a place to retreat to when the commotion gets to be too much.

It may be tempting to give more of your time to the boisterous, vocal extrovert child. She just naturally draws attention to herself. You may have to go out of your way to engage your introvert child. Find activities where the introvert and extrovert can challenge and support each other, for example, games that involve bursts of activity followed by periods of quiescence.

Teach your introvert that he can take a time out to collect himself whenever he feels like things have become "too much" in the moment. Teach your extrovert child that kids have different speeds and like to do things at different paces. You can encourage your kids to teach one another. The extrovert can help the introvert to become a better pseudo-extrovert, a skill he will need later in life, and the introvert can teach the extrovert to be more deliberate, a skill that will benefit her later in life.

A Parent's Guide for Introverted Children

If your child is an introvert, he will have special needs. You can teach your child to monitor his energy levels so he knows when to take a break and when to withdraw from a situation that is overstimulating. Crankiness is a good indicator that your child is feeling overwhelmed and he may not be mature enough to recognize this (adults often miss this too!). You can give him gentle encouragement and normalize the experience.

Your child may notice that he is different but not be able to articulate this difference. Even though he is cranky, he may not want to withdraw from the situation voluntarily or even with gentle encouragement. If he resists, you may need to get creative with distraction. Don't force it. Until they can learn self-soothing skills, young children will need your calm reassurance.

Invest in Your Kids

At almost any age, you can offer a mindfulness moment to your overstimulated child by asking him to focus on his breathing for a few moments. You are teaching your child skills he will need for a lifetime. He has probably noticed that other children function differently than he does, that some kids have endless energy to play and talk. Your child wants to keep up, but his temperament does not always allow for it. You can help children to appreciate their differences. As an introvert yourself, you may want to share some of your experiences of feeling overstimulated; needing to take breaks; and your value of privacy, silence, and the interior.

Your child may be more than just introverted; he may be high-reactive or highly sensitive. He will require extra special attention, but nothing outside the canon of good parenting. If your child is high-reactive, he is vulnerable to adversity, and also ready to thrive in exceptional ways when given the right encouragement.

FACT

The majority (at least 60 percent) of gifted children are introverts. According to studies at the Gifted Child Development Center (*www .gifteddevelopment.com*), 75 percent of children with very high IQs (above 160, which puts them the top 1 percent) are introverts.

Susan Cain interviewed child expert Jay Belsky about high-reactive children for her book, *Quiet*: "The parents of high-reactive children are exceedingly lucky. Belsky told me, 'The time and effort they invest will actually make a difference. Instead of seeing these kids as vulnerable to adversity, parents should see them as malleable—for worse, but also for better.' He describes eloquently a high-reactive child's ideal parent: someone who 'can read your cues and respect your individuality; is warm and firm in placing demands on you without being harsh or hostile; promotes curiosity, academic achievement, delayed gratification, and self-control; and is not harsh, neglectful, or inconsistent.' This advice is terrific for all parents, of course, but it's crucial for raising a high-reactive child."

Don't judge. Listen and appreciate difference. Try to see the world from the child's perspective. Don't invalidate. Know when to push and when to leave him be. Be patient. Embrace his style. Understand the challenge of novelty. Avoid the extremes of overprotection or pushing too hard. Try to normalize. Use positive reinforcement. Use mindfulness to help your child get comfortable with uncomfortable feelings. Role model. Create safe environments. Be gradual. Rehearse, plan, discuss, for example, visiting the classroom before the first day of school can provide some reassuring familiarity. Make sure your child has basic social skills.

▼ **DOS AND DON'TS FOR THE INTROVERT CHILD**

Do	Don't
Normalize	Blame or Label
Encourage	Push/Force
Praise	Criticize
Be patient	Compare

One of your principal jobs as parent (beyond providing food, shelter, and safety) is to teach your kids how to self-soothe. They learn this in part from watching you. How are your self-soothing skills? Do your kids see you mumbling angrily to yourself when you do something you're not pleased with? If so, they are learning from you. If your child is in an uncertain situation—wondering whether to join in with other kids to play—show him how to self-soothe. Provide gentle encouragement and perhaps he will learn to do the same for himself. You can teach your child to recognize the emotion, "I am afraid" without being beholden to it. You can teach your child to name the fear and move forward (at his own pace).

In their article titled "Introversion: The Often Forgotten Factor Impacting the Gifted," educators Jill Burruss and Lisa Kaenzig provide guidance for taking care of your introvert child at home:

- Your child needs a private space. Ideally, a private bedroom and if this is not possible a place the child can use. If at all possible, avoid putting an extrovert and an introvert together in a bedroom.
- Your child needs quiet time to recharge his batteries, and if the home landscape is loud, disorganized, or chaotic he will not be able to do this. Find a way to provide this respite to your child (and to yourself!).
- Model the values of solitude and the virtues of being alone. Burruss and Kaenzig stress, "If the child continually hears that being away from people makes one lonely, it sends a very strong message to them about what they should feel."
- Teach your child how to self-monitor and to say when he is at his limit of stimulation. Simply saying "enough" may be enough to give them a respite from participating in something that is becoming overwhelming. Be sensitive to your child's metabolism of social interactions, noise, and activities. He may not be able to recognize when he is overloaded, so you help him to recognize that. When kids get overwhelmed they associate negative feelings with the situation. By monitoring and modulating stimulation levels he won't form these bad associations and dread similar situations in the future.
- Large groups can be too much. Make sure he has small group activities so he can learn to be comfortable in a group. Small groups are

easier to handle. A good balance of solitary and group activities can help your child to function better in school, too.

- Share your own experience of being an introvert. This makes it seem normal and helps your child to accept his own introversion. Teach him the difference between introverts and extroverts in a way that values both.
- Teach your kids to value being an introvert and show them how to act extroverted when they have to. As an introvert, you know how to act like a pseudo-extrovert. Do you have any tricks you can show your child? Make sure he has time to recover after putting out energy in that unfamiliar way.
- Expose your kids to introverts in books and movies. Discuss books that feature introverts. Kids can benefit from some fictional role models.

Nurturing Resilience

Your child needs solitude. Watching TV does not qualify as solitude, even though the child may be alone. Parents over-expose their children to screen time (television, computers, iPads, and iPhones). The American Academy of Pediatrics recommends, "Television and other entertainment media should be avoided for infants and children under age 2. A child's brain develops rapidly during these first years, and young children learn best by interacting with people, not screens." A survey by researchers at Northwestern University found that only 38 percent of parents expressed concern about the amount of screen time their kids were getting; 55 percent were not concerned at all. The families were divided into high-, moderate-, and light-use. High-use "media-centric" (computers, tablets, smartphones) families spent on average eleven hours per day on screens. The children of these families spent four hours and forty minutes. Moderate households were five hours for parents and less than three hours for kids. "Media-light" kids spend about an hour and thirty-five minutes.

Solitude and Quiet Time

Solitude requires being alone with your own thoughts—not being fed the images created by others, hypnotized into an altered state of relaxed (or even agitated) complacency. Screen time may be a time of relative quiet for kids who are exposed to the open, noisy, relentless schedule of school, lunch, and recess. Yet there are better ways of nurturing privacy than plugging into screen time. Kids may need to be given permission to be alone. They may need to be praised for it, and they may need a role model. Are you showing them that you value privacy, quiet, and solitude? Have you shown them how to be "alone together"? You can be alone together reading, listening to music, or looking at art.

QUOTE

"Working at Apple was consuming too much time and energy and I had very little left over for being an adequately present and affectionate parent and partner, let alone for being an artist. The persona I had to develop to function adequately at the store was getting more and more difficult to maintain. I'm fine with developing personas to deal with certain social situations, but if I have to wear the same persona too much, like an ill-fitting mask, it starts to chafe."—Todd Sargood, artist

Just like their adult counterparts, introvert kids need space to think. They need time to restore. They are not lazy when they sit quietly. Their brains are probably churning, thinking through something that they have experienced, relating to something they have learned. When pressured, their minds may go blank. This can be consternating as an adult, but it can be a source of stress for kids. It may subject them to ridicule. Being embarrassed will make their minds even less effective. While you can't control what happens to your child outside the home, make sure to give her space within the home and to help her to accept the way her mind works. She can grow to appreciate how her mind is different once she realizes that it is not defective. Remind your introvert children often that there is nothing wrong with them. Once they learn how their minds work, they can relax and feel confident that their thoughts will come when they are ready to come.

An Introvert Manifesto for Young People

Introversion is a gift. Don't be afraid to be different. Don't be afraid to stand out or to disappear amid the wild extroverting around you. Know that you are solid even when you are treated as invisible. The world does not always recognize your gifts. You will need to nurture these gifts. Your mind works differently than other children—different is not inferior; it's just different. In her blog *Parenting from Scratch*, Kelly Bartlett recommends, "Five Things to Know about Raising Introvert Kids." Make sure your day has these things to help you to nurture your Introvert Edge:

1. Alone time: You need this and you shouldn't feel guilty for asking for this time.
2. Small talk: If you don't like small talk that doesn't make you shy. Aim for connection with people first and that will make you more comfortable speaking with them.
3. Give yourself time to process information, feelings, and thoughts. There is a lot going on beneath the surface and you shouldn't be put on the spot to speak about what's going on in your head until you are ready.
4. You prefer one-on-one play dates or small groups to big groups of kids. More is not necessarily merrier.
5. Let your mind wander. Bartlett says, "Any opportunity to think, pretend, get creative, solve problems, day dream or otherwise get inside their head is welcome. Great introverted activities include reading, writing, sketching, jump rope, roller skating, fishing, painting, bike rides, gardening, playing catch, swimming, hiking, swinging, climbing trees, puzzles . . . the list goes on."

Your introversion is a central part of who you are. If you can recognize your differences and nurture them, they will develop into strengths. You may not fit in with the way most other kids seem to be but there are more introverts out there than you realize. Many of your fellow introverts are good at pretending to be extroverts. It's good to be able to do that at times, but don't forget that it can feel really good to be yourself. Celebrate your difference. You have a lot to offer the world!

CHAPTER 13

Embracing Introversion in the Age of Narcissism

The self is celebrated, exalted, idolized, and idealized. Everyone's children are exceptional, special, and extraordinary. Author, storyteller, and humorist Garrison Keillor makes fun of this phenomenon in every episode of his *A Prairie Home Companion* radio show: "That's the news from Lake Wobegon, where all the women are strong, all the men are good looking, and all the children are above average." Of course, it's impossible for all children to be above average, or the concept of average would be meaningless. All children are unique, but not necessarily exceptional.

Understanding the Self-Esteem Trap

Jungian psychoanalyst and Buddhist Polly Young-Eisendrath documented the quest for specialness in her book, *The Self-Esteem Trap: Raising Confident and Compassionate Kids in an Age of Self-Importance*. She documents the changing tides in parenting styles and details how the current generation of young adults has been indulged in ways that would have been incomprehensible for their parents growing up in the 1950s, and before.

Polly Young-Eisendrath wrote the *Self-Esteem Trap* because she was at the end of her rope. "I had sat hour upon hour in my psychotherapy practice with my heart aching for anxious parents who worried that their teenage and older children lacked good sense and empathy for others, and then more hours with well-educated adults in their twenties and thirties who were already discontent with their desirable lives, and still more hours with young mothers bound to impossible ideals for themselves and their children. One day something in me snapped. 'Enough!'"

FACT

Mental disorders are common in the United States. According to the National Institute of Mental Health (NIMH), approximately 25 percent, or 57 million people, are diagnosed with a mental disorder in a given year. About 10 percent, or 20 million people, have depression and almost 20 percent, or 40 million people, have anxiety disorders.

Too much focus on the self—whether positive or negative—can cause problems. Dr. Young-Eisendrath has treated people who feel superior and feel bad about feeling that way. Problems with self-esteem can arise with a history of abuse, neglect, or criticism. Problems with self-esteem can also arise with a history of being overly praised. This is a fascinating phenomenon. Too much or too little praise results in problematic self-esteem. The balance is the middle.

Healthy Narcissism

Imagine what it must have been like for you being born. Prior to birth, you were in a dark, warm, and weightless environment. All of your needs were met instantaneously. You didn't get hungry, you didn't get diaper rash. You were bathed in a world of soft, rhythmic sounds.

Paradise Lost

Then one day, all of a sudden, you were evicted from this wonderful place into a bright, loud, and cold environment. Your first response is to cry. Who wouldn't? Now you must depend on your mother (or primary caretaker) in a different way. It is no longer instantaneous. You cry, and most of the time she is right there to feed you, change your diaper, rock you back to sleep. But sometimes you have to wait. Sometimes it seems like a long time—forever to your young brain. You cry and cry and nothing happens. Finally, she shows up and you forget how awful that waiting was. In her loving embrace, you overlook how angry, scared, and confused you were. If the ratio is right and mom is there most of the time, you are off to a good start. If mom is particularly good at reading your needs, you are very fortunate. Sometimes, you just want to be held and not fed. Sometimes you just want to be fed. Sometimes, you just want to be left alone. When mom is good at sensing your wants, you are in attunement. This is a happy place to be. You feel loved, secure, and your brain will wire itself up happily—especially in the areas that will regulate emotions, stress, and attention later in life.

FACT

Dr. Dan J. Siegel is a pioneer in the field called interpersonal neurobiology. He has written many books, including *The Developing Mind*, *The Mindful Brain*, *Mindsight*, and *The Pocket Guide to Interpersonal Neurobiology*. This is an interdisciplinary field that seeks to understand the brain, mind, and health and their foundation in relationships.

As an introvert baby, you had more needs for space than your extroverted brothers and sisters. There is a 25 percent chance that you were a high-reactive infant, which means your sensitivities were magnified. You loved to be held, but you didn't want to be held as much. Hopefully, mom noticed that and dialed it back. You didn't want to be on the go constantly. With any luck, mom gave you plenty of quiet, rest, and time without much to do. When she gave you what you needed you learned how to give these things to yourself. If she didn't, you may still be trying to figure how to take care of yourself.

The paradox of development is that the more successful the early narcissistic or mirroring period went, the less narcissistic you will be in adulthood. The more securely the sense of self develops the less concern there is with self. Too much or too little will lead to problems later on.

The Shadow Side of the Extrovert Culture

This is the age of narcissism, or what Dr. Young-Eisendrath calls the "Age of Self-Importance." Too much exaltation of self, including its latest expressions in social media has created a culture obsessed with the self. It is the problem with being special. Dr. Young-Eisendrath points out that the entire culture has bought into this myth of specialness and it is difficult to escape its grasp. It establishes the norms for parenting and the expectations for self, relationships, and happiness. She was trapped in it herself. "Inside the box we believe that everyone has something extraordinary to contribute to life and that being ordinary is an embarrassment." This pressure leads to too much self-focus.

Life should be fabulous, fun, and fantastic in every moment—an extrovert version of the good life. It is no wonder that almost everyone falls short of this ideal. It is well known that beyond a basic subsistence level there is no correlation between income and happiness. Once your basic needs are met, more money will not buy you happiness. Underlying the quest for happiness is the potential for feelings of emptiness, self-loathing, and anxiety. These are the shadow aspects of extroverted specialness. Too much self-importance is the culprit.

Coping with Disappointments, Setbacks, and Failures

Parenting styles have changed in the Age of Self-Importance. The parenting of previous generations could be characterized as benign neglect. Children were to be seen and not heard. Parents were strict and not particularly warm. They had high expectations and gave their children a lot of responsibility. Children were not the center of their universe.

As the baby boomer generation became parents, the pendulum swung in the other direction. Children became the center of attention. Since then, three styles of parenting have emerged. The first is called "laissez-faire parenting." These parents don't set limits and are chummy with their kids. They seek to be the opposite of their authoritarian parents. The next style of parenting is "helicopter parenting." These parents hover around their kids and do everything with them, believing that they and their children "always need to have pleasant, cozy, feelings." These parents stay friendly and close to their kids even as they go to college. Children, even as young adults, won't make decisions without consulting with their parents. Days may be spent exchanging text messages.

The third type of parenting is called "role-reversal." This is a more extreme version of helicopter parenting. "It's the full expression of the children-as-flowers fantasy; if you just give children the right nourishment, open affection, a lot of freedom and encourage their inner genius, they will flourish." If your kids aren't exceptional, then you have failed as a parent and shortchanged your child. Such parenting has fostered a generation of children who don't know how to take care of themselves (who live at home for prolonged periods of time), who are obsessed with self-importance (and are usually feeling inadequate), and are not prepared for the inevitable slings and arrows of life. They have been overprotected to a fault.

Preparing for Life

If you never do any physical work with your hands, you will not have calluses. Your skin will be tender and if exposed to something rough, you wind up with blisters. The emotional life has its version of calluses. If you don't expose yourself to challenges, adversity, and negativity, you'll never develop tough skin. These calluses allow you to handle more in the future. This is a paradox. The more you expose yourself, the more robust you become.

The Chinese character for "crisis" can also mean "opportunity." This ancient wisdom is still relevant today. Personality researcher Dan P. McAdams, author of influential textbook *Personality*, and more recently, *The Stories We Live By: Personal Myths and the Making of Self*, talks about the important role of adversity. Unhappy people focus on the crisis. The negative events of life make them feel deficient, defective, and deflated. They are seen as obstacles and not part of the natural order. Happier people see the opportunity in life's setbacks, disappointments, and failures. To be happy, you cannot be allergic to negativity. You must have calluses on your emotions yet not be callous—indifferent, disconnected, or numb. Your immune system protects you from illness, in part by producing antibodies to foreign invaders. The immune system learns from each exposure it has to things that should not be in the body. You have a psychological immune system too. It functions to protect you.

Happiness Is Waiting

In her TEDx Middlebury talk, Dr. Young-Eisendrath told the audience "happiness is not wanting things to be other than they are in this moment. Acceptance is integral to happiness. Instead of trying to micromanage your circumstances to fit with some preconceived notion of what happiness *should* be, you focus your attention on what *is* happening. Acceptance of the present moment helps to lessen shame. Things are not perfect for anyone. Everyone confronts adversity.

Having your share doesn't make you deficient. You can learn from adversity. You can grow from setbacks. You can meet challenges as they come to you. It helps when you don't compare yourself to others (or at least what others appear to be); it helps when you don't buy into the extroverted culture's images of happiness, success, and fun. When you let go of wanting things to be perfect, a freedom opens up where you can feel at home in any circumstance, not just the ones that go according to plan.

Be Authentic in Relationships

Dr. Young-Eisendrath cautions that love should not be taken for granted. She bristles against the cultural ideal of love as two streams flowing together. Love is more akin to two rocks rubbing up against each other. This friction smoothes the rough edges, but it is by no means a picnic. If the rocks touch hard enough, they may shatter.

A quick look at the divorce rate reveals a lot of broken rocks. The quest to avoid negativity can beset relationships too. When couples just focus on the pleasant, light, and passionate aspects of their relationship they fall into the trap of idealization. Challenge, heartache, and misunderstanding are integral to relationships, too.

FACT

The Center for Contemplative Mind in Society (*www.contemplative mind.org*) is located in Northampton, Massachusetts. Their mission is to transform, "higher education by supporting and encouraging the use of contemplative/introspective practices and perspectives to create active learning and research environments that look deeply into experience and meaning for all in service of a more just and compassionate society."

The extrovert culture fosters the over-emphasis on the positive—an idealized notion of relationships. It doesn't build a place for solitude. It doesn't value autonomy. It overlooks vulnerability. It runs the risk of being a sanitized version of connection. Perfectionism dominates. The ideal version of love is expansion without contraction. Reality, however, is expansion and contraction. If everyone is special, then their relationships should be special, too. When they turn out to be ordinary, disillusionment becomes a destructive force. People don't realize that disillusionment is a necessary part of any relationship. Its arrival is not the harbinger of an unforeseen problem but a sign that the relationship is maturing. Disillusionment forces the hand of acceptance. Dr. Young-Eisendrath says, "Loving a partner just as he or she is requires equanimity—that gentle, matter-of-fact awareness of what's actually going on."

Introversion as an Antidote to Narcissism

To avoid the self-esteem trap, you must be self-reflective in a way that transcends self-concern. Happiness is found through meaningful connection with others, by nurturing empathy, and by knowing yourself. If you are familiar with your interior, you know that it is not all peaches and cream.

The interior is a hotbed of emotions. You cannot know yourself very well unless you spend some time in silence. You can't appreciate the nuances of the human condition unless you have time in solitude to reflect. If you are constantly busy—as contemporary life demands—you may miss the wisdom available in the quiet heart. The way beyond narcissism is to get beyond the story of "me."

There are two main ways to transcend stories of self-importance. The first is to bring your attention to what is happening in the present moment. The second is to rotate that attention toward something bigger than yourself. Concern, care, and compassion for others are the antidotes to narcissism.

Dr. Young-Eisendrath prescribes six practices for "being ordinary." These are generosity, discipline, patience, diligence, concentration, and wisdom. If extroversion is the pursuit of *extraordinary*, then introversion is the embrace of *ordinary*. With the exception of generosity, each of these practices is more aligned with introvert tendencies. Both introverts and extroverts can be self-absorbed. Extroverts can be generous but they can also dominate conversations. Discipline focuses on reliability and responsibility. It's a natural fit for introverts who are conscientious and sensitive. So, too, with patience, diligence, and concentration. These are introvert qualities. Wisdom arises when you can accept the good and the bad in life with the even attention of equanimity and when you can enjoy life independent of circumstances.

CHAPTER 14

Navigating the Social Landscape

The most obvious difference between introverts and extroverts can be found in social situations. Extroverts are exuberantly social. They derive energy from engaging with others. Introverts are selectively social. They are deliberate and expend energy in social engagements. The extrovert is a public creature first; the introvert is a private creature first. This difference leads to many of the misunderstandings between introverts and extroverts and the erroneous impressions the culture (which, of course, is extroverted) perpetrates against introverts.

What Is Social Intelligence?

Introverts are neither antisocial nor asocial. They have different appetites for sociability and different versions of what they find meaningful in social situations. While gregarious extroverts appear more social, there may be a lack of depth to those connections. Introverts tend to prefer smaller groups of intimate friends to the social pack. Remember that introverts and extroverts differ in their preference for stimulation. Extroverts like the stimulating atmosphere of a big party with lots of conversations. The introvert finds the same social situation overstimulating and prefers one or two in-depth conversations to a series of "Hey, how are you? How was your summer?" type of exchanges.

QUOTE

"Whether you are surrounded by the singing of a lamp or the sounds of a storm, by the breathing of the evening or the sighing of the seas, there is a vast melody woven of a thousand voices that never leaves you and only occasionally leaves room for your solo. To know *when you have to join in*, that is the secret of your solitude, just as it is the art of true human interaction: to let yourself take leave of the lofty words to join in with the one shared melody."—Rainer Maria Rilke

Introverts and extroverts can have equivalent levels of social skills that are expressed in different ways. They will also communicate differently. Introverts and extroverts will take a different approach to anger. Extroverts are more prone to letting it all out—to express anger in the same enthusiastic, energetic way as everything else, and introverts are more prone to holding it in and processing it before talking about it. Introverts can get angry just like extroverts, and they often do. The gestation period for an emotion may be longer for the introvert and disconcerting for the extrovert. An extrovert would be more likely to express it and let it go; an introvert may mull it over for a while.

There is a classic Buddhist teaching story that goes like this: the monks were forbidden from touching women. Two monks were walking down the road and came across an old woman. There was a large puddle in the middle of the road and one of the monks picked her up and carried her across.

He was motivated by compassion. A few miles down the road, the other monk says, "I can't believe you touched that woman. It is forbidden." The compassionate monk replies, "I put her down miles ago, why are you still carrying her?" Blowing things up and holding them in are both imperfect strategies for dealing with strong emotions. Contrary to popular opinion, blowing off steam does not help you feel better. In fact, it can make the anger worse because you are not letting it go. Holding it in can increase stress, too.

The Four Horsemen of the Apocalypse

Dr. John Gottman is the author of *The Seven Principles for Making Marriage Work*, and he runs the "Love Lab," where he has conducted definitive research on couples' interactions. Couples spend the weekend in this lab, which is an apartment that has been rigged with cameras. Gottman believes that communication patterns predict marital discord and likelihood of divorce. Couples whose interactions are characterized by criticism, defensiveness, hostility, or stonewalling are at increased risk of later divorce. These communication styles are known as the "four horsemen of the apocalypse," because their presence is a reliable predictor of divorce. The introvert's silence and time lag to process might be seen by an extroverted partner as stonewalling. As the introvert, it can be helpful to negotiate for the time you need, and give your partner a clear sense of when you are going to respond. For instance, "I need some time to process this. Can we talk again in an hour?" Don't assume anyone—even another introvert—can read your distress. While it is painfully clear to you, it may not be apparent to others. Let them know.

Communication Skills

Mindfulness skills can help to manage anger and to tolerate dissent, discord, and drama; they can also improve communication. There are several communication methods that are based upon or consistent with mindfulness: Reflective listening, nonviolent communication (NVC), and Insight Dialogue. These methods can be helpful communication techniques for introverts and extroverts.

Insight Dialogue

Insight Dialogue is a process developed by Gregory Kramer that frames communication in a compassionate, kind, and effective framework. The steps in Insight Dialogue are Pause, Relax, Open, Trust Emergence, Listen Deeply, and Speak the Truth. These steps are grounded in mindfulness—attention to the here and now, with particular attention to the feelings in the body. To get beyond reactivity, based on old learned patterns and personality predilections, you must invite the *pause*. This means slowing down and looking before you leap. As an introvert, you may already be accustomed to this. For you, the challenge may be to pause before you withdraw or shut down. The next step is to *relax*. As you communicate about some difficulty, you notice tension in your body. By bringing attention to that tension, you can start to let it go. This helps to create a sense of *openness* to the other. Defensiveness gives way to curiosity about what is happening.

FACT

"Gregory Kramer, PhD, is the Founder and Guiding Teacher of Metta Programs and has been teaching Insight Meditation since 1980. He developed the practice of Insight Dialogue. The Metta Foundation was created in 1989 to offer programs and teachings to support life that is balanced, wakeful and compassionate. Its central offering is the meditation practice of Insight Dialogue, based on a relational understanding of early Buddhist teachings." (*www.metta.org*)

Trust emergence is letting go into the unknown and uncontrolled territory of authentic dialogue. You don't know what is going to happen next and the invitation is to trust what emerges without trying to micromanage it. When you micromanage, authentic communication cannot happen. In order to get anywhere with communication, you must *listen deeply*. This makes the act of listening a meditation. Your object of focus is the words and the very *being* of the other. You give your full attention and keep bringing your attention back to the other whenever it moves away (into the future planning what you are going to say next, or thinking back on something that was already said, and so forth). *Speaking the truth* is the final component. As the Buddha suggested, it is not enough to just speak the truth, the communication should also be beneficial. What is the purpose of your utterance? Is it to show off? Is it to shame? Is it to be right? Can you let go of being right to say what is authentically so for you? The authentic communication may surprise you.

Nonviolent Communication

Nonviolent communication (NVC) is a method and movement started by Marshall Rosenberg. "Violent" or life-alienating forms of communication that undermine effective communication involve moralistic judgments, making comparisons, denial of responsibility, and confusing demands with desires. Moralistic judgments may include blaming, name-calling, overgeneralizing or otherwise implying that the other person is wrong. Such judgments put people on the defensive and thwart effective communication. Making comparisons is another form of judgment that fosters defensiveness and distracts attention from the real issues at hand—your feelings. Denial of responsibility can also involve blaming or not taking account of your contribution to the situation. It is other-focused instead of self-focused and self-focus is crucial to NVC. Finally, NVC involves communicating your desires as needs and not making demands on the other.

The steps involved with NVC are Observe, Feel, Need, and Request. In *observe*, you pay close attention to the particular event that you are having feelings about. You avoid generalizing, criticizing, and blaming and instead make mention of the specifics of the situation. To do this, you must pay close attention to what is actually happening. In the *feel* step, you articulate what you feel in relation to what has happened or is happening. To do this step, you must have a broad and deep feeling vocabulary. You must be able to know and to articulate the feelings that you are having. Then you can address your *needs*. These are the values, beliefs, and desires that are giving rise to your feelings. By expressing needs you are taking responsibility for your feelings and you can avoid blaming, projecting, and other counterproductive communication strategies. Now the stage is set to make a *request* that can be received with openness.

A shorthand version of the Insight Dialogue and NVC approaches can be a simple "ouch" when something is said that hurts. The "ouch" communicates your feelings and alerts the other to something important that has occurred. Because it is your feeling, it is not blaming, and it implies a request to stop the offending behavior.

FACT

The Center for Nonviolent Communication (CNVC) was founded by Marshall Rosenberg and has a presence in 65 countries. "NVC begins by assuming that we are all compassionate by nature and that violent strategies—whether verbal or physical—are learned behaviors taught and supported by the prevailing culture." (*www.cnvc.org*)

Reflective Listening

Both NVC and Insight Dialogue are consistent with what the influential psychologist Carl Rogers called "unconditional positive regard." Another simple technique based on Rogers's humanistic psychology is reflective listening. When one partner speaks, the other listens actively. It is hard to listen to another when you don't agree or they are saying something that is upsetting you. This gives rise to reactivity and defensiveness. Listening does not mean agreeing. It gives the other an opportunity to be heard. When you listen and your partner finishes, you relate back what you just heard to let them know that you understand what the concern is. This is the key to active listening. Now you have a chance to speak. You can use a timer for this process if needed and take turns so that you and your partner can both be heard.

Protecting Yourself from Energy Vampires

Extroverts draw energy from socializing and introverts spend it. Some extroverts can also take energy from you. These people are known as energy vampires—sucking the life out of you. These are extroverts who are exceedingly dull, self-absorbed, or needy. Not all energy vampires are extroverts, but it can be challenging to find yourself stuck in a conversation with someone who does not stop talking. Being sensitive to the needs of others, you probably don't want to exit in the middle of a story, and this person keeps telling lengthy story after lengthy story. If the energy vampire is interested in your story, you may find being interrogated is stressful, too. This extrovert interviews you, firing question after question.

The extrovert interprets your silence as an opportunity to keep talking. He is not likely to appreciate that you are processing and need that silent time to do so. To get a word in edgewise, you have to force yourself, and this is draining, too. Is there a way to gracefully exit a conversation that is steam-rolling you? If you really had to pee, you would beg out of the conversation. Why can't you beg out for a less "legitimate" reason—that you are bored to tears? Or you are about to collapse from fatigue? There isn't a language for this introvert self-care behavior. Society doesn't sanction such forthright-ness. As a compromise between accommodating and brutal honesty, you can simple say, "Excuse me, I must beg your pardon," and then leave. In extreme cases, the person may continue talking. Certainly, you can imagine this on the telephone. How many times have you held the phone out from your ear as you roll your eyes? How many times have you walked away from the telephone and returned to find the person prattling on at the other end? It is hard not to be rude in situations with energy vampires—"Pardon me, you are sucking the life out of me; would you mind stopping?" When you are in this kind of situation, try to keep some attention on your breathing. Imagine a protective boundary around you where the words of the vampire just slide off.

Becoming Invisible

H. G. Wells's classic the *Invisible Man* is an attractive fantasy for introverts. The Invisible Man could enter any situation unobtrusively. He could be left alone. Unfortunately, a side effect of the potion he ingested to become invis-ible was megalomaniacal madness. If he hadn't become mad, he might have enjoyed being a pure observer of the world around him. For the intro-vert, seeking invisibility is a necessary refueling of energy and not neces-sarily a denial of self. To be invisible is to be relieved of social demands in the moment. It is a respite from the incessant expectations of others to be happy, "on," and part of the fun. How do you become invisible without drinking dangerous concoctions? Adopt the role of the observer—become an anthropologist doing a field study of the humanity around you. Become an archeologist studying the relics at hand.

Your breath and body provide what might be thought of as a cloaking device. In *Star Trek*, the enemy Romulans and Klingons have cloaking technology. They are able to make their ships invisible. While cloaked, however, they cannot fire weapons. Your cloaking device is an interior stance, a turning inside when the moment becomes too much. At first, when you ground yourself in the feelings of your breath and body you won't be able to fire—that is, talk. With practice you'll be able to be enjoy the protection of the cloaking device of mindful attention to the body while you communicate. You can be invisible and engaged at the same time.

Social Media for Introverts

A metaphor used in understanding how to network in social media is the cocktail party. You would not go into a party with a megaphone to get your message across; so too, in social media. You don't shout—post messages about what you want to promote. Instead, you engage in conversations. This is your strength as an introvert—initiating and sustaining deep connections.

FACT

There were almost 1.5 billion social network users in 2012, which was a near 20 percent increase over 2011. Almost two-thirds of U.S. Internet users are active in social media. There are over 500 million Twitter accounts, and 900 million users on Facebook.

The Internet presents interesting challenges and opportunities for Introverts. It is a way to connect that may be less taxing than face-to-face communication. But you may find that "being on" Facebook is similar in feeling to "being on" in a conversation. At least with Facebook and other social media platforms, you have more control.

The Internet has changed privacy. People now post their private lives online through Facebook, Instagram, Twitter, and other social media applications. This is the age of privacy lost, a devaluing of the quiet, intimate, private space of the interior. It is an age where people want to get noticed by friends and strangers. On the one hand, the dynamics of the Internet appeal to introverts. You can sit in the comfort and privacy of your home and participate or not, participate according to your preference and energy. Don't feel like chatting on Facebook? You can turn off the chat function. You can't do that at a real party without looking aloof at best or misanthropic at worst. On the other hand, the pressures of social media may feel like just that—pressures. Facebook, Twitter, and Google Plus are arenas where you have to be "on" in some way. This can make social media feel like a burden. Find your places in social media—the points that you wish to enter—and don't feel guilty about not participating when you don't feel like participating. It's just like any other social intercourse—it takes energy to engage. Your energy is valuable. How do you want to spend it?

Party Survival Guide

An upcoming social event may recall the words of the classic Clash song, "Should I Stay or Should I Go?" The Clash warned that if you stay there will be trouble, if you go there will be double trouble. Damned if you do, damned if you don't. If you go, you may be drained; if you don't go, you may have an acute case of FOMO (fear of missing out), or someone important to you will be disappointed. At times, you may feel like you can tap into your extrovert reserve and go to the party as a pseudo-extrovert. At other times, all you will feel is dread.

ESSENTIAL

Avowed introvert and author of *Quiet Influence: The Introvert's Guide to Making a Difference*, Jennifer Kahnweiler says, "I recognize a powerful shift occurs when I flow into the less prominent side of my personality. When I choose to embrace my internal energy, I gain deeper insights, delve into my creativity, and become more centered."

How do you decide? Consider the gravity of the social occasion. How important is it that you attend? Is it important to your work or your career? Is it important to some cause that is important to you? For example, a black-tie affair for a nonprofit you support. How invisible and anonymous will you be there? Will there be places to escape to? Spots to hide out? Are you locked in, such as at a formal dinner, or can you make a showing then disappear? Can you come and go as you please? Is this a recurring or onetime event? Is someone counting on your being there? How is your energy level? Do you have a reserve you can draw on? Have you been going out a lot or not much at all? Is it a good time to push yourself?

QUOTE

"It may seem impossible to be authentic and engaging while promoting yourself. You're bored by people who talk too much about themselves, and you don't want to be a bore. But if you don't talk about yourself, you'll have to rely on others to do so. This can leave you feeling powerless and disappointed—not to mention invisible."—Nancy Ancowtiz from *Self-Promotion for Introverts*

If you decide to say no, you want to be as tactful as possible. Experts disagree on whether you should be blunt or tell a white lie. Which will you choose? Part of that choice depends on whether you want future invitations. If you don't, then let it be known that it is not your thing. Feel free to be blunt. If your reason is situational, you may want to make excuses and tell that white lie. You may also be able to be truthful without turning off your host. Can you take this as an opportunity to embrace your introversion and tell some version of your truth? "Thank you for the invitation. It means a lot to me. However, I need to decline."

You don't have to make excuses about "being wiped" or having something else already planned. You can just say that you don't want to attend. If you get pushed for more of an answer, you can say, "I need to take care of my energy and that is why I am declining. I am not in a place where I will enjoy myself. Thanks again, and I hope you have fun." While you may refuse most social invitations, there will inevitably be some social occasions you cannot duck—weddings, bar mitzvahs, and work functions. Here is a guide for surviving parties:

- The best way to survive a party might be to say no to the invitation.
- If you know you have a big event coming up, conserve your energy leading up to this event. Bring fresh energy.

- Like elite athletes, you can use visualization to improve your performance. Create a picture in your mind of the event you are going to attend (if it is in an unfamiliar place you may want to do a dry run if that is possible). See yourself being in this place in a relaxed manner. Imagine the feeling of being calm in that situation. Recall other times when you enjoyed being in a similar situation. Call to mind success and also imagine the worst-case scenario. Can you survive that? It would be unpleasant but you *could* survive.

- Don't drink the Kool-Aid. Don't buy into the extrovert ideal. You don't have to be the life of the party; you don't have to have the best time of your life. Your job is to show up. Try to make at least one meaningful connection.

- When you are at the party, give yourself permission to leave after a certain point, once you have made a sufficient appearance.

- Be embodied. As you walk into the party, remind yourself that you have a right to be there and that you do not have to be a performer. Give yourself permission to be an observer. Give yourself time to warm up. Ease in gradually.

- If it is a big party, you may have more anonymity. Survey the room and find a place where you can camp out.

- Channel the anthropologist Margaret Mead. Adopting the anthropologist's mindset can be very useful at parties and, indeed, all social functions. Instead of being caught up in performing, you adopt the role of observer. Imagine that you are attending the party with your clipboard, recording careful observations. When you are observing others, you won't be preoccupied with yourself and how you feel or how you are coming across to others. The more elaborate the party, the keener your observations can become. What are people wearing? Watch their body language. Listen to the rhythm of the conversations and hear the din of the room as a musical performance. Observation provides protection. It is a place to hide in plain sight. You might even want to bring your journal and take notes on what you see (perhaps when you are taking care of yourself with strategic exits from the extrovert circus). You can also practice being an archeologist. Imagine that this is a new culture that has just been discovered. What can you learn about it by studying the artifacts that are present (you probably do this anyway)? Examine the books, magazines, and artwork, the architecture, and interior design. This can be a helpful break from introductions and small talk.

- Take frequent breaks. Find your respite places. Look for egress into nature; locate the restrooms, the staircase leading to a less crowded area. Walk outside if possible. Get some "fresh air."
- Pace yourself. If this is a party where you know a lot of people, you can find meaningful ways to connect. If the setting is a group of strangers, abandon the tyranny of meeting everyone.
- Have several versions of an elevator pitch ready to respond, especially with strangers. Mix it up and have fun with it. In business, elevator pitches are usually sixty seconds long or about 200 words. In social settings, you could focus on about thirty seconds for the casual introduction or about 100 words. Practice your pitch. It will do in a pinch.
- Find something to do other than relentless socializing or hiding out. Does the host need help with something? Animals and kids may be more approachable targets.
- Use your smart phone. Practice info-mania if you must (obsessively checking e-mail, status updates, and voicemail). Your phone can be a refuge and also a lens to view the party. Take pictures. Step outside to make calls, write text messages or e-mails.
- Take your own car or arrange alternative transportation if you come with a friend. You may have a different appetite than your ride and want to escape earlier. Be willing to take a cab if that is the best way to take care of yourself.
- Practice mindfulness. You can focus on your breathing whenever you get tense or locked up. In those moments, your breathing will be tighter, shallower, and more rapid. By focusing attention on breathing, you can help the breath to soften, deepen, and slow down. This will activate your parasympathetic (calming) nervous system and deactivate your sympathetic (arousal) nervous system. Remember that every breath you take reflects your emotional state. Take your emotional pulse. Where are you?
- Don't beat yourself up. Things will not go perfectly. You will not be the most eloquent speaker; you will not say everything you could have possibly said. Try to let go of perfectionism and embrace being good

enough. Aim for 80 percent. Giving yourself permission to be imperfect can help you to relax and actually facilitate your being closer to "perfect."

- Schedule recharging. After exerting yourself at a party, you will want to nurture your energy. It takes additional energy to self-reproach; don't waste energy on beating yourself up for not being more of an extrovert. Plan an activity (or no activity) that will help you to recoup. Going to the party expended energy; it's now time to restore the bank account or put water back in the well.

Practicing the Art of Chitchat

Some people naturally have the gift of gab. You may marvel at these people—"How can he do that?" Or you may be repelled—"Aargh, what a bore." While some seem to be born with the ability, it is a learnable skill and one that you can practice. When you enter into a social situation where chitchat will be happening, you'll want to be prepared. Keep up with some news and popular culture so you can be topical. Be prepared to discuss what is interesting to you. Practice opening lines and transitions to keep the conversation going (that is, if you *want* the conversation to continue). You can practice speaking in front of the mirror or with a trusted friend. Remember to speak aloud if you are practicing at home alone. There is no substitute for projecting your voice.

People love to talk about themselves. You can always engage extroverts by asking them questions. Put on your reporter cap and interview. Asking questions provides cover, and besides, you are a good listener. Practice your exit strategy. Have phrases prepared. Don't just slink away. Don't be afraid to take note cards with reminders. You might need prompts if it is an over-stimulating situation.

Surviving the Holidays

The holidays (especially the stretch between Thanksgiving and the New Year) are stressful for everyone, particularly for introverts. Holiday stress starts with anticipation. You know you are going to be put in situations that are going to be taxing and they may be unrelenting compared to your normal life. You won't have the freedom to disappear that you exercise in your regular life and at most parties. It's hard to excuse yourself from Thanksgiving dinner, telling everyone "I've just had enough."

Getting there is another dimension of stress. You may be forced into an airplane stuck for hours next to someone who won't stop talking ("Is there a way to jump off this plane?!"). You may have to drive for hours to your destination in a crowded car with kids and spouse. A drive alone may be a welcome delight, but the family packed into the car can be a nightmare. Then you have to deal with the actual holiday festivities. Family visits can trigger a lot of emotions. Almost every family has "issues." There was a cartoon that depicted a conference for "functional families." There was only *one* person in the audience. One family therapist quipped that a dysfunctional family was "any family that had more than one member." It is hard to arrive at the family gathering without expectations, hopes, and desires. If you are attached to the outcome, you will experience a lot of misery. If you can let go of your hopes, you can protect yourself from disappointment.

QUOTE

"There must be quite a few things that a hot bath won't cure, but I don't know many of them."—Sylvia Plath

Hosting presents its own set of challenges. You have people in your home and you are forced into being "on" for prolonged periods of time. You can take refuge in the kitchen or in cleaning up. Delegate as much as you can to other family members. Don't be afraid to disappear for little energy tune-ups. Here are additional suggestions:

- Get engaged with meal preparations and the like. Having something to do can be a respite from relentless socializing.
- Check your expectations at the door. You've been through this a thousand times before. Don't get caught up with expecting family members to be reasonable, quiet, and to drink moderate amounts. Expect the worst and be relieved if it's not that bad.

- Plan some solitary time—go for a quiet walk, or walk ahead or fall back behind the pack in a group walk.
- Take your headphones, especially for the car or airplane.
- Try to get sufficient sleep. The commotion will be more stressful if you are sleep deprived.
- Practice little bits of mindful breathing throughout the day.
- The festivities will make a hefty withdrawal from your energy savings account. Conserve before; restore afterward.
- Perhaps you can take that hot bath that Sylvia Plath recommends.

CHAPTER 15

Close Relationships

Intimate relationships are a crucible. They can be especially challenging for introverts when paired with either extroverts or other introverts. Communication challenges are common for the introvert-extrovert couple. Even though your spouse is your safe person, you will sometimes be in polar opposite places regarding energy, need for communication, and desire for stimulation. If you don't understand each other's temperaments, conflicts can abound.

The Dating Scene

A recent Vermont Public Radio commentary by a twenty-something introvert extolled the virtues of online dating. This woman found her fiancé through the online process and felt that approaching dating this way suited her temperament. Going to bars to find dates can be a challenging environment for an introvert. They may be crowded, loud, and chaotic. Speed dating is another venue that is probably not the best setup for an introvert. If it takes you time to warm up and settle down, the speed of speed dating will leave you speechless half the time. By the time you are ready to talk, your next partner will be sitting in front of you. Online dating avoids these pitfalls, but by dating you will have to confront your introvert tendencies more than staying single.

Image credit: Michaela Chung, Introvert Spring (*www.introvertspring.com*)

Unlike a blind date, you can get a lot of information beforehand with online dating. Of course, you still have to go out on dates, but these may go smoother with some backstory. Don't be surprised if people misrepresent themselves online; it's a common complaint. As with any dating situation, people are going to be put their best foot forward and disillusionment will likely follow any idealization. Keep your expectations in that context and you'll avoid a lot of frustration.

FACT

There is an online dating website devoted to introverts: The Introvert Dating Site (*www.introvertdatingsite.com*). Match.com has Tips for Dating an Introvert (*www.match.com/magazine/article/12181/*) that covers: flirting, conversation, communication, socializing, and conflict. And also Tips for Dating an Extrovert (*www.match.com/magazine/article/12180/Tips-For-Dating-An-Extrovert/*).

How does an introvert meet someone if online dating is not yet their thing? The key to meeting people is to circulate as much as possible in your community. This, of course, can be difficult for you if you prefer quiet activities at home. You are more likely to meet an extrovert out in the community, because that's where extroverts are found. You are more likely to find introverts in the relative anonymity and controlled environment of Internet dating. You may want to be with an introvert because he or she will understand you implicitly without any need to explain yourself. An extrovert, however, can draw you out, complement you, and challenge you to grow.

How to Get Along with an Extrovert

There is a very good chance that you are in close relationships with one or more extroverts. Introvert-extrovert pairs can make great complements to one another and can also be the source of much friction. The extroverted partner can draw you out into the world, maintain the social calendar, and make life fun. You, as the introvert, can add a sense of groundedness, calm, and deep significance. Sometimes, though, these different ways of being in the world can be at odds with each other. One partner wants more of one kind of socializing while the other wants less. You will probably have to be explicit about your style and what you need. You will have to teach the extroverts in your life the unique contribution of introverts.

The extroverts in your life are not mind readers. You will have to tell them what you are thinking and feeling. When you are in conversation, the challenge is to hold a space for yourself where you don't get sucked into the conversation and lose energy. You may need to request time to pause and reflect. This time needs to be requested explicitly, otherwise the extrovert may interpret your silence as your not having anything to say. Conversation with extroverts needs a version of Miranda rights. "You have the right to remain silent. Anything you say (before you are ready to say it), can and will be used against you in the court of relationship." Your internal process can be a rich source of information—your feelings can guide you in conversation, but this richness will be missed if you don't cultivate silence. Tell your partner, "Listen, I know this is important to you and I really want to address this, but I need some time to think this over before I respond."

Work to Home Transitions

After a long day at work, especially if you have been forced to be a pseudo-extrovert, the last thing you want to do when you get home is socialize. Your extroverted partner just wants to keep the party going. How can you navigate this territory? Your partner may feel resentful that you spent your social quota at work. You just want to unwind.

Extroverts may not *get* what it is like to be an introvert and to feel drained from being socially overstimulated all day at work. While it may not be true that men are from Mars and women are from Venus, it is more likely the case that extroverts are from Mars and introverts are from Venus (assuming Mars is a party-planet and Venus is quiet). As the introvert, you must be sensitive to how your needs for solitude affect your extroverted partner. Just as they may not be able to *get* what you need, you may not *get* how they can't *get* you. Solitude needs to be negotiated and you just can't assume that your needs are obvious. Your partner may feel lonely, resentful, or deprived of your best attention. They may feel taken for granted.

QUOTE

"When romantic partners first meet, their introverted or extroverted temperament may not be apparent. And even if their temperaments are noticeable, in the honeymoon stage of a relationship, differences are often seen as refreshing and exciting. However, as the initial glow fades, those *same* differences become tiresome and irritating."—Marti Olsen Laney

Even if you spend a lot of time with your partner raising children and running a household, it is important to spend deliberate and fun time together. This is called "date night." Commit to going out and doing something fun once a week, preferably on the same night each week. Make it a serious commitment. If you have to cancel, reschedule. You may want to alternate doing quiet versus loud activities or do a mixture of both each evening—dinner with friends and then a movie. It can be an interesting experiment to learn something new with your partner. This puts you both on equal footing of being novices and you can enjoy stretching yourselves together.

Introverts and extroverts may have different styles for dealing with conflict. The extrovert may want to engage, confront, and process in real time while the introvert may want to withdraw or avoid conflict. This can lead to painful relationship dynamics. One partner wants to be heard, and the less she is heard the more she approaches. The other partner feels overwhelmed and the more demands that are placed upon him, the more he withdraws. It's a vicious cycle that leaves both partners feeling dissatisfied.

Managing the Mix

Practice asking for what you need from the extroverts in your life. Let them know when you are at your limit and need to withdraw (rather than just withdrawing and doing a vanishing act that leaves them assuming you are surly, aloof, or that something is wrong with you).

It's a caricature to think that all extroverts are shallow and happy and all introverts are deep and sullen. You each have something to offer. An extrovert can help draw you out into the world and you can draw them into the interior. Introvert to introvert relationships can become insular with neither party drawing the other out. Extrovert to extrovert relationships can become competitive.

The introvert-extrovert coupling, while challenging, also presents many opportunities. You can grow together when you take a stance of curiosity rather than judgment toward each other's differences. Occasionally, it can be helpful for your relationship with an extrovert and for your own growth to push yourself outside your comfort zone. Let's say your extroverted partner has an important social function—one of those gala fundraisers where you meet and greet countless strangers. It's the kind of social event that makes you want to run for the exit. You can use mindfulness skills to help you cope with such an event. You can bring your observation skills and observe. You can let go, surrender into the energy of the evening, and see where it takes you.

Intimacy with Fewer Words

The male introvert-female extrovert pairing presents a particular test because the man is not in the traditional bold action-oriented role. Another consternating variation is when one partner (either sex) has to be a pseudo-extrovert at work all day and comes home to an extroverted partner. The introvert is exhausted from performing all day and just wants some down time. If the extroverted partner does not understand, this can lead to conflicts. In the traditional sex roles, the man comes home having given all his best energy to work and may not be that comfortable talking about his feelings and his female partner experiences him as distant. She presses for more connection and he withdraws further. The more each tries to get their needs met, the more defensive they both get.

Fluctuating Energies

Introverts in relationships with introverts can find a wonderful comfort together without the demands of being extroverted. The challenge for introvert couples may be boredom, confinement, or complacency. The relationship may become stagnant. While both partners may be introverts, each will have their own levels of introversion and their energies may fluctuate throughout the day and over time.

ESSENTIAL

Seven really irritating extrovert behaviors: (1) They are too happy for Happy Hour and expect you to be, too; (2) the party never stops and you are a party pooper if you leave early; (3) their part of the conversation sounds like a Facebook status update; (4) strangers get included in your dates; the whole world is a potential friend; (5) your silence means they get to speak more; (6) you hate talking on the phone and they call you to update you on the trivialities of their day; and (7) they think something is wrong with you if you are not smiling and jumping up and down for joy (pensive is not okay or is threatening).

As the introvert in a relationship you cannot assume that your partner knows when you are feeling underpowered and need to recharge. It is important for you to recognize when your energy is flagging and not only to communicate this to your partner but to do something about it as well. Energy maintenance is *the* key task for introverts, and taking care of your energy can be a boon to your relationship. For example, don't just disappear when you need to withdraw. Communicate to your partner what's happening. Let him or her know what is going to happen: "I need to go meditate for a little while to restore my energy. I'll be back in forty-five minutes, and then we can talk" (or go out or whatever it is that your partner wants to do).

Expressing Feelings

Is it difficult for you to express your feelings? An extrovert may say whatever is on her mind, but introverts like to ponder things and sometimes have difficulty committing to words. The words may seem inadequate to express the depth of what you feel. Practice expressing appreciation for your partner. You may think your feelings are obvious because you feel them so intensely, but never assume that your partner can read minds (or feelings). You may have to push yourself through the discomfort to become more familiar with the give and take of verbal banter.

Introverts can bring a world of silence to a relationship. Intimacy does not always have to be verbal. Indeed, most of human communication is nonverbal, and couples can be intimate without exchanging words. Introverts enjoy the company of solitude—having private space among people.

Perhaps this means just sitting on the couch with your partner reading or watching television.

You can also find this space in a coffee shop where you read or write in the presence of others who are reading and writing. Look around the coffee shop; chances are introverts are overrepresented in this group. Writing is often preferable to speaking. You may find the synchronous (chatting) or asynchronous (posting) or interactive Tweeting aspects of social media more comfortable to approach. You can opt in or opt out depending on your energy in the moment.

Harmony

Asian cultures place an emphasis on harmony. Confucius and the Buddha have been strong influencers of these traditions. Asian cultures regard space differently than Western cultures. If the West is *in your face*, then the East is eyes cast down and away. Indeed, different cultures have different norms for personal space. Americans have the least amount of personal space. In cultures like Japan and China, there is more respect for personal space and a wish not to intrude upon, offend, or waste the time of another. Of course, there are loud-mouthed extroverts in every culture, but the norm is more interior and focused on group harmony.

The ancient manuals of Buddhist psychology known as the Abhidhamma reveal an interesting facet about the importance of harmony. In this system, mindfulness is not a standalone factor. It is one of the nineteen "beautiful mental factors." Mindfulness is not just about paying attention, when it occurs it co-occurs with a host of other mental factors. These include *hiri* and *ottappa*. *Hiri* is the social conscience; it is concerned with the well-being of others and seeks not to do anything that would harm someone else. *Ottappa* is a private ethical conscience and seeks not to do anything that would cause harm to self. For instance, if you get angry and berate your spouse, this is *ahirika* (the negation of *hiri)*. If you get angry with your spouse, and instead of expressing it, you ruminate, then *anottappa* has occurred (the negation of *ottappa)*. To be fully present in the moment, you need to be not causing harm to self or others. Tranquility is another factor that is always present when the mind is engaged with mindfulness. To learn more about the Buddha's psychology, visit the Barre

Center for Buddhist Studies in Barre, Massachusetts that offers courses and workshops (*www.bcbsdharma.org*).

FOMO

Fear of missing out (FOMO) is a new cultural phenomenon that seems to have been birthed by the digital age. Now you don't have to imagine what everyone else is doing, you just have to look at their Facebook feeds. There is a tension between self-care and opportunity. If you go to the party you are dreading going to, you will feel depleted. If you don't go, you may simmer with anxiety wondering what you are missing out on. Meanwhile, you are feeling bad because everyone else seems to be having a good time except you.

FOMO takes you out of the moment and into comparison-land. It creates a trap of contingency where you can only be okay if conditions are just right, everyone likes you, et cetera. FOMO can be the source of a deep abiding anxiety that only gets worse as the world becomes more connected. You probably carry around a personal computer in your back pocket that connects you to the Internet and social media. The world's information is at your fingertips. You are always missing out on something.

FACT

There are two types of people: optimizers and satisficers. Optimizers seek the best of everything they do. They research a purchase, agonize over it, and are less likely to be satisfied in the end. Satisficers seek "good enough." Once they reach a sufficient level of satisfaction, they are happy and tend to remain so.

When you get caught up in the web of possibilities and feel lacking, FOMO disconnects you from your interior strength. As an alternative, you can give yourself permission to be present to this moment. You can bless your choice to be alone and to enjoy this sacred (and needed) time. You can remember that there will always be another opportunity tomorrow when your energy might be in a different place. Remember that it is the quality of experience rather than the quantity of experience that is most important. Breathe through any anxiety that lingers. Know that this will pass.

Healthy Balance

As an introvert, you must navigate the balance between talking and being daily. The multifaceted demands of a cocktail party are well suited to extroverts' brains. They can handle multiple loads on their attention; they can scan and integrate and perform under those conditions—and rather than feeling like a performance, it is a natural, energizing environment for them. By contrast, introverts will find the same stimulation overwhelming—too many things going on at once.

An experiment by psychologist Avril Thorne had introverts and extroverts talking to one another. When introverts talked to introverts they chose weightier topics compared to the extrovert-extrovert pairs, who talked more about lighter topics. When the pairs were mixed, however, an interesting synergy emerged. Extroverts have a tendency to draw introverts out, to make the conversation lighter. The study showed that introverts do like to talk although they tend to talk about different things. Introverts crave simplification and quieter surrounds. They will find home base when they can narrow attention into a single conversation.

You probably take talking for granted; after all you've been doing it since you were eighteen months old. However, the most basic of human tasks like talking, reading, and writing require astonishing complexity. The brainpower that goes into navigating a simple conversation is formidable and something the most sophisticated computer cannot yet replicate. Multiply that conversation by all the factors that are present at a social function like a dinner or cocktail party and you have a situation that requires an even greater amount of brain power. Extroverts thrive in these situations and introverts are overextended—fish out of water.

CHAPTER 16

Guardians of Solitude Lost

The great early twentieth-century poet Rainer Maria Rilke knew a thing or two about solitude. In the *Book of Hours* he said, "I am alone in the world, and yet not alone enough to make every hour holy." For introverts, solitude is the precondition for "holiness." Rilke, a likely introvert, notes the intrusions on his aloneness—social obligations, and other important matters that kept him from the art of writing. The value of solitude has been lost in this extroverted culture. To be alone is sometimes considered to be pathetic. Solitude is confused with loneliness.

The Importance of Solitude

Rilke said in one of his letters from the collection *Letters on Life*, edited and translated by Ulrich Baer, "I have little to add except the following, which is valid in all cases: the advice, perhaps, to take solitude seriously and whenever it occurs to experience it as something good." He recognizes that the majority of people may not appreciate the value of solitude and that a key component to human relationships is denying the inevitable space that separates even the closest human beings. The collective culture fears solitude and maintains a suspicion of those who crave it ("What are they doing alone?"). Extroverts can't understand why introverts want time apart—from their perspective, the more the merrier. Alone time for an extrovert may feel like exile, an uncomfortable place tinged with anxiety, boredom, and restlessness.

QUOTE

"How many of us are taught the value of solitude skills? How many of us are taught to protect our boundaries, to foster imagination, to be alone? How many of us are encouraged to withdraw from social activities and nurture the life of the mind?"—Laurie Helgoe

American culture also promotes an idealized notion of relationship as the merging of two people. Just listen to any popular love songs to find ample evidence of this. The goal is to *complete* yourself with the other person, to find your "soul mate," and to merge into one another to become *one*. Psychologists would view this fusion as unhealthy. A *Saturday Night Live* skit portrayed a couple enjoying this culturally sanctioned *fused* form of love. "You found that one special someone and you never want to be apart." They did everything together. The punch line was their use of a special double commode, "The Love Toilet" that allowed them to continue being together always!

The other extreme is unhealthy, too—being cut off from others. Introverts know how to take refuge. To be a healthy introvert, you seek a balance in the middle of merging on the one side and cutting off on the other. Introverts want meaningful connections with others in the context of solitude. They are not loners, but need "me" time. Without the possibility of solitude—both physical and emotional—the introvert can feel trapped, exposed, and ill at ease. You have probably experienced this yourself. When the demands of others, whether kids, spouses, or bosses feels like too much, you want to withdraw to restore your energy. You may feel guilty for having this need even though it is not your choice. It is, after all, how you are built. Relationships need an explicit agreement around solitude and this can be a difficult negotiation in an introvert-extrovert couple. You need to be aware of your need for solitude, prioritize it, and sustain it. Better to be proactive and take the time and space to restore before you get tapped out and cranky.

The Place for Solitude

Rilke recognized that the need for solitude has to be protected. The crowd does not prioritize solitude. Therefore it is imperative to bring separateness into a relationship by mutual consent—thus each partner appoints the other. Indeed, Rilke thinks this appointing process is the highest honor that can be bestowed in a relationship. To be the *guardian of solitude* is a crucial task in a relationship.

QUOTE

"I consider the following to be the highest task in the relation between two people: for one to stand guard over the other's solitude. If the essential nature of both indifference and the crowd consists in the non-recognition of solitude, then love and friendship exist in order to continually furnish new opportunities for solitude. And only those commonalities are true that rhythmically interrupt deep states of loneliness."—Rainer Maria Rilke

Solitude is like punctuation in writing. Writing has built in pauses: commas, periods, paragraphs, and chapters. It would be difficult to read a run-on sentence that went for pages and pages. Your mind would get weary. You would gasp for air, as if you were swimming to the surface of the water from a great depth. Relationships are like writing—they need pauses, too—this is the value of solitude. Connection requires the pause of solitude otherwise it becomes a run-on sentence. You get on each other's nerves. As an introvert, without solitude in your relationship, you will feel trapped, claustrophobic, and resentful. Solitude is not disconnection—it is the space that allows connection to be possible. Real connection *requires* solitude. You may find it difficult to have your solitude. Your partner may not understand. They take your need for space as a personal rejection. Quantity of connection gets confused with quality of connection.

Everyone wants to be witnessed, heard, and validated. For introverts, it just takes a little bit of silence to do this. Solitude will not always feel good. That's an idealization. But solitude is necessary like air. It is not a luxury. Solitude is the core of connection. It should not be confused with loneliness, isolation, or disconnection.

Making Solitude a Priority

The culture of extroversion is so pervasive it is hard to see objectively. Laurie Helgoe shares a scenario that highlights the ubiquity and absurdity of the extrovert domination. Imagine that you are depleted from a week of being "on" and you are looking forward to a quiet Friday evening at home. You bump into a friend who invites you to a party. You decline and your friend gives you a concerned look like there might be something wrong with you. "Why wouldn't you want to go out?" your friend thinks. "TGIF!" It's time to celebrate the weekend with parties, dinners, and drinks. What if you reversed this scenario? When you bump into your friend, you tell her that you are going to a party. She now gives you a look of concern and says, "You've been waiting all week for some time to yourself, why would you compromise that?"

The poet David Whyte echoes a similar sentiment. It is okay to decline weekend plans to paint the house or watch a football game, but it might be regarded as weird to decline those same plans to work on your poetry. The extrovert culture does not value the interior and along with that goes poetry, reflection, and just being. You can call in sick to work when you have a cold, but you can't call in sick when your soul is exhausted and you need time to recharge your batteries. Solitude is not prioritized.

Image credit: Michaela Chung, Introvert Spring (*www.introvertspring.com*)

The late Kurt Vonnegut said the only thing more difficult than telling your parents that you are gay is telling them that you want to be an artist. The life of the mind is not valued in the extroverted, action-oriented, money-making circus that is contemporary life.

QUOTE

"We have a verb for interacting with people—socializing—but have no single, affirmative verb to describe being alone."—Laurie Helgoe

Perhaps a new term is in order? "Solituding" is a mouthful, but gets at this essential activity. Solitude is seen as pathology or an indulgence, but it is not necessarily either of these. Solitude, as Rilke said and the Buddha observed 2,500 years ago, is a key part of being human.

The Buddha advocated a balance of solitude and community. The interior was valued and made central through meditation. Yet meditation took place in communal form. The *sangha*, or community of practitioners, was one of the three gems of his teachings. Presence together in silence. Today, you have the "uncomfortable" silence not a shared one.

ESSENTIAL

Activities that nurture solitude: meditating, contemplating, praying, pondering, daydreaming, journaling, walking, reading, writing, painting, drawing, breathing.

Solitude is on the periphery. It is viewed with suspicion—a depressed place of painful emptiness or the place where misanthropic serial killers plot their maleficence. What if solitude were placed at the center? Being social would then be seen as a deficiency in solitude, a potential imbalance to be guarded against. Solitude is not profitable. Madison Avenue cannot sell solitude as much as it can sell stuff. Some of that stuff you can enjoy in solitude, but that is not the way it is presented. When you are comfortable in solitude, you may not need so much stuff. When you can enjoy your own company or the simple pleasures of nature, you are not spending that much money. Breathing is free. You don't need any props, accouterments, or gadgets.

Intrusion is the norm for personal space. You may find that you need to build a wall around yourself to get the solitude and privacy that you crave. It's not just a simple request. It's an ordeal, especially if you are surrounded by extroverts who don't want solitude or don't get how important solitude is for you.

Solitude in Connection

Solitude is the practice of what child therapist Donald Winnicott termed "being alone together"; it is integral to the ability of the child to self-soothe. Ideal child development occurs from a place of secure attachment. The capacity to be alone in the context of an attuned connection lays the groundwork for healthy brain development, especially in the prefrontal cortex that is responsible for social, emotional, and self-awareness capacities. The prefrontal cortex of the brain undergoes a critical period of development early in life. When children don't get solitude in the context of connection they become insecurely attached and either cling to or cut themselves off from other people.

QUESTION

What are the nine functions of the prefrontal cortex (According to Dr. Dan Siegel)?
(1) Body regulation (monitoring the body, controlling physiological reactions), (2) Attunement (the capacity to pay attention to and connect with another), (3) Emotional balance (neither rigid or chaotic), (4) Fear modulation (turning off false alarms), (5) Response flexibility (being able to pause), (6) Empathy (understanding what someone is feeling), (7) Moral sense (overriding impulses in order to be good), (8) Intuition (listening to the body), and (9) Insight (self-understanding).

Between Fusion and Disconnection

The cultural ideal of love is a skewed, unhealthy one. The idea of two becoming one, of the soul mate, of completion would make any family therapist cringe. A healthy relationship is between two whole people who can enjoy connection and separation. Before there was a field of marital therapy, the poet Rainer Maria Rilke offered a profound insight into the dynamics of close relationships:

> *It is a question in marriage, to my feeling, not of creating a quick community of spirit by tearing down and destroying all boundaries, but rather a good marriage is that in which each appoints the other guardian of his solitude and shows him this confidence, the greatest in his power to bestow. A togetherness between two people is an impossibility, and where it seems, nevertheless, to exist, it is a narrowing, a reciprocal agreement which robs either one party or both of his fullest freedom and development. But, once the realization is accepted that even between the closest human beings infinite distances continue to exist, a wonderful living side by side can grow up, if they succeed in loving the distance between them which makes it possible for each to see the other whole and against a wide sky!*

If you are an introvert in a significant relationship with an extrovert, you cannot count on that extrovert to become the guardian of your solitude. You will have to request this for yourself and negotiate your needs for privacy. This solitude does not necessarily mean physical separation. It is allowing things to be as they are. Your partner leaves you alone, gives you a quarter of silence. This peace can be granted in many ways. You can enjoy solitude sitting on the couch together and reading. You can be deprived of solitude even when great physical distances separate you. Your partner cannot be the guardian of your solitude if her emotional needs are intrusive, demanding, and relentless. Solitude is having space to *be* yourself and space to be *by* yourself.

QUOTE

"I never found the companion that was so companionable as solitude. We are for the most part more lonely when we go abroad among men than when we stay in our chambers."—Henry David Thoreau

Raising a Family

There are standard cultural scripts that most people adhere to: go to college, get married, have children, move to the suburbs, and then retire. If you don't do these things, you stand out as an outlier. If you choose not to have children, people may not understand. As an introvert, you may be less inclined to have children or certainly find the intrusions into privacy and the difficulties (and sleep deprivation) of child rearing more stressful. Of course, it is not practical for half of the population to not procreate, and you likely will have or already have children.

The challenge is to nurture your solitude in the midst of relationship and family. You will have to take extra special care of yourself during these years. Knowing your limits will help. Knowing when you need to withdraw to restore will help. Having things scheduled in your life that feed your energy will help.

Many couples, especially with the pressure of raising children, lose sight of their relationship. Even though they spend a lot of time together, much of this time is strategic—geared toward the household management. Couples can benefit from "date night," a dedicated weekly outing that is pleasurable. If you are coupled with an extrovert, you may need to take turns doing an activity that is considered "fun." For you, fun may be a quiet dinner and a movie. For your extrovert partner, fun may be going to club or a party. Whatever you choose to do, this is time to enjoy one another outside of the responsibilities of family, home, and work. Don't talk about issues.

Date night can help couples remember why they love each other and got together in the first place. Without something like date night, couples can take each other for granted and lose the connection that binds them together. You may also need to recruit surrogates—friends who can stand in to fulfill important needs. If your partner is an extrovert, spending regular time with an introverted friend can be a replenishing necessity.

The Value of Vulnerability

There are two types of vulnerability. The first arises when you are exposed in a way that compromises you. The second arises when you meet the moment with uncertainty, when you jettison your preconceptions in favor of openness, even when that openness is raw, scary, and intense. You can think of these as bad and good vulnerability.

Solitude is often feared. It is an unknown territory where the true needs of the self may lurk in shadows. Given enough time and quiet, these needs will be revealed. The culture is one of doing, not being. You are inundated by messages to keep busy and to live life to the fullest—which translate as doing and buying a lot of things. If you get quiet, you will encounter your vulnerability. The poet and corporate consultant David Whyte speaks to vulnerability in his book, *The Three Marriages: Reimagining Work, Self, and Relationship:* "If I spend any time in silence, any time watching the way my mind works, I will find that there is a way in which we withhold the very thing from ourselves that might provide us with the possibility of happiness. . . . What we withhold from ourselves is the willingness to understand our own imperfection. The strategic, intellectual self, looking in from the outside, cannot have the experience of sheer physical vulnerability that the deeper internal self must gain to walk through the door of self-compassion."

Whyte suggests that imperfection is the gateway to wholeness when you can accept those imperfections and learn from them. It is this willingness to confront vulnerability that gives you the Introvert Edge. Extroverts keep themselves too busy to realize these vulnerabilities. Your access to the interior brings you to this place and it takes a modicum of nerve to open yourself in this way. On the other side of this vulnerability is happiness. Nothing happens without silence. Quiet opens the possibility of happiness but this is not a happiness born of convenience. Rather, it is a risky venture into uncertainty. What will you find in that silence? Demons, regrets, and fears, likely, but also angels, hope, and courage. You may have to sit in a space of uncertainty—of not knowing—and avoid the tendency to seek a quick fix. You will have to overcome the culture's tendency to problem solve.

QUOTE

"The great omission in American life is solitude; not loneliness, for this is an alienation that thrives most in the midst of crowds, but that zone of time and space, free from the outside pressures, which is the incubator of the spirit."—Marya Mannes, writer, author, and critic

Safety for the introvert requires space, time, and quiet. When you don't have these things, you can feel the bad kind of vulnerable. At the same time, when you have space, time, and quiet, you can experience the good kind of vulnerability.

Brené Brown, PhD, conducts research on vulnerability. She gave a TED talk to about 500 people on the "Power of Vulnerability" and during this talk she revealed a personal episode of vulnerability. In another TED talk called "Listening to Shame," she reports having a "vulnerability hangover" after giving that first talk. She holed up in her home for three days. When the talk was posted on YouTube, she was mortified because she thought another 600 or 700 people would see it. She told a friend, "If 500 turns into 1,000 or 2,000, my life is over." Little did she know millions would see it! (9,508,882 views as of May 2013). This exposure ended her life of being "small." She says, "vulnerability is not weakness and that myth is profoundly dangerous." She defines vulnerability as "emotional risk, exposure, and uncertainty. It fuels our daily lives . . . vulnerability is our most accurate measurement of courage."

To live as an introvert in an extroverted culture requires this act of courage. As an introvert, you are open to vulnerability. As poet Mary Oliver says in her poem "Wild Geese," "let the soft animal of your body love what it loves." This openness is a liability when it is seen as weakness instead of courage. American culture promotes the message: "Never be vulnerable." Good luck with that. It's easy to drink that Kool-Aid and buy into the weakness myth. Brown says, "Vulnerability is the birthplace of innovation, creativity, and change." But the culture does not want to hear about vulnerability, does not want to admit that it is central to everything.

The Physical Space of Solitude

It can be valuable to have an actual physical space to retire to when you need solitude—a sanctuary of solitude or SOS. It is a place where you can experience what T. S. Eliot described as the "silence between two waves to the sea." Do you have one? What is your ideal space? When you envision this space, you will discover clues about what is important to you. Features of an SOS include:

- A dedicated space that is private. It has a door that you can close.
- You visit it often, daily, perhaps even multiple times per day.
- Avoid feeling stressed there. You want this space to be associated with calm, repose, and good feelings. Don't make this space in your home office if you can avoid it, because you pay bills in there and deal with other matters of consequence. Don't have arguments with your spouse or children in there (hey, what are they doing there in the first place? This is your space!)
- Fill it with objects (art, artifacts, and furnishings) that are meaningful for you and associated with a sense of relaxation.
- Paint the walls a soothing color.
- Keep it uncluttered. While you want it to contain meaningful objects, you don't want it to be cluttered; you want it reflect the calm feelings of tranquility, peace, and spaciousness.
- Focus on the space as well as the objects in the space. In your special room, you can spend time appreciating the open spaces that surround the things. This space represents the uncluttered, clear, openness of

solitude. You can focus on the space around things anywhere to bring a portable sense of solitude to any situation.

If you are fortunate enough to have a private office at work, bring some of these same features to this space as well. You can designate some part of the office as your SOS, even if your office is a cubicle. If you work in a communal or open-office space, the SOS challenge will be greater. You may have to be creative. Perhaps your SOS is in the space overhead. Perhaps by focusing on the space around the other people, you can find your SOS in the sea of open space of the entire office. Don't be limited by the concept of four walls.

QUOTE

"No man should go through life without once experiencing healthy, even bored solitude in the wilderness, finding himself depending solely on himself and thereby learning his true and hidden strength."
—Jack Kerouac

Any space can become an SOS. Perform a cleansing ritual that will help you to claim the space. In Asia, incense is burned. In Native American traditions, a sage stick is burned to "smudge" the space clear of old energies and ready it for your energy. If you can't actually burn something in your space, you can do a mental smudging, perhaps bow to the four directions as a way of asserting that space as your own.

A meditation space can double as an SOS. Many meditation spaces have a shrine that holds special objects infused with good memories. The altar serves as a reminder of what is important—the sacred in the ordinary. A meditation space is by default an SOS, and contemplative practice is another important way to nurture solitude.

The SOS is not a luxury; it is integral to your well-being and maintains the Introvert Edge. The SOS should be a living space—always changing and constantly being infused with calm, positive energy. You can recharge your batteries in the SOS and should do so often.

The Case for the Interior

There are ancient practices within most faith traditions that have prized the interior experience of meditation. In the present day, meditation is growing in popularity as life gets more stressful and as people struggle to find meaning in contemporary existence. One popular form of meditation is the secular practice of Mindfulness-Based Stress Reduction (MBSR).

Teachers of MBSR often joke that the course could be called Mindfulness-Based Stress *Induction*—at least at the beginning. If you have not been in the habit of looking inside, then once you do you will find a lot of things that you have been avoiding, and this will temporarily raise your stress levels.

Meditation is the practice of paying attention to the interior—the subjective experience of being alive. The focus can be on a sound (mantra) or on the process of breathing and other bodily sensations. It can also be on sound or other senses. The key is to concentrate and monitor attention and keep the mind from its busy, talk-based mode (known as the default mode network in neuroscience research).

Students in an MBSR course will learn to focus on breathing and bodily sensations as the place to return from thinking about the future and the past. The breath is a good place to concentrate. You can't forget to bring it with you—it is always available. Breathing occurs in the body and in the present moment. Each breath you take is colored by your emotional state in the moment, so focusing on the breath is like keeping your finger on the pulse of your emotional life—a very useful thing when you are trying to be less stressed. Participants in MBSR classes show measureable and beneficial changes in stress levels and also their brains after eight weeks of practice. You can start today by paying attention to your breathing right now.

CHAPTER 17

The Portable Introvert: Contemplative Practices to Develop the Interior

The good thing about being an introvert is that you can carry it with you wherever you go. You can keep your Introvert Edge, even when you are not in optimal conditions. The portable introvert can breathe in the noisy commotion of the extroverted circus. When you learn to nurture, preserve, and deepen your contemplative interior the din won't drain you of precious energy.

The Contemplative Introvert

The seventeenth-century philosopher and mathematician Blaise Pascal was most certainly an introvert. He said, "All men's miseries derive from not being able to sit in a quiet room alone." This quote could be the contemplative introvert's manifesto.

First, sitting is stillness. Stillness opens the door to contemplation, reflection, and introspection. If you are too busy doing things, keeping occupied, or simply moving, there is no chance for that space of stillness to take hold. The room is quiet. No talking, no distractions, no television, radio, or music. Just the sounds of breathing and the ambient sounds of the room. A clock ticking. Birds outside the window. And there is solitude, aloneness. Not loneliness, but welcome seclusion. You will be able to hear yourself think in this scenario. This thinking would go beyond the constant ruminations of your storytelling mind. Instead, you might have the opportunity to discover how you actually feel about a particular situation, issue, or person. You may uncover your personal truth with less distraction and less interference from fear-based defense mechanisms. You can become intimate with your own mind and heart (and find that they are one).

QUOTE

"Within you there is a stillness and a sanctuary to which you can retreat any time and be yourself."—Hermann Hesse, author

Try making your hands lie still at different points throughout your day. What do you notice? You can try this now. Let your hands rest. This exercise is recommended by Jan Chozen Bays in her book, *How to Train a Wild Elephant.* What do you notice? Probably an urge to move them! Why does misery arise from the busy, distracted doing-ness? Pascal wrote his bon mot long before the "culture of personality" emerged in the United States in the 1920s. Long before the seventeenth century in the sixth century B.C.E., the Buddha recognized a similar sentiment. Although the Buddha might have recommended sitting in silence together as his followers did.

Nurturing Your Introvert

Sustenance for the introvert can be found inside the body and mind. The body can be sitting still in a meditation hall or trail running in the woods. Nourishment can be found in the quiet meditation can bring. Energy can be found in the practice of meditation, yoga, tai chi, qigong, or prayer. These contemplative practices can nurture your introvert energy needs. Without constant refreshing, you risk exhaustion. The world will become irritating as it presses its demands upon you, your patience hanging from a string. To know what nurturance you need, you have to be tuned in to mind and body. These needs will change moment by moment and phase by phase of your life. It's never a one-size-fits-all solution.

The Tree of Contemplative Practices

You can likely find contemplative practice instruction and groups in your area. When you are learning these disciplines, you will enjoy periods of silence. The instructor may be speaking, but you practice in silence. When you practice at home, you cultivate intimacy with your interior—the place from which your Introvert Edge draws its power.

The Center for Contemplative Mind in Society has a wonderful image— The Tree of Contemplative Practices. There are eight categories of contemplative practices: activist, relational, movement, ritual/cyclical, stillness, generative, and creative. All of these are ideal for introverts and extroverts who want to develop their introvert qualities.

Activist Practices include: Pilgrimage to areas where social justice issues are highlighted, work and volunteering, vigils and marches, and bearing witness. Creative Practices include: contemplative arts, improvisation, music and singing, and journaling. Generative Practices include: *lectio divina* (reading scripture, prayer, and meditation), visualization, beholding, and loving-kindness meditation. Movement Practices include: labyrinth walking, walking meditation, yoga, dance, qigong, aikido, and tai chi chuan. Relational Practices include: council circle, dialogue, deep listening, and storytelling. Ritual/Cyclical Practices include: ceremonies and rituals based in spiritual or cultural traditions, establishing a sacred/personal space, and retreats. Stillness Practices include: meditation, quieting the mind, silence, and centering. There is a world of richness to explore!

The Tree of Contemplative Practices

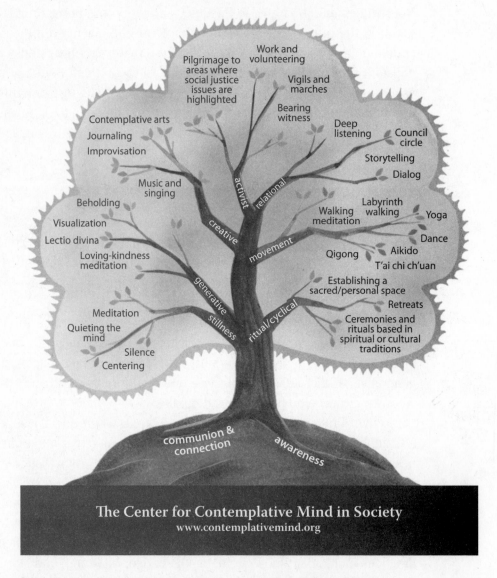

Reprinted with permission from the Center for Contemplative Mind in Society

Mindfulness and Meditation

Since 1979, when Jon Kabat-Zinn introduced Mindfulness-Based Stress Reduction (MBSR) to the patients at the University of Massachusetts Medical Center, the introverted practice of meditation has become a staple of major medical centers around the country and the world. Mindfulness-based interventions have over thirty years of research supporting their benefits in helping people cope with chronic illness. Neuroscientists such as Richard Davidson at the Waisman Center at the University of Wisconsin-Madison have done groundbreaking research showing that mindfulness practice can lead to observable changes in both the structure and function of the brain. You don't need to be a monk in a remote monastery practicing for thirty years; these changes are seen with as few as eight weeks of practice.

Mindfulness practice embodies the soul of introversion—sitting still. There's not a lot of action at an MBSR class, just a lot of sitting and some talking and listening, and gentle movement. There is even less stimulation in a silent meditation retreat where participants spend their days in sitting and slow walking meditation (and slow eating and no talking). The extrovert in search of stimulation would find the enterprise boring. The prolonged practice and silence of a retreat can even be challenging to an introvert who craves silence and slowness.

FACT

The Center for Mindfulness in Medicine, Health Care, and Society was founded in 1979 by Jon Kabat-Zinn and others. Over 19,000 people have taken Mindfulness-Based Stress Reduction (MBSR) courses there and thousands of professionals have been trained to deliver MBSR through the OASIS Institute. (Center for Mindfulness)

Mindfulness interventions are not only available in medical centers, they are being taught to veterans and active-duty service members, educators and their students, corporations, health care professionals, and even prisoners. There are numerous different therapies that have stemmed from MBSR. These include: Mindfulness-Based Cognitive Therapy (MBCT) for treating depression, Mindfulness-Based Eating Awareness Training (MB-EAT) for treating eating disorders, Mindfulness-Based Relapse Prevention (MBRP) for treating substance abuse, Acceptance and Commitment Therapy (ACT), and many others.

Mindfulness Revolution

The popularity of these interventions reflects a Mindfulness Revolution. Congressman Tim Ryan (Democrat-Ohio) has documented and furthered this revolution in his book *A Mindful Nation: How a Simple Practice Can Reduce Stress, Improve Performance, and Recapture the American Spirit.* He speaks to the return on investment of teaching young children how to manage their minds. "We don't need more gadgets or fly-by-night programs in our school systems. If we teach children to follow their breath—and return to it when they get distracted—we are teaching them how to concentrate. . . . For an incredibly small investment, we can prevent incredible future costs and heartaches in our communities."

Folk wisdom says, "What you resist persists." When you try to push out negative emotions, that effort and the attention that comes along with it can actually make the negative feelings worse. Either extreme of pushing away or ruminating upon can intensify the feeling. Mindfulness seeks to make contact with the conditions of the moment as they are with an open curiosity—in other words: acceptance. This keen attention takes the story of "me" out of the experience and thereby changes how that experience is experienced. What might have been distressing can now be interesting.

Qigong: The Embodiment of Tao

Qigong (or Chi kung) is an ancient Chinese practice that seeks to bring mind, body, and breath together in the moment through deliberate gentle movement. Qigong is a moving meditation and an invigorating form of exercise. Taoist and Buddhist practitioners developed it to offset what would be known as "Zen sickness" today. It is stressful to engage in intensive sitting practice (zazen) day after day; the movement of qigong gave these monks meaningful breaks and allowed them to continue their practice.

Qigong literally means working with qi through time. "Qi" or chi translates as energy. It is sometimes referred to as the life force energy or it can be thought of as the electromagnetic and other forces that surround you at all times. "Gong" refers to accomplishment, skill, or work. Therefore qigong refers to work with or cultivation of qi—energy. According to the National Association of Qigong: "The gentle, rhythmic movements of qigong reduce stress, build stamina, increase vitality, and enhance the immune system. It has also been found to improve cardiovascular, respiratory, circulatory, lymphatic and digestive functions. Those who maintain a consistent practice of qigong find that it helps one regain a youthful vitality, maintain health even into old age and helps speed recovery from illness. Western scientific research confirms that qigong reduces hypertension and the incidence of falling in the aged population."

QUESTION

What can acupuncture treat?
Acupuncture is effective in treating most musculoskeletal pain, carpal tunnel syndrome, fibromyalgia and myofacial pain, headache, arthritis, and postoperative dental pain. In addition, acupuncture is effective in treating many internal disorders including gynecological, gastrointestinal, respiratory, fatigue, chemotherapy nausea and vomiting, stroke rehabilitation, asthma, and menopausal symptoms. Acupuncture can also be a useful adjunct to be included in a comprehensive management program. (Source: Arthur Makaris, *www.completechinese medicine.com*)

Qigong and kung fu master Arthur Makaris describes the different components of qigong. Qigong works with energy located in different parts of the body and paying attention to how this energy connects to the wider world. There are three basic energy centers or *dan tiens*. These are regions where mental, emotional, and physical energies intersect. The lower *dan tien* corresponds with the region just below the belly button and represents *jing* energy—reproduction, sexuality, and fertility. The middle *dan tien* fills the abdomen to the solar plexus and represents *qi* energy—digestion and aerobic activity. The upper *dan tien* corresponds with the region around the heart and represents *shen* energy—mental activity.

Collectively, *jing*, *qi*, and *shen* are known as the Three Treasures. If you draw a circle around the entire body, the middle point will be at the lower *dan tien*. The arms trace another circle. The midpoint of this circle is the upper *dan tien*—in the region of the solar plexus. Balance is achieved by bringing attention to all the energy centers—connecting to earth, sky, and self. The energy centers and channels explored in qigong are similar to those used in acupuncture.

Tai Chi Chuan

Tai chi chuan or (tai chi) is a martial art form (part of kung fu), that overlaps with qigong. It involves gentle, sweeping movements and draws on the power known as "chi"—the electromagnetic energy that suffuses the body and the world. It literally means the "fist of the supreme ultimate" (that is, chi or qi). It was developed in the fourteenth century.

QUESTION

What are the five styles of tai chi?
Chen, Yang, Wu, Sun, and Wu Yu-Xiang or Wu (Hao).

The practice seeks to harmonize the energies of yin and yang. Tai chi practices came from an introverted culture and were devoted to explore the connection between the interior and the exterior world. Tai chi masters can mobilize tremendous amounts of energy—harnessing the power of chi. Some have been said to be able to move an object just by putting their hands close to it without actually touching it. Tai chi nurtures the introvert interior and also provides an effective means for interacting in the world—a confidence, grace, and power in movement. There are many different forms of tai chi. You can probably find a course in your community or you can read books. There are many free videos on YouTube that provide instruction.

Yoga

Yoga has exploded in popularity, and there are dozens of different forms available: Hatha, Ashtanga, Bikram, Jivamukti, and Kripalu to name just a few. Like qigong and tai chi, yoga seeks to unite body and mind in movement (in fact, *yoga* means "to yolk" or "bring together"). Most yoga classes include a brief meditation at the end. In antiquity, yoga was a way to prepare the body for intensive meditation. Today yoga has placed more emphasis on the external forms. Still, when you practice yoga, you are acquainting yourself with your interior.

Classes vary by the instructor and the practice tradition. Some yoga practices are extroverted. They are nonstop, athletic, and performed to the barking instructions of a drill sergeant–like instructor. What else would you expect in an extroverted culture? Perhaps these vigorous forms explain yoga's current popularity. Bikram yoga is practiced in rooms that are heated to 105°F with 40 percent humidity. Power Yoga seems to be the perfect practice for ambitious extroverts. More contemplative styles, such as Jivamukti and Kripalu, will suit the introvert. At the very least, yoga will get you closer to your body, providing physical fitness and powers of concentration. While the movements may be vigorous, the classes, which are usually an hour and a half, provide a welcome respite from the other activities of your day.

Reading in the Age of Information

Reading is a lost art. The publishing industry is changing dramatically. Large book chains are going out of business. If you are lucky, you have an independent bookseller nearby. Video and the Internet have taken a huge bite out of reading. Books still sell, but people spend less time reading. Why bother when there's so much fun stuff to do? Who needs to read when you can watch endless hours of video on YouTube, Netflix, or HBO On Demand? If introverts ruled the world, the center of public life would be the library—a quiet place to read, research, and think. Unfortunately, funding for libraries has been cut.

Reading is a natural activity for introverts. Reading brings you into an imaginary world created by the author (or exposes you to stimulating ideas in nonfiction or poetry). Reading provides a cloak of invisibility. People are less apt to bother you when you are engrossed in a book. Reading can be a place to recharge your batteries. Does video do the same for you? Notice whether you feel more or less energy when reading compared to watching television or a video. Book readings can be a stimulating (but not too stimulating) Artist Date to take yourself on.

Reading is integrally connected to writing and writing is naturally connected to introversion. Stephen King says in his memoir *On Writing* that a writer has to read a lot. If you don't have time to read, you don't have time to write. Reading provides a respite from outer activity while keeping the mind engaged. Reading signals to others that you are busy and they will be less likely to disturb you.

Going Off into the Wilderness

Humans did not evolve in crowded cities. If you live in a city, you are still an integral part of nature. Think about the iron in your blood. Where did it come from? Scientist Darryl Reanney says in his book *Music of the Mind*:

> *It was smelted into being in the fiery furnace that was the brilliant core of a giant star; it was flung across space by the violence of a supernova when that star exploded in an apocalypse that had the brilliance of a million suns; it congealed in the rocks of a just-born planet; it was rubbed into soil by wind and water and the action of microbes; it was taken up and made flesh by a plant; and now it lives in a red cell, circling the rivers of your blood, helping you breathe and keeping your consciousness afire, here, now.*

You are part of that, and evolutionary biologist extraordinaire Richard Dawkins cautions that there is likely a molecule in your next glass of water that passed through the bladder of Oliver Cromwell (and every other famous person in history).

QUOTE

"I'm an introvert. . . . I love being by myself, love being outdoors, love taking a long walk with my dogs and looking at the trees, flowers, the sky."—Audrey Hepburn

Going back into nature can help you to hear yourself think and open a space where you don't have to think. Of course, reality permeates all things—those natural and human made. If you are like most people, you travel in a car to work and are then engulfed in an office building for the rest of the day. You return home in your car and tread across a little lawn before you re-enter your home. That's not enough nature. Golf courses are an integration of human and natural landscape. Golfing your local or club course in the twilight hours can be a wonderful place of solitude (golfing at other times could put you in touch with other golfers, some of whom love to talk).

Make sure you get enough contact with nature and go into the wild world any time you feel overwhelmed, depleted, or dispersed.

Recharging and Renewal: Introvert Utopia

Imagine your ideal scenario for self, love, and work—the whole of your life. How do you spend your time from morning till night?

- When do you want to utter your first word during the day? Perhaps you start the day with an hour of silence.
- Your day starts with coffee, movement, and contemplation. The day looms on the horizon but attention dwells in the present moment.
- You take the train to work, engrossed in a good novel or the latest treatise by Malcolm Gladwell, Jonah Lehrer, Michael Pollan, or Steven Pinker.
- You arrive at the office and close your door. Now you review your e-mail, voicemails, and look ahead at your schedule for the day.
- You work in uninterrupted silence with only one meeting scheduled for the day. At lunch, you take a mindful walk or when you feel like it, sit with a coworker and talk about ideas. Or you meet a friend and talk through a problem that you are trying to solve at work.
- At the end of the day, you feel tired but not depleted. You are ready to connect with friends and family. On the days that you don't feel like socializing, you look forward to a quiet evening at home, reading, writing, or playing the piano. Perhaps you meditate again in the evening.
- You take the dog for a long mindful walk in the woods near your home. Or you walk the city streets with an iPod playing your favorite music (the ear buds give you a cloak of invisibility).

- You enjoy the spaciousness of your home. You relish the quiet—only noises that you put there are present. Your partner is with you, but is serving as the guardian of your solitude. You feel connected without being intruded upon. You experience that wonderful living "side by side" that the poet Rilke talked about.
- You go to sleep feeling relaxed and satisfied with how the day went. You look forward to the next day; you feel connected with the projects and people that give life meaning. You are within your purpose and following your bliss.

How closely does your life resemble this introvert utopia? This version of utopia may not fit with yours; can you create your own version? What can you do today, tomorrow, and the next day to bring yourself closer to experiencing this utopia?

CHAPTER 18

The Tao of Introversion: Finding Yin in a Yang Culture

The Tao is a philosophy of balance—a concept that seems to be lost on this extroverted culture. The Tao is symbolized in the familiar yin-yang symbol—the dynamic equilibrium of opposing forces of expansion and contraction, masculine and feminine, light and dark. The Introvert Revolution is bringing more "yin" energy into the culture, reclaiming the silent interior from the incessant, hurried activities of the extrovert circus.

Lessons from Taoism on Balance

Taoism is an ancient philosophical system that arose in China 2,500 years ago. It seeks the balance between opposing forces like action and stillness. Its emphasis on the balance between polar forces is a good model for understanding the dimension of extroversion and introversion.

The *Tao Te Ching* is the teaching of Lao Tzu, a contemporary of Confucius. Famously, Lao Tzu (perhaps highlighting the differences between introverts and extroverts) said, "Those who know do not talk/Those who talk do not know."

The Tao is the word given to the nameless. It is often translated as the "Way" or the "Teaching." According to the *Shambhala Encyclopedia of Eastern Religions*, the Tao is "the all-embracing first principle, from which all appearances arise. It is a reality that gives rise to the universe." The goal is to unite oneself with the Tao. This is not an intellectual task, but a contemplation of the unity of all things, the simplicity that can be found in all things, and the emptiness of all things when concepts are removed.

QUOTE

"Difficult and easy complement each other. / Long and short contrast each other; / High and low rest upon each other; / Voice and sound harmonize each other; / Front and back follow one another." —Lao Tzu, *Tao Te Ching* (translated by Gia-Fu Feng and Jane English)

Nothing exists without its opposite. No one is a pure introvert or extrovert. You are a balance. Your center of gravity will lie somewhere along this continuum, but life will demand both sides of the energy/action equation. There are situations where you will have to tap into your extrovert. Afterward, you will need to restore your introvert. Without this recharging, you will be out of balance.

Gia-Fu Feng and Jane English's beautiful translation of the *Tao Te Ching* has a verse that reflects balance. Lao Tzu says:

That which shrinks
Must first expand.
That which fails,
Must first be strong.
That which is cast down
Must first be raised.
Before receiving
There must be giving.

Your energy will expand and contract. You will fall down and need to restore yourself. If you have "failed" it means you have been successful. Everything is in balance. Exhalation follows inhalation.

Dispersion and Collection: The Balance of Yang and Yin

The symbol of the Tao is one of the most universally recognized symbols. It is a circle bisected by a curved line in the shape of an "S." One side is black, the other white. There is a small white circle in the black and a small black circle in the white. This is yin and yang. Yang is the masculine, expansive, and dispersive energy represented by the white part of the circle. Yin is the feminine, contractive, and collected energy represented by the black part of the circle. Yang is extroversion and yin is introversion. Like the symbol of the Tao, when you are an introvert you have extroverted tendencies, and vice versa. The Tao symbol captures the balance of introversion and extroversion. It recognizes that one resides within the other.

Cycles of dispersion and collection happen in every moment, day, and phase of life. Breathing is a constant running through your days. The expansion of the inhalation is followed by the contraction of the exhalation. Energy expands throughout the day and contracts at night. Within the day, energy fluctuates. As an introvert, your days will see more contractions than your extrovert counterparts. You energy is more sensitive, reactive, and attuned to the events of your day. When you are in a "yin" period of collection, you are restoring your energy. Soon, your energy will disperse again. When you have been in a "yang" period of dispersion, you are expending your energy.

Soon, if you know what's good for you, you will seek to move back to collection and let the yin energy restore balance. The little energy "eyes" in each half of the Tao symbol provide further encouragement. When you are dispersing, there is that little circle of collected energy in the midst of the outgoing activity. This can be a pocket of meditative calm in the midst of a chaotic situation. Likewise, when your energy is collecting, there is that little circle of dispersive energy. This can be the energy that makes your meditation practice go—the juice that sustains a sense of calm.

Grounded

Yin is grounded in the earth; yang reaches for the sky. The introvert is comfortable with the ground, digging deep into its moist darkness. The ground is the fertile birthing place for creativity and transformation. Solitude is the "fertile void" that holds meaning.

The poet David Whyte refers to Moses and his introverted modesty in the poem, "The Opening of Eyes (After R. S. Thomas)" from his collection *Rivers Flow:*

> *That day I saw beneath dark clouds,*
> *the passing light over the water*
> *and I heard the voice of the world speak out,*
> *I knew then, as I had before,*
> *life is no passing memory of what has been*
> *nor the remaining pages in a great book*
> *waiting to be read.*
>
> *It is the opening of eyes long closed.*
> *It is the vision of far off things*
> *seen for the silence they hold.*
> *It is the heart after years*
> *of secret conversing,*
> *speaking out loud in the clear air.*

It is Moses in the desert
fallen to his knees before the lit bush.
It is the man throwing away his shoes
as if to enter heaven and finding himself astonished,
opened at last,
fallen in love with solid ground.

Many Rivers Press, Langley, Washington, printed with permission from the publisher

The poem starts with dark clouds—the reality of life. It's not some bright, sunny, cheerful day (in other words, not a day according to the cult of positive thinking). Yet, there is light that reaches down and touches the water. He hears the "voice of the world speak out." These words are not actual words; they are like the Tao—the nameless reality of the world around and within. He says, "Life is no passing memory of what has been." Life is lived in the present moment. Memory is imagination; it is not life here and now. "Nor the remaining pages in a great book / waiting to be read." Again, life is lived in the present moment and not in anticipation of the future. This, too, is imagination. The only reality is right here, right now—in the sky and on the earth.

Coming into the present, the subject of the poem opens his long-closed eyes. He wakes up out of a sleepwalking trance to beautiful reality around him. Like the Tao, things are seen for the "silence they hold." Then it is the heart's turn to open. The heart has not been still but secretly conversing for years—waiting, gestating, readying itself to speak aloud. This pregnancy, if you will, happens every day for introverts. You listen, take the words deep within, and process them. The response may not come to you right away.

FACT

David Whyte has written seven books of poetry and three books of prose. He is a traveler and leads tours that combine the natural world, fine meals, conversation, and poetry and talks by David. He and his groups have explored the Galapagos Islands, English Lake District, and West Ireland among other destinations. You can learn more at davidwhyte.com.

Introverts are connected to solid ground. In this poem, Moses is humbled. He comes to his knees. He is awed by the burning bush—the astonishing presence of the divine in nature. He is humiliated—brought to the ground, to the humus. This is not seen as something to avoid or be embarrassed by. The grounding is a moment of transformation.

Each time you come to ground, this transformation is at your feet. To get there, you must "open your eyes," and value the silence. The heart must speak aloud what is true for itself. In the biblical story, the burning bush witnessed Moses's confession, received his humility, and blessed him with loving release. To get to the ground, he not only comes to his knees, but he throws away his shoes. These shoes may be the encumbering stories of identity—the shoulds and shouldn'ts that bind to anxiety. Something must be shed to reach this point of openness. And the entry point to the metaphorical heaven does not come from some angelic transcendence up to the sky but in coming to the ground. Extroversion reaches for the sky; introversion touches the ground. Moses is realizing his introversion. He is coming to ground, coming to acceptance of his way of being in the world.

The key to life is neither found in the memories of the past nor in the anticipations of the future; it is found in the present moment and a vision of yourself that transcends all of your previous conceptions. This vision holds "silence" and opens the heart to its truth—a truth born out of silence.

Slowing Down

The world is moving faster and faster. Communications are ubiquitous; their speed is instantaneous. Fast food restaurants (to use the term *restaurant* loosely) infest the suburban landscape. No one has time for anything. Work encroaches on time and energy, raising kids has become a nonstop frenetic chauffeuring service from soccer practice to a dozen other activities. There is no time to pause and be, to just sit and breathe. It is no big surprise, then, that stress has become a huge problem.

Introverts are known for not thinking on the spot, for not being quick witted. They need time to process. Psychologist Marti Olsen Laney says in her book, *The Introvert Advantage*, "I found my thoughts were like lost airline baggage; they arrived some time later."

ESSENTIAL

Brattleboro, Vermont, hosts an annual Slow Living Summit. The "Slow Living Summit is a gathering focused on sustainable living, resilient communities, and the personal, inner transformations that are necessary for both" (*www.slowlivingsummit.org*). Slow living is a response to the extroverted, stressful, hectic pace of life.

Speed is valued. FedEx moves at the "speed of business." And if you are not moving at that speed, you may just get left out. The faster things go, the more money can be made. The International Slow Food movement, founded by Carlo Petrini in 1986, arose as a response to the speed culture (or a culture that seems to take speed). It seeks to counteract the culture, economics, and health consequences of fast food. Petrini told the *New York Times* (in a piece written by Mark Bittman): "People in rich countries need to regenerate our way of thinking to give value to food, which has been lost in the last 50 years. As a result, we have a systems crisis: by using more energy than we produce to grow food—and we're using 76 percent of our water for agriculture—we're reaching the end of the planet's resources. And young people understand we can't survive with this and are beginning to act." It's not clear whether Petrini is an introvert. Nonetheless, his vision for the world is consistent with conscientious, mindful, and compassionate values that are important to introverts.

Unplugging

You probably carry a smartphone with you at all times, with access to the Internet and all the entertainment and information the Web brings. News that once took weeks to travel across country is now accessible in real time. The amount and speed of information can be overwhelming. Can you give yourself permission to unplug when you need to? Remember that as an introvert you are more prone to stimulation. Bad stories in the news can be unsettling, and you may find it harder to let go of the images of death, disease, and destruction, especially if you are an HSP (highly sensitive person). You may feel a responsibility to take it all in, and this, too, can feel overwhelming.

Internet technology allows introverts to connect without forays into the noisy commotion of the "real" world and this can be a wonderful thing. The downside is that this information can encroach on your silence, solitude, and serenity. It may feel automatic to let that energy in to your world, but you can say "enough."

Today, if you don't respond to a text message within thirty seconds, your friends will think that you either hate them or something terrible has happened to you (because why *wouldn't* you respond immediately?). The expectation of immediacy can be an incursion into your quiet. Can you let your friends know that you won't be available like that? Can you set aside your technology for regular media fasts? Can you imagine the world that Thoreau lived in? He was not far from Boston when he sought respite at Walden Pond, but he could not be reached by telephone, he could not watch television, and he could not surf the Web. Unplugging gives you the chance to experience a bit of Walden whenever you remember and give yourself permission to do so.

The Silence Between Two Waves of the Sea

In the *Four Quartets*, T. S. Eliot speaks of the "silence between two waves of the sea." The sea moves with inexorable force just as life does. If silence can be found in the tumult of the sea, you can find silence in the midst of anything. The key is not to make your sense of well-being in the moment contingent upon conditions being a particular way. This lack of contingency grants you freedom. Of course, quiet, calm, and cooperative settings are wonderful, but sometimes, all too often, the environment is chaos. People are talking, honking horns, and moving at the speed of light. How can you find peace in the midst of the craziness? Find your breath. If you are breathing, you can find peace in any moment. It is the portable "silence between two waves of the sea" and is available in any moment—in every moment.

FACT

T. S. Eliot was well acquainted with Buddhism and other Indian philosophies, which influenced works such as *The Wasteland* and *Four Quartets*. Themes of living in the present moment, stillness, and impermanence can be found.

It's easy to get caught in the trap of contingency. It's probably an old habit that will be hard to shake. Contingency robs you of happiness in the moment because it says things should be other than they are. It takes you away from the experience of what is happening and places your attention in a complaint. The center of that complaint is a frustrated desire—wanting things to be different than they are. When you can recognize that desire and let it go, you can find peace in the moment, no matter how imperfect that moment is. Your access to the interior is a great gift and it is also a double-edged sword. The same tendency that makes you contemplative can also make you get caught in your head—ruminating. Developing the capacity to step out of the flow of thinking, complaining, and storytelling gets you off the painful edge of that sword. From storytelling, you can move to experiencing the moment with interest. Can you relinquish your agenda for how things should be in this moment? This is not to say you should passively accept conditions as they are but accept conditions when they are beyond your control. If you are sitting in a room and feel cold, get up and close the window if it is open. However, if you are at a bus stop and feel cold, you can't close the window. If your happiness is contingent on being warm, then you will be unhappy. If you can get beyond that contingency, then you can be happy even when you are cold.

CHAPTER 19

Going Beyond Introversion and Extroversion

What is a self and what is a personality? Is there even such a thing as a self? Is there some essential you? Some true self? An essence? While researchers debate whether personality is some fixed thing or arises from the situation or is some combination of the two, there is another perspective offered by Buddhist psychology. The Buddha pointed out that humans have a mistaken notion of self, and when they cling to this erroneous self, all kinds of trouble ensues: dissatisfaction, stress, anguish, and even suffering.

A Buddhist View of the World

Buddhism was born in Asia, a usually introverted part of the world. The Buddha lived and taught in northern India. The Buddhist monk, Bodhidharma, brought his teachings to China, and then, centuries later, the Japanese Zen master Dogen Zenji brought them to Japan, where they became Zen. The teachings of the Buddha spread around the Asian world and became the Buddhist religions. The Buddhist view of the world is closer in spirit to the introvert view of the world. Buddhists tend to be quiet, contemplative, and deliberate.

There are certainly extroverted Buddhists. Just watch the charming film *The Cup*, by Tibetan Buddhist teacher and filmmaker Dzongsar Khyentse Rinpoche. The troublemaking preteen protagonist is anything but introverted.

FACT

There is no one "Buddhism," but many different Buddhist religions that have developed from the Buddha's original teachings. Popular forms include Theravada, Zen, and Tibetan Buddhism. In contrast to the religions, secular Buddhism is a growing movement forwarded by Andrew Olendzki, Mu Soeng, Stephen Batchelor, John Peacock, and others.

The Buddha's insights into human psychology are just as relevant today as they were 2,500 years ago, and they can give you insights into how to be a more effective introvert in the extroverted world. The teachings can do this by showing how all notions of self are "constructed" by the mind.

The Constructed Self

The twentieth-century Englishman turned Taoist scholar Wei Wu Wei (aka Terence James Stannus Gray) asked, in his often quoted poem, "Why are you unhappy?" The answer to that question may surprise you. You might be unhappy because you are preoccupied with a self that does not exist (or at least does not exist in the way you think it exists). All the energy that goes into defining and defending this constructed self creates agitation, anxiety, and angst. The Buddha noticed that life contained a lot of difficulty. It is not just big-ticket items like sickness, old age, and death; this difficulty shows up in every moment that you are alive. Most of this stress, anxiety, misery, or dissatisfaction can go unnoticed—it becomes part of the background story of life.

QUESTION

In the legend of the Buddha, what were the four signs that prompted him to go on his spiritual quest?
Birth, sickness, old age, and death.

Can you have a relatively fixed personality and still have no essence? The Buddha taught that a notion of a fixed self, some essential self would give rise to all of the suffering that you experience because there is a "me" that suffers. If you can get beyond that sense of "me" then there is no one to be anguished. The source of anguish, according to the Buddha, is desire. You want things that you do not have and you don't want things that you do have. All that pulling things in close or pushing them away creates anxiety. When things are going well, you'll worry about them not going well. The biggest source of stress comes from your sense of identity. When instead of focusing on "me" you direct your attention to the experience of now, you can be free from this "constructed self." You can take it apart by paying careful attention to this moment.

Introverts Are Misfits, but Everyone Suffers

Introversion and extroversion represent a central continuum of self, but what is self? Neuroscientists have yet to find a "self" in the brain. Whatever self is, it seems to emerge out of all the different processes such as consciousness, attention, memory, and feelings that are taking place in the moment. Yet, there seems to be something that is essentially "you"—a solid self that never changes. The Buddha suggested that any sense of a concrete, unchanging self was a mistaken idea—an illusion that arises out of the basic processes of being alive. Suffering clings to any notion of self that is abstracted from moment-to-moment experiences. This may be a hard notion to understand given the central importance self takes in this culture. Self is indispensible. Self is sacrosanct. "What do you mean there is no self?"

FACT

The Buddha is known for saying life involves a lot of "suffering." The term that gets translated into suffering (or stress, anguish, dissatisfaction) is *dukkha* and this literally means "bad wheel." The Buddha used the metaphor of a bad wheel on an oxcart to capture the pervasive nature of dissatisfaction, anguish, stress, or suffering.

This mistaken notion of self arises out of the mind's tendency to tell stories. All good stories have a main character. In this case that is you. You are the hero (or villain) of your stories and the more time and energy you put toward thinking about these stories, that is, the more you think, remember, and ruminate, the more energy you are putting into these stories. They become real, but they are only stories stemming from memory and imagination. The self is a fantasy—it is remembered and anticipated. It is confirmed by constant self-reference. As an introvert comfortable with the interior of the mind, you are at risk for stress, anxiety, and even depression if you spend too much time there.

Self Is a Metaphor

If you look at the self as a more fluid process rather than a solid object like a book (the book image is apt because a book is a tangible object that contains stories and that is what the self appears to be—a story-containing and story-generating thing) you will be less prone to stress, anxiety, and suffering. The following is a metaphor to help you understand this difference.

Imagine a tower made of glass panels. These panels are louvered so they can be moved from an open (parallel to the ground) to closed position (perpendicular to the ground). When the panels are closed they are vulnerable to the wind because there is more surface area for the wind to touch. The wind blows and the tower strains under the force. If the panels are open, there is only the thinnest edge set against the wind and the energy of the wind moves through the tower instead of against it. The tower remains steady, unperturbed. This is what the fluid self has to offer—a way of being that changes your relationship to the energies of the world. You get pushed around less because you are less defensive. You spend less energy defending yourself because situations can move through you instead of against you. There is more space for enjoyment because there is less preoccupation with what the self is getting or not getting. You can focus on the moment-by-moment process of becoming with interest rather than "What does this mean for me?"

QUOTE

"Just as a solid rock is not shaken by the storm, even so the wise are not affected by praise or blame."—The Buddha

As an introvert, you are familiar with the internal landscape and equipped to make this shift from a solid to a fluid sense of self. The challenge is to relinquish the stranglehold on the story of "me." Your ability to focus and delve into a problem provides the raw skill that can be applied to this more subtle consideration—what is self? Turn your attention toward the energy of this moment rather than abstract notions of "me" and the stories that follow. Bring mindfulness to everything that is happening in this moment in your body and in your senses and try to be with this experience without comparing it to other experiences, judging it, and without putting it into a narrative.

The Buddha Was an Introvert

The Buddha was likely an introvert. When he was eight years old, he fell into a spontaneous meditation under a rose apple tree. He did this after experiencing compassion for the worms that got killed during the plowing of the fields. The Buddha may have also been an HSP (highly sensitive person). After leaving home at the age of twenty-nine to seek philosophical truths about the nature of mind and reality, he spent many solitary years in the forest practicing intense forms of yoga. Such activities would have been unbearable for a card-carrying extrovert. He left his wife and newborn son behind.

FACT

The historical Buddha lived in what is now Northern India. He lived for eighty years. It was previously thought the Buddha lived between 563 and 483 B.C.E. Buddhist scholar Richard Gombrich has uncovered errors in this estimate and places the life of the Buddha between 485 and 404 B.C.E.

After he had his awakening (or enlightenment), he was not sure people would understand what he had experienced. Nevertheless, he decided to teach and he attracted many followers. Buddhist scholar Richard Gombrich in his insightful book, *What the Buddha Thought*, points out how remarkable it was that the Buddha's introverted method caught on: "A great deal of modern education and psychotherapy consists of making people aware that they are responsible for themselves. In fact, we consider that it constitutes a large part of what we mean by becoming a mature person. It is amazing that someone should have promulgated this idea in the fifth century B.C.E., and hardly less remarkable that he found followers."

Indeed, he did find followers—thousands of them. The people of the time found themselves in transition from an agricultural to an urbanized and mercantile economy. These changes made life stressful and people were hungry for meaning in their lives. In contrast to the Brahman priests who offered rituals and served as intermediaries to the gods, the Buddha suggested that meaning could be found within—a very introverted idea.

The Buddha was a public figure—giving thousands of sermons over his forty-five year teaching career. His public excursions were always followed by periods of quiescence. Meditation preceded and followed talking and talking was kept to a minimum. He encouraged his followers to engage, "right speech." Right speech was saying what was true, but it was also a directive to say what was useful. Talking should be true, relevant, and useful. The Buddha had no use for extroverted chitchat, small talk, and banter. He saw it as a waste of time and energy.

Sitting in Silence Together: The Buddhist Sangha

The *sangha* was one of the three most important things the Buddha taught, one of the three jewels or gems. The other two were *buddha* and *dharma*. Buddha was each person's capacity to awaken. Buddha literally means one who has woken up, and each person can do this. The Buddha was also a role model. He had traversed this path. He found a way beyond suffering. Dharma refers to the Buddha's teachings (his collected works, as it were) and also to the fundamental truths or natural laws he taught. One of these truths is impermanence. All things are in a constant state of change at some level.

QUOTE

"People with opinions just go around bothering each other."—The Buddha

While solitary meditation was a mainstay of his method, the Buddha's followers practiced together. This was the *sangha*—people sitting together in silence. People have been doing this in formal and informal settings for 2,500 years and the *sangha* is one of the oldest continuous human institutions. The communal practice balances the more severe tendencies of solitary practice by connecting people. Practicing in common silence allows anonymity and connection simultaneously—an ideal scenario for most introverts. You can find these Buddhist practice communities all over the world and probably in a community near to you. They can be affiliated with a formal Buddhist institution like Zen or they can be informal secular practice centers. The tradition for Buddhist practice centers is to offer sitting and basic teachings free of charge. The Buddha never charged fees for his wisdom.

CHAPTER 20

A Field Guide to Becoming a Pseudo-Extrovert

It seems like extroverts are the majority. Everywhere you look, you can see people in groups. What you may know from your own experience is that many introverts are forced to behave like extroverts at work, school, or in their families. You may choose to do this to create harmony, or it may be done unconsciously to fit in with the prevailing energy of the apparent majority. Here's a guide on how to do that more effectively.

Life as Performance

When you look at behavior, extroverts are the clear majority. There is a growing recognition that introverts are here in great numbers and have much to contribute to this extroverted society. However, the revolution is just starting and you will find yourself still needing to behave like an extrovert sometimes.

Hamlet the Extrovert

If Hamlet were alive today working in the contemporary office, he might have revised his soliloquy to this: *To conform or not to conform, that is the question. Whether 'tis nobler in the mind to suffer the slings and arrows of extroverted fortune (paychecks, accolades) or to take arms against a sea of expectations (being bright, cheerful, and chatty). And by opposing end them? To die; if I don't get some solitude. No more; and by a sleep to say we end the overextension and the thousand unnatural shocks that introverted flesh is heir to,· 'tis a consummation, devoutly to be wish'd. To die, if I don't have some quiet. To sleep, perchance to restore my energy: ay, there's the rub. For in that sleep of restoration what dreams may come? When we have shuffled off this pseudo-extrovert coil. Must give us pause; there's the respect that makes calamity of so long life.*

ESSENTIAL

Many performers are introverts. This is puzzling because they *look* like extroverts—outgoing, bright, energetic. The extrovert role can be a comfortable place for introverts precisely because it is a role—they can hide in plain sight. However, introverted actors, teachers, and entertainers pay a price for their performances. Rest and recovery must follow expenditure.

Buying In to Extroversion

The extrovert matches the American Ideal. Advertisers are always trying to sell you something and much of this fits the extrovert lifestyle. You buy appliances and products to make your life more convenient and efficient so you can get back to having fun. You buy over-the-counter and prescription drugs to keep you in action. If you aren't bouncing off the walls with happiness in every moment, you may be depressed and in need of medication ("ask your doctor . . .").

The pursuit of unrelenting happiness is stressful. It is also unnatural. Life is not as it appears on television and in the movies. An Audi commercial that aired during a recent Super Bowl tells a tale of overcoming introversion. An adolescent is going solo to his prom. His mother tries to normalize his going stag, but his little sister thinks he's a loser. His father throws him the keys to the superfast, super sexy Audi and the kid is transformed from a shy, retiring introvert into a confident badass extrovert. He parks in the principal's parking space, walks into the crowded prom and plants a kiss on the prom queen right in front of the prom king (who then proceeds to give the hero a black eye). He leaves the party smiling ear to ear. The tagline: "Bravery is what defines us." This commercial was one of the most popular that aired during a recent Super Bowl. You can bet that introverts and extroverts alike could appreciate this tale of transformation, disinhibition, and power. It reflects and creates the cultural ideal of the bold extrovert.

Negotiating Purpose

Day after day, do you find yourself being expected to participate in the cheerful, enthusiastic, kinetic world of the extroverted culture? Being on when you'd rather be off; being with people when you'd rather be alone? Do you find yourself acting? Pushing yourself beyond what feels comfortable? How do you handle this dilemma? "To conform or not conform, that is the question." Conformity comes at an energetic cost; nonconformity sets you apart, subjects you to misunderstanding, ridicule, or negative evaluation. There is a cost either way: if you act or if you are true to yourself.

QUOTE

"The last introvert in a world of extroverts. Silence: my response to both emptiness and saturation. But silence frightens people. I had to learn how to talk. Out of politeness."—Ariel Gore, author and founder of *Hip Mamma*

Studies have shown that people can fake extroversion reasonably well. You may have to fake it to function at work, to get promoted, and to fit in. Introverts can be very skilled at pretending to be extroverts—pseudo-extroverts—but end up paying an energy tax for those exertions. It helps if you really believe in the cause—the reason why you are stretching yourself in this way.

Susan Cain cites the work of Brian Little and what he calls "core personal projects." It feels better to become a pseudo-extrovert for a job, a relationship, or a cause. *The Purpose Driven Life* by Pastor Rick Warren is one of the best-selling books of recent times. People crave purpose, and having a purpose can move you to transcend your introversion. This may seem like a paradox—being true to yourself by acting. But pseudo-extroversion can be an authentic expression of who you want to be when it fulfills ends that are consistent with your core values.

Working the Room

The conversations at parties (a networking event is a party) are like a contact sport for introverts. The fast-paced melee of verbal interchange can be dizzying. If you are not in the mix, you will probably feel awkward, outside. Ultimately, it is exhausting. Performing as an effective pseudo-extrovert can be a necessary skill to have in the extroverted culture.

QUOTE

"All this talking, this rather liquid confessing, was something I didn't think I could ever bring myself to do. It seemed foolhardy to me, like an uncooked egg deciding to come out of its shell: there would be a risk of spreading out too far, turning into a formless puddle."
—Margaret Atwood

Self-Monitoring

Pseudo-extrovert skills are enhanced by being able to assess the social situation at hand and to modify your behavior to fit that situation. This is called, ironically, "self-monitoring," and is based on the work of psychologist Mark

Snyder. The term "self-monitoring" is a little misleading. People good at self-monitoring are actually good at monitoring the demands of the social situation. A better term would be "social monitoring." People who are not as good at self-monitoring are actually more responsive to their own feelings and less concerned with the situation around them. Self-monitoring has one aspect in common with mindfulness—attending to the environment or what neuroscientist Dan Siegel calls the eighth sense (environmental and social awareness).

High self-monitors are good actors, and if you want to increase this tendency, you will have to work at becoming a better actor. You may think this is inauthentic if you are a low self-monitor. Monitoring allows you to adapt by conforming to the situation at hand. Is it acting or genuine? For this, you'll need to acknowledge your inner feelings, and then go beyond them, to figure out what the current situation requires. It's a willingness to stretch yourself for a purpose, perhaps a core personal project. High self-monitoring is akin to the Asian personal identity of ensembled individualism that is highly attuned to the needs of the group and subordinates individual desires for the benefit of the group.

Assimilate or Accommodate?

Life is always a balancing act between assimilation and accommodation. The Swiss psychologist Jean Piaget showed that these two principles propel cognitive development in children. For adults, behavior in a situation will fall somewhere on this continuum. At the extreme of accommodation, you morph yourself to fit the situation, jettisoning your own needs, desires, and aspirations. At the extreme of assimilation, you force the world to fit your framework. You may come across as rigid, selfish, or arrogant. Balance is found in between—knowing when to adapt and when to preserve. It all depends on what is important to you and what you are willing to sacrifice and to what end that sacrifice is offered.

A Brief Guide to Pseudo-Extroversion

Alcohol deserves its reputation as a social lubricant. It disinhibits. It's liquid extroversion. If you rely on alcohol to be a pseudo-extrovert and you have to do it frequently, this could lead to a drinking problem. You'll need other strategies.

The take-home message is to be prepared. Being social is much like a performance, just as public speaking is a performance for which you would prepare. Having an opening line and a few things ready to say can prevent you from looking like a deer in the headlights. Yes, it's prepared, perhaps even canned, but it is strategic and serves your goal of getting through that cocktail party. The party may be very important to one of your core personal projects, so the preparation and effort will be worth it. Being prepared can help you to be less stressed and actually perform better. When you know you have something to fall back on, you can feel more confident being in the open space of conversation.

QUOTE

"The problem is acceptance, which is something we're taught not to do. We're taught to improve uncomfortable situations, to change things, alleviate unpleasant feelings. But if you accept the reality that you have been given—that you are not in a productive creative period—you free yourself to begin filling up again."—Anne Lamott, author

Conversations are much like writing. When you read an author's work, you are seeing a highly edited version of their writing. What you don't see are all the terrible first drafts that Anne Lamott talks about in her book on the craft of writing, *Bird by Bird: Some Instructions on the Writing Life*. If the writer can't give herself permission to write a bad first draft, the creative process will be stifled. If you can't give yourself permission to have imperfect conversations, the process of opening and connecting will likewise be stifled. In other words, don't get hung up on the early miscues that occur in connecting with people. You need time to warm up. Keep trying and eventually you will have a lovely, readable "text" with that person.

Here is a list of some pseudo-extrovert strategies:

- Be prepared: take notes, practice in front of the mirror.
- Self-monitor.
- Align with your values.
- Pace yourself.

- Smile.
- Be attentive to posture; strike a pose that feels confident or reminiscent of a confident time.
- Find one person to have a sit-down conversation with rather than approach an existing configuration.
- Interview: Ask questions of others—people love to talk about themselves.
- Use props. Rehearse things to say and even bring notecards with you to review. Since it may be harder for you to think on your feet in the moment, make sure to write things down when you visit your doctor, lawyer, mechanic, or anyone else where you may have a short amount of time to communicate.
- Be patient.
- Breathe.

Practice Public Speaking

While you probably hate public speaking, there are occasions where you will have to do it. You may have to give presentations for work or you may, ironically, be an introvert author needing to promote your own book. Public speaking is the top fear that people have. There is something primal about having a room full of eyes on you. It is reminiscent of life on the savannah where a set of eyes on you may have meant some creature was interested in having you for dinner. Now, of course, this ancient fear gets transferred to people being judgmental, bored, or disappointed by your presentation. Most people—introvert and extrovert—need to prepare for public speaking. As an introvert, you'll need to put extra effort into preparation. Here are some tips:

- Be prepared (probably not a problem for you as introverts tend to be vigilant).
- Practice in front of the mirror; video or audio record yourself.
- Practice in front of a friend or two.
- Remember that your sense of time is probably heightened—a short pause may seem like an eternity. If you record yourself or practice in front of a friend, you can get feedback.

- Make a space for being nervous. A moderate amount of arousal can actually improve your performance. Don't react to the anxiety and make it worse. Feel the sensations in your body and check in with your breathing.
- Make sure you are breathing in a helpful way. Practice diaphragmatic breathing. Diaphragmatic breathing engages the diaphragm—the wall of muscle that separates the lungs from the abdomen. When the lungs fully engage with air, the diaphragm expands, making it seem like your belly is filling with air. To find out if you are breathing this way, place one of your hands on your chest and the other on your belly and breathe. Watch which hand moves. Try to breathe with only the belly hand moving. It might be easier to notice this if you lie down on your back. The full diaphragmatic breath can help to keep you calmer in a tense situation.
- Find a local Toastmasters chapter. Toastmasters is an international, nonprofit, peer support organization devoted to developing public speaking skills.

Finding Your Style

You may have a reputation as a party pooper. Your disinclination toward unwieldy social gatherings no doubt cemented this reputation. The extroverts in your world need to be educated on the energy flow of introverts, how they process stimulation, and how a party like the one you were just invited to is about as attractive as sitting in the dentist's chair. Even as you say no to the invitation, there may be a part of you that is afraid that you will miss out on something special—meeting your soul mate or making a key business connection. There is a tension between self-care and opportunity; FOMO (Fear of Missing Out) can rear its ugly head.

Remember that introverts can have just as many social skills as extroverts although they are expressed in different ways. Introverts like and connect with people. Just because you are an introvert does not make you a misanthrope. Extroverts may set a high standard of enthusiastic social intercourse, but you don't have to copy this. Find your own style. Think about how your world is peopled. Are you satisfied with the connections you have with a select group of individuals? How would you like your world to be peopled? Do you want to go deeper? Do you need to find folks with more common interests?

FACT

Toastmasters boast a membership of 280,000 people participating in one of 13,500 clubs in 116 countries. Groups are peer run and members practice speaking assignments and receive feedback. There are ten self-paced speaking assignments to practice. (*www.toastmasters .org*)

Some Enchanted Evening

Introvert entrepreneur Guy Kawasaki teaches *enchantment* skills in his book *Enchantment: The Art of Changing Hearts, Minds, and Actions*. How do you come across as enchanting? The first step is to smile, and he suggests a real smile. A real smile wrinkles your eyes whereas a fake smile just moves your mouth. The next suggestion is to "use real words." That is, use simple words in the active voice. Keep it brief and sprinkle it with well-known metaphors. Another step is to "dress for a tie." Overdressing or underdressing can be a sign of disrespect. Dressing equivalently creates a more egalitarian vibe.

A solid handshake is another asset. Smile, utter a greeting, grip the hand firmly and don't hold it for too long (no more than two to three seconds). He then suggests not imposing your values and accepting others. He says, "enchanting someone by imposing your values is rare and usually has the opposite effect." Acceptance recognizes that people have strengths and weaknesses and that everyone "is better than you at something and people are more similar than different."

Balance and Restore Your Energy

Whether or not you try to be a pseudo-extrovert, extrovert-like demands will be placed upon you. Do you have energy recovery spots? Like Wi-Fi hotspots, they only work if you are in the vicinity. Your energy recovery spots will only work when you occupy them. You will need strategies to restore your energy after expenditures in the rings of the extrovert circus. You probably already have some of these down—finding a hiding place, canceling plans, taking a nap, and going into the interior with meditation, yoga, or qigong. The next step is to claim your energy recovery spots without guilt.

In an ideal world, you would never have to stray from your introvert comfort zone. You would socialize when you felt like socializing; you would retreat when you felt like that. Your energy would be robust. You would have time to think and a quiet space to ponder great thoughts. It's safe to say that you don't live in this utopia. There are times, all too often, that you have to extrovert yourself. Life can be anything but quiet. Your mind is squeezed by competing demands. If you are clear about what is important to you, your excursions into extroversion can be viewed as the price you pay for having your introvert time. You just have to make sure that you get to enjoy that goal that you've extended yourself for in the first place. When you are clear about what you want, you can use this wanting to negotiate for time with family, friends, coworkers, and bosses.

Look at your current work situation. Do you have a good balance between introverted and extroverted activities? What is the ratio of reading and writing to meetings and teamwork? What is the ratio of thinking to talking? If the balance it tipped toward extroverted activities does your life outside of work help you to establish balance? If not, you are at risk for burnout. In other words, do you have enough energy recovery spots in your life?

Finding and Occupying Your Voice

Your voice—your wanting—may have gotten lost in the accommodations that are forced upon you every day. If you are obligated to be a pseudo-extrovert every day, you may have lost touch with how you truly are. Before reading this book, you may not have even considered that reclaiming your voice was an option. The time is ripe now to stop and to repossess your voice.

You have lived your entire life in the extrovert circus. It seems normal—just the way life is. You may have become so accustomed to acting like an extrovert that you have lost touch with your introvert way of being. All you know is that you are frazzled, distracted, and exhausted. The Introvert

Revolution is giving a voice to introverts to reclaim their power. The Introvert Edge lifts you from disenfranchisement to celebrating your introvert gifts.

FACT

"Glottal fry" is the tendency for the voice to crack when it is used in a lower register. This is a common phenomenon and puts strain on the vocal cords. It results from insufficient energy in the voice that causes the vocal cords to vibrate. If your voice is cracking, you need to put more energy into it.

Discover Your Wanting

How can you find what your true wanting is beyond the expectations of others, society, and even yourself? The first way is to think back to what you wanted to be when you were a kid. This can provide important clues. The second way is to pay attention to the work you are drawn to. Many careers and jobs are multifaceted. Which ones give you juice? This is another set of clues. The last suggestion is to notice what you envy. This can provide another set of clues. Everyone has a particular wanting. Sometimes this is called your "calling," "passion," or "core personal projects." Whatever it is called, the key is to align your life with what brings you the most satisfaction. Chances are this wanting will also be aligned with your skill set. What are you good at? What brings you joy and satisfaction? These are additional important clues. The great mythologist Joseph Campbell urged, "Follow your bliss." This is bound to reveal your wanting.

Smiling

You can replicate this simple experiment. Take a pencil and purse it in your lips. This will cause a bit of a frown. Notice how you feel. Now take the pencil and put it between your teeth. This will force a smile. Now, how do you feel? If you are like most people, you will feel better when you smile—even if it is a forced smile. It is as if your brain doesn't know the difference. It is as if the brain is saying, "You are smiling so you must be happy." This can be a useful strategy for faking it until you can make it and it also has the added advantage of projecting a more positive energy. As an introvert, your energy will likely be more interior and you may come across as aloof. If you smile, you send out an invitation to the world around you that is open, warm, and welcoming. Smiling dispels aloofness.

Try another experiment. Walk down the street with a neutral expression. Now walk down the same street smiling, with your head up, and engaging people with eye contact. See if you notice a dramatic difference in these two experiences. Smiling changes the internal and external energy. It is an essential tool in your pseudo-extrovert arsenal that can help to give you the Introvert Edge when you need it the most.

Embodied Cognition

What you do with your body can affect your mind. There is a newly emerging field called "embodied cognition" that explores how the body affects thinking, judgment, and emotions. Researchers Barbara Isanski and Catherine West define embodied cognition as "the notion that the brain circuits responsible for abstract thinking are closely tied to those circuits that analyze and process sensory experiences—and its role in how we think and feel about our world."

Consider this well-known demonstration by the popular neuroscientist V. S. Ramachandran. Imagine two forms. One has curved lines, the other straight, pointed lines. Which one is named Kiki? Which one is named Bouba? Ninety-eight percent of people identify the curved lined figure as Bouba, because Bouba sounds smooth and curved. Kiki sounds sharp. Embodied cognition affects every sensory system. If research participants are subjected to a rejection, they judge the room as colder (hence, the origin of the "cold shoulder"). When excluded from a game, research subjects preferred hot soup and coffee afterward. Holding a hot liquid in your hands makes you more likely to rate the people in your life as more caring. The Macbeth effect is the urge to wash your hands when your morals are threatened or the other way around—washing your hands can reduce the tension of moral dilemmas. Holding a heavy clipboard gives ideas more importance (hence, a *weighty* idea or a *heavy* concept).

FACT

Your brain can tell the difference between a fake and real smile in another person (a fake smile does not affect the eyes). Detecting real smiles is accomplished by mirror neurons. However, the brain does not appear to be able to detect the difference between your own fake and real smile. Studies have shown that your own forced smile makes you feel good.

Embodied cognition suggests that smiling may not be a superficial trick. Practice and see what happens.

CHAPTER 21

For Extroverts Only

There is some extrovert in every introvert and some introvert in every extrovert. There are no pure cases. You can enjoy the Introvert Edge even if you are an extrovert. You can enhance your life by tapping into the power of solitude, the depths of quiet, and drawing strength from your interior. By embracing your natural introvert qualities, you can create greater balance in your life. This balance will be more important as you grow older.

Give Introverts a Break

You may have never realized that introverts live in the world in a very different way than you. You may have assumed if someone was not as cheerful, enthusiastic, and energetic as you that they must be depressed, neurotic, or sleep deprived. Your introvert counterparts need your understanding and, in turn, you can benefit from their way of being in the world. You can embrace the Introvert Edge to become a better-balanced extrovert. You can become more thoughtful, insightful, and poised. You can invite a space of silence, stillness, and peacefulness into your life.

QUOTE

"They say that extroverts are unhappier than introverts and have to compensate for this by constantly proving to themselves how happy and contented and at ease with life they are."—Paulo Coelho, bestselling author

When you notice yourself getting impatient with someone for taking time to respond to a question, think introvert first. When your friend refuses an invitation, think introvert again. Introverts are not inferior; they are different. Extroverts are the poster children for great cultural optimism. They have boundless energy, can-do attitude, and fearless ability to look before they leap. Not everyone can leap with you. Give the introverted members of your family, office, and friends a break. Consider slowing down for a moment. Don't interpret every pause as an invitation to keep on talking. Look within. A *Psychology Today* cover article, "Revenge of the Introverts" has a set of recommendations for "What Not to Say to an Introvert":

- "Why don't you like . . ." (insert people, parties, et cetera). Introverts like them fine—on *their* terms.
- "Surprise . . ." Don't hit introverts with surprise changes in social configurations, like "I've invited so and so along." Don't encroach on their personal space with surprise visits.
- "Don't demand immediate feedback." Introverts take longer to process information.

- "Don't ask why they are not contributing in meetings." Introverts may want to contribute in alternate ways to meetings or need time to prepare their thoughts.
- "Don't interrupt."

Beth Buelow, introvert coach, says, "We hate people telling us how we can be more extraverted, as if that's the desired state."

Finding Balance

As the famous psychologist Carl Jung said, there is no such thing as a pure introvert or extrovert. You are mixture of both. If you are predominately an extrovert, you will benefit from tapping into your introvert tendencies, even if these are buried deeply within you and haven't seen the light of day for a long time. There are many activities that can help you to be more introvert-like. Writing and meditation are two potent practices for exploring the interior, and the two can even be combined.

Even though the workplace tends to be dominated by extrovert norms, extroverts need to be mindful of recharging their energy too. Extroverts are energized by new adventures, social contact, and talking. If your job involves solitary time, quiet engagement, and sedentary hours, you will find yourself needing to boost your energy. If you are not getting what you need at work, are you making those connections after work? Are you having enough adventures? Susan Cain in *Quiet* encourages extroverts:

If you're a buzz-prone extrovert, then you're lucky to enjoy lots of invigorating emotions. Make the most of them: build things, inspire others, think big. Start a company, launch a website, build an elaborate tree house for your kids. But also know that you're operating with an Achilles' heel that you must learn to protect. Train yourself to spend energy on what's truly meaningful to you instead of on activities that look like they'll deliver a quick buzz of money or status or excitement. Teach yourself to pause and reflect when warning signs appear that things aren't working out as you'd hoped. Learn from your mistakes. Seek out counterparts (from spouses to friends . . . to business partners) who can help rein you in and compensate for your blind spots.

Everyone has blind spots. Yours may come from exuberance, whereas an introvert's may come from caution. All human beings are works in progress. Life can be a learning experience when you adopt an attitude of openness. You can grow from adversity when you seek to accept what is happening to you.

Midlife

In *The Inferno*, Dante talks about the perils of midlife. He finds himself in a dark wood, where the way is truly lost. Whether you pay attention to them or not, darkness, uncertainty, and "stuckness" are inescapable facts of life. Uncertainty permeates everything, even when you move through life with confidence, bravado, and energy. The elemental uncertainty is death. You know you are going to die but you don't know when. This is a curious phenomenon for human beings. Midlife may bring this awareness into focus when you recognize that there may be fewer days ahead of you than behind. As life moves on, the statistical likelihood of that moment of death becomes greater. The longer you live, the more opportunities for loss, disappointment, and failure. These dark elements of life can be great teachers, but are often met with fear, loathing, and defensiveness. Midlife can also be a time of being stuck. The arcs started in youth have played themselves out—you've raised a family, had a career (or two), now what?

QUOTE

"Midlife is the time to let go of an overdominant ego and to contemplate the deeper significance of human existence."—C. G. Jung

Midlife is a time for pausing, reflecting, and reappraising how you lived your life to date. Are you on the right track? Where do you want to go? As an extrovert, you may enjoy taking risks in business, recreation, and relationships. You may enjoy living on the edge. Is this sustainable? Your body may not be able to do what it once did. The time of midlife is a time to invite in some of your introverted qualities. They may be dusty, but they are within you. They may be remote, yet they are accessible. As you slow down (even if only a little) as you age, this is a good time to bring attention to the interior. Extroverts tend to move closer to being introverts as they enter middle age. They start to draw on their inherent but perhaps underdeveloped introvert qualities. Action is balanced with stillness. Expansion is balanced by contracting. Collection follows dispersion.

Tap into Your Natural Introvert

Journaling practice is a great way to start a conversation with yourself and to draw out your natural introvert. Journaling creates a space of aloneness and quiet. It brings you in contact with your thoughts and provides a space for reflection on things other than the to-do list. Journaling helps to slow things down. It can be helpful to journal anytime, especially in the morning before the day gets underway. When you write, try to write without any restrictions. Don't edit, worry about penmanship, grammar, or spelling. Just write whatever comes to mind. Keep your hand moving at all times (or your fingers if you are typing on a keyboard).

Mindfulness 101 for Extroverts

You may find silence an alien landscape. If your surroundings are silent, your mind may still be quite active. Another level of silence is to quiet your mind through meditation. One simple approach is to focus on your breathing —the physical process of breathing—and return your attention to these sensations whenever it moves into the future or the past. Whenever thinking resumes, gently escort your attention back to breathing. Repeat this process as needed. This simple practice is known as mindfulness meditation, and it can be a useful adjunct for helping you to develop your Introvert Edge. This breathing exercise can make even the most mundane task interesting because you are setting aside the "judging" component of your mind, that is, the part of your mind that generates commentary such as "This is so boring, I wonder what's on television?" You recognize that as a thought and you bring your attention back to your breath. If you are prone to boredom, mindfulness practice can be a beneficial tool. You can think of it as a cure for boredom. Anytime you find yourself in a situation where you might otherwise be bored, focus your attention on your breathing. Investigate breathing with curiosity, interest, even fascination. Each breath is different. Can you appreciate its uniqueness?

Seek Solitude

Spending time in solitude is another way to access the introvert. Small hits of solitude and silence are provided by meditation practice. Chances are, you haven't spent much time in silence. Your days are filled with activities, talking with friends, and entertainment. Take a solitary walk in the woods. Look at the trees, the flowers, and the sky. Try to find something new in each moment. Notice what being alone feels like. If it is uncomfortable, can you investigate this feeling the same way you investigated your breath? You can even practice solitude with another person. Spend some time with another person, perhaps on that same walk in the woods, without speaking. Notice what this space of silence feels like in a social situation.

Opening Up

Extroverts can learn how to become more compassionate and empathetic in their communications from introverts. You start through listening. Listening requires attention, patience, and forbearance. The conversation is a process of exchange of ideas, emotions, and a sense of presence. The introvert is naturally keyed into these elements, and you may have to work harder to get there. You probably have lots of great ideas, associations, and stories that you would like to share. You can practice first by listening. Set aside your agenda for getting it all out and focus on what the other person is saying. Assure yourself that you will eventually get to say everything that you want to say or that it is not of dire importance that you get every word in.

QUOTE

"The cure for boredom is curiosity. There is no cure for curiosity."
—Dorothy Parker, writer

The introvert can find entertainment in any situation, even ones that may seem dull from the outside. This is part of the Introvert Edge. If you can invite silence, stillness, and solitude into your days you can get this edge too.

Aim for empathy. Try to take the other person's perspective. What is she thinking? What is she feeling? Embrace patience. Allow moments of brief silence to punctuate the conversation. Reflect back on what you have heard from your speaking partner rather than just trade stories. Avoid the tendency to "fix" the problem your friend is sharing with you (unless he has explicitly asked for you to help him to fix it). Often, people just want to be heard, to have someone witness their pain. They don't want their problem to be fixed. Your offer of help, while well meaning, can feel unempathetic to the person with the situation.

If your speaking partner is your significant other who also happens to be an introvert, she will welcome the newfound space in the conversation. She will enjoy the unhurried pace and the moments of silence. She will appreciate your taking in what she has to say without jumping to a solution. You may not be ready to become a professional counselor, but these introvert tendencies can help you to communicate in a more compassionate way and to feel more connected to the people you care about.

Pacing

Introverts can show you how to slow down, to access the depths, and to mine the riches of the interior. How well developed are your introvert qualities? What can you learn from the introverts in your life? Folk wisdom says to stop and smell the roses. It's hard to do this if you are moving too fast. Life becomes a blur. There is a freedom that comes from movement *and* from sitting still.

QUOTE

"All men's miseries derive from not being able to sit in a quiet room alone."—Blaise Pascal

What do you notice when you slow down? What does it feel like to contain your energy? Three principles of mindfulness are silence, containment, and engagement. They work together to help you to appreciate life in the moment. Silence opens you to a vast internal world of sensations, images, and feelings. Containment gives you choice in how to express impulses. Not every feeling needs to be voiced; not every thought needs to be articulated; not every impulse needs to be acted upon. How much trouble would that save you? When you can bring silence and containment to the moment, you can engage more fully with it. There is nothing between you and the moment. You are right there, undistracted by running around. You can find lots of stimulation within if you give yourself the chance to slow down.

Can you, once in a while, sit in a quiet room alone? It's an important skill to have because sometimes you may have to sit alone. By being able to embrace solitude, you won't need to depend on having company all the time—you can make your own company. Most introverts enjoy the company of others and also know how to entertain themselves. In fact, they crave it, require it, and seek it out often.

An Introvert Guide for Extroverts

You can enrich your life by connecting with your introvert qualities. You can balance activity with rest, dynamism with stillness, and speaking with listening. Here are things you can do to develop your introvert self:

- Go on a solo date. Take yourself to an art gallery, museum, or concert.
- At your next party, focus on having one or two lengthy conversations instead of many brief ones.
- Try meditation, yoga, qigong, or tai chi.
- Start a journaling practice. Take your journal to a public place. People watch and write down your impressions.
- Spend a Saturday in silence. Refrain from speaking, texting, and social media. Read, meditate, and eat slowly.
- Spend time with a single task. Avoid the temptation to multitask.
- Do something outside of your comfort zone.
- Relabel boredom an opportunity for discovery.
- Get familiar with all the speeds of life: slow, medium, and fast.

- In your next conversation, spend more time listening than speaking.
- Start your day with a few moments of stillness before you spring into action.

Behaving like an introvert may be a new experience for you. It can open a new dimension to life—a slower, deeper, and deliberate way of moving through the world. You can enjoy the rich interior presence of senses, connect with your thoughts, and just spend some time *being* rather than doing.

CHAPTER 22

Owning Your Quiet

There is a power that comes with silence, solitude, and quiet. People are starving for this quiet even if they have not yet articulated it. Mindfulness revolutionary Jon Kabat-Zinn noted, "I am keenly aware, and reminded daily, of the huge subterranean yearning in people everywhere for authenticity and personal agency, for silence and stillness and peace of mind." Your Introvert Edge embraces this silence, stillness, and peace of mind. You have an inner introvert, whether you are an avowed introvert, an extrovert, or somewhere in the middle.

Starting the Conversation: Asking the Right Questions

Everyone can benefit from accessing their inner introvert and bringing its power into work, relationships, and creativity. Your inner introvert may be feeling neglected, beaten up by the exuberant expectations of extroverted society. Your inner introvert is a rock star waiting to rock the world. You don't need to apologize any longer for being an introvert. You don't need to hide any longer. The Introvert Edge is yours to claim. It's time to own your introversion, and take your rightful place in society.

QUOTE

"We are not consumers. For most of humanity's existence, we were makers, not consumers: we made our clothes, shelter, and education, we hunted and gathered our food."—Matthew Fox, author and theologian

Doing is the working language of American culture. It's the American Way. If *doing* is the coin of the realm, then *being* gets lost. You belong to the group known as human beings, but in reality, humans are more "doings" than "beings." The Introvert Edge reclaims the power of being, over the mindless preoccupation with doing. The beginning of the conversation with yourself starts with asking questions:

- Am I getting what I need at work?
- Can I ask for what I need, if my needs are not being met?
- Am I getting what I need at home?
- Can I ask for what I need, when my needs are not being met?
- Am I in the right work?
- Am I in the right relationship?

The latter two can be hard questions to ask because you may not want to hear the answers. They are important, nonetheless.

Giving Yourself Permission

Claiming the Introvert Edge starts with giving yourself permission to be who you are—an introvert and proud of it. You don't need to apologize for being the way you are; you don't need to explain yourself to others. You will need to make your differences and needs clear to others. You will have to tell the truth about what you want. In *Introvert Power*, Laurie Helgoe provides a succinct script you can use to respond to an extrovert's invitation: "I see that you really want me to come. I like that part, and I'm sorry to disappoint you. But what I really want is some time to myself." Simple, succinct, and truthful.

You don't need to apologize for wanting something different. You don't need to make excuses or blame it on being too busy. The broader culture does not seem to value this wanting. There is a bias against mental wellness. You can call out sick from work if you have a cold, but you are not supposed to call out sick if you are emotionally weary. You can call out sick, but you can't call out well.

You don't have to lie by saying there is something wrong with your energy. How many times have you refused an invitation by saying that you were "spent," "burnt," "tapped out," "exhausted," or "fried"? These statements may be true, but do you really want to go to that event or is it just another one of those extrovert affairs you'd rather skip? You don't need to be energy compromised to say no. You can just say, "I don't want to." Saying no more often may actually help you to preserve your energy so you don't become spent, burnt, tapped out, exhausted, and fried. It is okay to be proactive. It is okay to protect your energy.

From Chaos and Rigidity to Integration

Neuroscientist Dan Siegel defines the mind as a "relational and embodied process that regulates the flow of energy and information." You have a unique mind that requires some special care instructions. When you are feeling exhausted, irritable, dull, anxious, impatient, or shut down, your energy may be out of balance. It is time for you to restore yourself. Being overwhelmed in social settings will move your energy toward disorganization—toward rigidity or chaos. When you shut down into rigidity, you feel walled off, exhausted, and blank. When your energy spins out into chaos, you feel anxious, impatient, and irritable.

QUOTE

"Each of us needs periods in which our minds can focus inwardly. Solitude is an essential experience for the mind to organize its own processes and create an internal state of resonance. In such a state, the self is able to alter its constraints by directly reducing the input from interactions with others."—Daniel J. Siegel

Rest, contemplation, and connection are the best ways to restore balance. You need time with activities that will restore you from the chaos and rigidity of what Siegel calls "integration." Integration is a holistic, healthy flow of energy. The best way to take care of yourself is to have a repertoire of self-care actions you can take ready at hand. You may have to squeeze something in a few minutes of break at work or it may be a longer self-care ritual at home. These rituals can include breathing, exercise, journaling, connecting with a good friend who gets you (probably another introvert), taking a nap, just being alone, and so forth. Whatever works for you is the key.

Don't just rely on your memory, which may be fried when you need it the most. Make a list of the things you can do and when you need to do them. For example, a few minutes of mindful breathing, yoga postures, or qigong moves can go a long way in restoring your energy. Find what things work for you and give yourself permission to do them. Recognize that you need to do them when you have moved out of integration—in a sense you have dis-integrated, and you need to remember that you can take care of yourself and need to take care of yourself.

Remember that you are not an extrovert and if you pattern yourself on the extroverts around you, depletion is sure to follow. This is the "price" you have to pay for the advantages of being an introvert. Your energy requires more care than the extroverts (that is not exactly true; it is easier in this culture for extroverts to get their needs met; in another culture it would not be so difficult). And the benefit of this care is rich access to your interior, something extroverts find alien territory. Energy maintenance is best done proactively. Don't wait until you are completely wiped to turn to your self-care list.

Punctuate your day with micro-restoration activities (or lack of activities that drain you) like just sitting still for a few moments.

Downtime

Elite athletes preparing for competition require downtime or they run the risk of developing overtraining syndrome. The body becomes physiologically depleted and shuts down. It is a serious condition that can derail an athlete's competitiveness. Introverts are like elite athletes. You cannot go all out every day and not break down. You need downtime, where your mind and body are in a restful pattern. You need to be "off" from the demands of the extrovert world. "Off" will mean different things for different introverts and different things to you at different times. Elite athletes have the good fortune to have their full-time job be training, self-care, and competition. You probably have a job, family, and other responsibilities. Self-care is in competition with everything else. It seems like it is getting harder and harder to have downtime in the frenetic world of the digital age. It doesn't matter what everyone else is doing. If you don't take care of your energy, you are going to break down. Simple as that.

Sleep Is the Foundation of Your Energy

Because introverts have unique energy needs, you need to make sure you have the solid foundation of rest that comes from good sleep. You live in a sleep-deprived society and this pattern may work for extroverts but it crushes introverts. If you are not getting enough sleep, you are digging yourself into an energy hole that will be difficult to get out of. You may not have even learned good sleep habits because sleep is undervalued in this culture. Getting sufficient sleep is the goal. People need an average of eight hours per night. Your sleep needs may be more or less. If you are a short sleeper, you can be rested after six or seven hours. However, if you are a long sleeper, you will require nine, ten, or even more to feel sufficiently rested. How much sleep do you *actually* need? That's a different question from how much sleep you get or how much sleep you think you need. Figure out how much you actually need. Experiment with different lengths and see where you feel most rested.

All diurnal creatures have what is known as a circadian rhythm. This rhythm results in fluctuations in energy and body temperature throughout the day. For most people, the circadian low occurs between 2:00 and 4:00 P.M. (and A.M. since it is a 12-hour cycle). Most people will feel a little dip in their energy during this low. If you feel sleepy to the point of wanting a nap, then you are likely sleep-deprived. If you are spending your days as a pseudo-extrovert without sufficient restorative breaks, you are at risk for energy spin out.

ESSENTIAL

Some tips for optimizing sleep are: Go to sleep and wake up at consistent times; sleep in a dark, cool, and comfortable environment; only use the bedroom for sleeping and sex (reading may be okay, but television can be stimulating, especially for introverts and may interfere with your sleep quality); don't eat or drink large amounts before bedtime; don't do vigorous exercise too late in the evening.

Be mindful of caffeine intake. This can disrupt your sleep. You may need even more sleep than you think, especially when you are taxing your energy throughout your day. Respect sleep. It is the foundation of your energy. If you don't take care of it, you will be fighting your energy. It's a double whammy. Your energy is drained by the kinetic interactivity of your workday—just trying to keep up in the extrovert circus. If your energy is already compromised, these exertions will be even more difficult. Even if you don't have to be a pseudo-extrovert during your day, your energy will need to be restored. The challenge of energy maintenance is compounded by inadequate sleep.

Following Your Bliss

In the film *Finding Joe*, filmmaker Patrick Takaya Solomon explores the ideas of mythologist Joseph Campbell, who famously urged a generation to "follow your bliss." What brings you joy? What do you love to do (when you give yourself permission to do so)? The process of following your bliss starts with the recognition that you are entitled to this. You don't have to ask permission from your boss, partner, or children—only yourself. Once you grant yourself permission to discover your bliss, the process of discovery begins. A simple thought experiment could get you started. In an ideal world where money and other people's expectations were not obstacles, how would you spend your days? This is an important clue. What did you love to do as a child? Perhaps a dream that you have abandoned long ago? What activities bring you into the moment and make your "talking head" go away—an activity that absorbs you and where your full attention is right there with the task leading to joy and a sense of timelessness? This experience is known as *flow* and it happens in situations where there is just the right combination of skill and challenge. It also happens in situations you love to do.

Practicing Your Passion

Once you have issued the permit and done the discovery, now the challenge is to live this passion. How can you make your ideas a reality? What do you have to communicate to others? What risks do you have to take? You may feel vulnerable communicating your passion to someone who may not understand it or, worse, ridicule it. You may want to practice "coming out" to someone who is likely to be sympathetic—perhaps another introvert. What do you have to let go of to make your passion a reality? There is bound to be at least one person who is going to be disappointed, disapproving, or let down by your decision to move in this new direction. Can you stay true to what you need? It will be more difficult at first, and your resolve will be tested during this transition. People may accuse you of being selfish, crazy, or misguided. Can you remain faithful to your own truth?

QUOTE

"We must let go of the life we have planned, so as to accept the one that is waiting for us."—Joseph Campbell

If your job is the obstacle, can you change it? When it is impossible to modify your job and impractical to find a new one, finding your passion may fall to volunteerism or what you do for your leisure time. By starting on the margins, the call of what is true will grow louder and louder until you have to respond—"To take the one hand you know belongs in yours"—as the poet David Whyte says in his poem, "The True Love," This is your own hand extended to itself—embracing your passion and finding your bliss.

Taking Pride in Your Unique Skills

Extroverts are WYSIWYG—what you see is what you get. Introverts are enigmas. You have strengths that may be going unappreciated. You have the power of thoughtfulness, contemplation, and depth. You don't wear your heart on your sleeve; you don't verbalize every thought you have. The philosopher and mathematician Blaise Pascal cautioned, "All men's miseries derive from not being able to sit in a quiet room alone." You know how to "sit in a quiet room alone." It's one of your greatest strengths as an introvert. If you can combine the quiet room with a quiet mind, you can experience a profound peace, tranquility, and even bliss. The solitude of the hushed room can facilitate contemplation, meditation, and prayer. You are not afraid to be alone with your own thoughts, feelings, memories, and fantasies. You are not shy about exploring the silence that occupies your mind beyond all the talk, stories, and images.

Recommendations for Society Hooked on Extroversion

This culture is addicted to extroverted optimism. A change could start in schools, as kids may need more quiet time. Indeed, there is a movement to bring mindfulness into schools. Teaching mindfulness to kids can help to establish introvert qualities in introverts and extroverts alike. Introverts, instead of being made to feel less than, can be celebrated, admired, and respected. Children can be taught balance at an early age, and carry this wisdom forward. A society that embraces introversion won't be afraid of uncertainty. It will be comfortable there. The workplace can support introverts, by creating quiet spaces such as napping lounges (as some forward-thinking companies have done). Everyone should have the opportunity to interact, or not interact, according to their energy in the moment. Here is a quick guide for counteracting hyper-extroversion:

- Dial it back. Not everything has to be over the top.
- Contemplate.
- Create.
- Seek balance.
- Slow down.
- Do nothing (sometimes).

America has not always been the land of the extroverted. This has been a trend over the past 100 years. Things have gotten out of balance. There is too much frantic activity. There is no time to enjoy life. The extrovert culture has bitten off more than it can chew. Anxiety disorders afflict a huge swath of the population (over 20 percent) and stress is at near epidemic proportions. It is estimated that stress costs industry $200 billion annually including medical costs, absenteeism, low productivity, and turnover.

Introverts and extroverts handle stress differently. Extroverts act out—blow off steam, vocalize, distract. Introverts act in—withdraw, ruminate, rest. Perhaps the demands of extroverted society are not entirely to blame for today's stress epidemic. The Information Age of digital technology also contributes. But compare work norms in the United States with those of a Scandinavian or European country: longer workweeks, fewer benefits (such as maternity/paternity leave), and an older retirement age. Scandinavia is the land of introverts. The Scandinavian countries of Sweden, Norway, Finland, Denmark, and Iceland are among the top nations for quality of life. See the difference?

ESSENTIAL

Ten companies that allow napping at work: 1. Google, 2. Ben & Jerry's, 3. AOL, 4. Zappos, 5. Nike, 6. Pizza Hut, 7. British Airways, 8. Time Warner, 9. Newsweek, 10. MetroNaps (manufacturer of napping pods). Source: guycodeblog.mtv.com/2013/02/19/napping-at-work/

Imagine if introverts were in charge. Life would move at a slower pace. Self-care would be a priority. The workplace would not be a potboiler of stress. There would be shorter workdays and workweeks, and longer vacations. Your energy would be valued—top corporate assets. Conversations would never have *awkward* silences. Silence would be honored.

Actions You Can Take Today

Since introverts are not yet in charge, you may not be able to find your place of quiet at your current workplace; you may not be able to find solace in your current relationship. Can you make modifications? Can you make your needs a priority? Do you have the courage to consider change? Here is a quick reference guide for introverts:

- Normalize your introvert. There is nothing wrong with you!
- Practice speaking (singing, acting).
- Solitude is not a luxury.
- Recharge while you discharge (mindful communication).
- Change when all else fails.

QUOTE

"Interestingly, we belong to life as much through our sense that it is all impossible, as we do through the sense that we will accomplish everything we have set out to do."—David Whyte

The first step is to come to terms with your introversion. This is how you are. While you can *act* like an extrovert you can never become one. Even though it may seem fabulous to be an extrovert, you can learn to accept, love, and even celebrate your way of being in the world. Since you will have to speak, you can practice speaking. Learning to project your voice can make speaking less stressful. Solitude has to be the basis for your self-care. It is not a luxury, and you cannot ignore it. You can learn to practice mindfulness while you are in high-energy output situations. Staying in the present moment can help you preserve more of your energy as you do the extroverted tasks of your day. Change may be necessary when you recognize your life is out of balance. Your life may require more than just embracing your solitude. You may have to renegotiate the terms of your job, your relationship, and your inner life.

The Path of Integrity

If you want to be happy, you must listen to who you are and move toward acceptance. If your reflex is to say "no" (in an effort to protect your energy), practice saying "yes." If your reflex is to say "yes" when you should say "no" can you set the limit? When is it the right time to say yes? How do you know when it is the right time to say no? You know by knowing yourself. When you give yourself permission to be who you are, you give yourself the Introvert Edge. When you have faith in what you experience and no longer buy into the expectations of the culture, you can feel the freedom of being yourself.

Integrity has two meanings and both apply—character and wholeness. To embrace your Introvert Edge is to find the path with character for yourself—pursuing what is true, right, and beneficial for your particular life. To have integrity is to be whole—complete. Loving your Edge brings you to wholeness. You are complete without apology. You are whole without regret. A great burden can be lifted from your mind when you know there is nothing wrong with you. You are free when you see your introvert qualities as gifts instead of liabilities. You grow into the space of silence that is your birthright.

Delight in Speaking Softly

There is a delight in finding your own voice, even when that voice is quiet, or silent. You may actually want to say less when you set aside the expectation that you "should" be saying more. There is a delight in going against the grain of expectations. Whether it is society or your loved ones, you are living in a world of expectations, demands, and responsibilities. The person often forgotten in the litany of expectations is you. You have the right to take care of yourself, and if you want to be happy, you will need to make your needs a priority.

QUOTE

"You have a grand gift for silence, Watson. It makes you quite invaluable as a companion."—Sherlock Holmes to his faithful assistant, Dr. Watson

Protecting your energy and nurturing your creativity may have always been viewed as luxuries, if they were considered at all. Is it a luxury to spare yourself from soul numbing denial of what is most important to you? Now you have the opportunity to delight in being the way you are and expressing this through work that is important to you and in alignment with your true values—your Introvert Edge.

The Courage in the Dark

You can find balance in the union of forces: dark and light, yin and yang, contraction and expansion. The dark can be your teacher, your guide. The darkness can be "sweet" as poet David Whyte shares in his poem the "The Sweet Darkness" from the collection, *River Flow:*

When your eyes are tired
the world is tired also.

When your vision has gone,
no part of the world can find you.

Time to go into the dark
where the night has eyes to recognize its own.
There you can be sure
you are not beyond love.

The dark will be your home
tonight.

The night will give you a horizon
further than you can see.

You must learn one thing.
The world was made to be free in.

Give up all the other worlds
except the one to which you belong.

Sometimes it takes darkness and the sweet
confinement of your aloneness
to learn

anything or anyone
that does not bring you alive

is too small for you.

Many Rivers Press, Langley, Washington, printed with permission from
the publisher

"The world was meant to be free in." What a powerful statement. And
to be free you must learn to trust yourself—to trust your introverted way of
being. The prerequisite for this freedom is "the sweet confinement of your
aloneness." As an introvert, you already have access to this interior space
and have tasted its sweetness. The last stanza is a manifesto for introverts.
You are probably well practiced at engaging with things and people that are
"too small for you." This smallness depletes your energy, diffuses your attention, and makes you want to pull your hair out.

ESSENTIAL

Tara Brach is the founder of the Insight Meditation Community of
Washington in Bethesda, Maryland. She is one of the many featured
teachers on Dharma Seed, a website that offers thousands of free
talks by meditation teachers. You can listen to one of Tara's nearly 400
talks at *www.dharmaseed.org/teacher/175/*

Darkness is found in the quiet spaces of stillness. Darkness is found in
the interior of meditation. If you can allow yourself to be less busy and find
a place of repose, you can invite the shadows in. In fact, they will come
on their own—given the opportunity to find you not doing something that
distracts your attention. In the dark you will find recognition, validation,
and comfort—"the night has eyes to recognize its own." Here, you find a
home with expanding possibility—"a horizon further than you can see." The

darkness will teach you the most important lesson: "The world was meant to be free in." To be free, you must accept everything. For true happiness, nothing short of radical acceptance will do.

Radical Acceptance

Tara Brach makes this abundantly clear in her influential book *Radical Acceptance: Embracing Your Life with the Heart of a Buddha* and more recently in *True Refuge: Finding Peace and Freedom in Your Own Awakened Heart.* She says, "The belief that we are deficient and unworthy makes it difficult to trust that we are truly loved." Freedom comes from acceptance and recognition that you *are* worthy. Like Tara Brach, David Whyte assures you that "you are not beyond love." He encourages you to give up everything except the one world "to which you belong." How do you find this world? "The sweet confinement of your aloneness" is the prerequisite to discovery. It is the precondition for learning that "one thing." The quest is to be alive— fully alive without reservation.

Things get in the way; people get in the way. It's easy to allow obstacles to derail the connection to your truth. It's easy to get caught up in the busyness of work, raising a family, and staying sane. Life can often be "solitude lost" if you don't protect your aloneness. This aloneness doesn't have to be isolated. It is a place where you can hear yourself think. It is having sufficient quiet to know that you are a living creature living on this third planet from the sun, in this galaxy of galaxies with its 100 billion stars. If you are not careful, life will contract you. Others will place their demands upon you. The stress of life will squeeze the silence from your mind. Joy will be absent and peace will shy. The first lines of the poem recognize the fatigue that afflicts modern life. The dark, sweet silence is where you find your home. The sweet darkness is where your energy becomes whole, robust, and available.

Coming Home

Your passion doesn't have to conform to the expectations of others. It can be a quiet engagement with something that you love. It doesn't have to be a billboard announcing your activities to the world. Following your bliss is the process of coming home. When you embrace your Introvert Edge, you come home into yourself. The Nobel Laureate Caribbean poet Derek Walcott speaks to this coming home in his poem "Love after Love." He says, "the time will come when with elation you will greet yourself arriving in your own door, in your own mirror. . . . You will love again this stranger who was yourself."

QUOTE

"We are introverts and we are going home."—Laurie Helgoe

When you reach acceptance, you have come home into your experience. You are empowered to be an introvert and you can get along better with extroverts and other introverts. Your home is your comfort. It is a physical space of solitude and it is a place within you—a safe place you can retreat to in any moment. Home is found in the exterior and interior sanctuary. It can be nothing more than feeling okay to sit back and watch; to rest when you don't feel like jumping in. Being home means not having to explain yourself to *anyone*—including yourself. You don't need to apologize for being an introvert. You don't need to hide your introversion. You can celebrate it. Extroverts will be envious of your ability to sit still, of your singularity of focus, and your rich inner life.

The Introvert Edge is yours for a lifetime.

APPENDIX A

Introvert Author Web Resources

The Power of Introverts
Susan Cain, author of *Quiet: The Power of Introverts in a World That Can't Stop Talking*
www.thepowerofintroverts.com

Dr. Laurie Helgoe
Laurie Helgoe, author of *Introvert Power: Why Your Inner Life Is Your Hidden Strength*
www.drlauriehelgoe.com/home.html

Marti Olsen Laney
Marti Olsen Laney, author of *The Introvert Advantage: How to Thrive in an Extrovert World, The Hidden Gifts of the Introverted Child,* and *The Introvert and Extrovert in Love*
www.hiddengiftsoftheintrovertedchild.com

Introvert Zone
C. Black, author of eBook: *I'll Be in My Room*
www.introvertzone.com

Jennifer Kahnweiler
Jennifer Kahnweiler, author of *Quiet Influence* and *The Introverted Leader*
www.jenniferkahnweiler.com/blog/

Adam S. McHugh
Adam McHugh, author of *Introverts in the Church: Finding Our Place in an Extroverted Culture*
www.adamsmchugh.com

C Level Strategies
Lisa Petrilli, author of *The Introvert's Guide to Success in Business and Leadership*
www.lisapetrilli.com

Introvert Energy
Nancy Okerlund, author of *Introverts at Ease*
www.introvertenergy.com/index.php

APPENDIX B

Introvert Blogs

Introvert Spring
Blog by Michaela Chung
www.introvertspring.com

The Introvert's Corner
Psychology Today blog by Sophia Dembling,
author of *The Introvert's Way: Living a Quiet Life
in Noisy World*
*www.psychologytoday.com/blog/
the-introverts-corner*

Self-Promotion for Introverts
Psychology Today blog of Nancy Ancowitz, with
career advancement tips, quips, and insights for
the quieter crowd
*www.psychologytoday.com/blog/
self-promotion-introverts*

The Quiet One
Blog by Marisa @ The Quiet One, Living (and
Loving) My Introverted Life
www.quiet-one.com

Introvert Retreat
Celebrating Inner Life in the Outer World
www.introvertretreat.com

Quietly Fabulous
Blog by Susan Steele: We are introverts. We are
awesome.
www.quietlyfabulous.com

Brave Introvert
Blog by Teri, Finding My Voice in a World That
Won't Stop Talking
www.braveintrovert.com

Introverted and Loving It
Blog by Becki Jaspin Noles
www.introverts.net

APPENDIX C

Books Cited

Ancowitz, Nancy. *Self-Promotion for Introverts: The Quiet Guide to Getting Ahead*. New York: McGraw Hill, 2009.

Aron, Elaine. *The Highly Sensitive Person: How to Survive When the World Overwhelms You*. New York: Broadway, 1997.

Aron, Elaine. *The Highly Sensitive Child: Helping Our Children Thrive When the World Overwhelms Them*. New York: Three Rivers Press, 2002.

Beulow, Beth. *Insight: Reflections on the Gifts of Being an Introvert*. Introvert Entrepreneur, 2012.

Black, C. *I'll Be in My Room*. Introvert Books, 2013.

Brach, Tara. *Radical Acceptance: Embracing Your Life with the Heart of a Buddha*. New York: Bantam, 2003.

Brach, Tara. *True Refuge: Finding Peace and Freedom in Your Own Awakened Heart*. New York: Bantam, 2013.

Burkeman, Oliver. *The Antidote: Happiness for People Who Hate Positive Thinking*. New York: Faber & Faber, 2012.

Cain, Susan. *Quiet: The Power of Introverts in a World That Can't Stop Talking*. New York: Broadway Books, 2013.

Cameron, Julia. *The Artist's Way*. New York: Tarcher, 2002.

Csikszentmihalyi, Mihaly. *Finding Flow: The Psychology of Engagement with Everyday Life*. New York: Basic Books, 1998.

Dembling, Sophia. *The Introvert's Way: Living a Quiet Life in Noisy World*. New York: Perigee, 2012.

Eliot, T. S. *The Four Quartets*. New York: Mariner, 1968.

Fischer-Schreiber, Ingrid. *The Encyclopedia of Eastern Philosophy and Religion*. Boston: Shambhala, 1994.

Gladwell, Malcom. *Blink*. New York: Back Bay Books, 2005.

Gleitman, Henry. *Psychology*. New York: Norton, 1986.

Goldberg, Natalie. *Writing Down the Bones*. Boston: Shambhala, 1986.

Gombrich, Richard. *What the Buddha Thought*. London: Equinox, 2009.

Gottman, John. *Seven Principles for Making Marriage Work*. New York: Three Rivers Press, 1999.

Hanh, Thich Nhat. *Miracle of Mindfulness*. Boston: Beacon, 1975.

Helgoe, Laurie. *Introvert Power: Why Your Inner Life Is Your Hidden Strength*. New York: Sourcebooks, 2013.

James, William. *The Varieties of Religious Experience*. New York: Penguin Classics, 1985.

Jung, C. G. *Psychological Types*. Princeton, NJ: Princeton University Press, 1971.

Kabat-Zinn, Jon. *Full Catastrophe Living*. New York: Delta, 1990.

Kahnweiler, Jennifer. *Quiet Influence: The Introvert's Guide to Making a Difference*. San Francisco: Berrett-Koehler Publishers, 2013.

Kahnweiler, Jennifer. *The Introverted Leader: Building on Your Quiet Strength*. San Francisco: Berrett-Koehler Publishers, 2013.

Kawasaki, Guy. *Enchantment: The Art of Changing Hearts and Minds*. New York: Portfolio Trade, 2012.

Kozak, Arnie. *Wild Chickens and Petty Tyrants: 108 Metaphors for Mindfulness*. Boston: Wisdom, 2009.

Kozak, Arnie. *The Everything Guide to Buddhism*. 2nd edition. Avon, MA: Adams Media Corporation, 2011.

Kramer, Gregory. *Insight Dialogue: The Interpersonal Path to Freedom*. Boston: Shambhala, 2007.

Lamott, Anne. *Bird by Bird*. New York: Anchor, 1994.

Laney, Marti Olsen. *The Introvert Advantage: How to Thrive in an Extrovert World*. New York: Workman, 2002.

Laney, Marti Olsen. *The Hidden Gifts of the Introverted Child*. New York: Workman, 2005.

Laney, Marti Olsen. *The Introvert and Extrovert in Love: Making It Work When Opposites Attract*. Oakland, CA: New Harbinger, 2007.

McAdams, Dan. *The Stories We Live By: Personal Myths and the Making of the Self*. New York: William Morrow, 1993.

McHugh, Adam. *Introverts in the Church: Finding Our Place in an Extroverted Culture*. Downers Grove, IL: IVP Books, 2009.

Mitchell, Stephen. *The Selected Poetry of Rainer Maria Rilke*. New York: Vintage, 1989.

Okerlund, Nancy. *Introverts at Ease: An Insider's Guide to a Great Life on Your Terms*. North Charleston, SC: CreateSpace, 2011.

Petrilli, Lisa. *The Introvert's Guide to Success in Business and Leadership*. C-Level Strategies, 2011.

Mood, John J. L. *Rilke on Love and Other Difficulties*. New York: Norton, 1994.

Rosenberg, Marshall. *Nonviolent Communication*. Encinitas, CA: PuddleDancer, 2003.

Tzu, Lao. *Tao Te Ching*. London: Wildwood House, 1982.

Wagele, Elizabeth. *The Happy Introvert: A Wild and Crazy Guide to Celebrating Your True Self*. Berkeley, CA: Ulysses, 2006.

Whyte, David. *Songs for Coming Home*. Langley, WA: Many Rivers Press, 1989.

Whyte, David. *Where Many Rivers Meet*. Langley, WA: Many Rivers Press, 1990.

Whyte, David. *The Fire in the Earth*. Langley, WA: Many Rivers Press, 1992.

Whyte, David. *The Heart Aroused: Poetry and Preservation of the Soul in Corporate America*. New York: Crown Business, 1996.

Whyte, David. *The House of Belonging*. Langley, WA: Many Rivers Press, 1997.

Whyte, David. *Across the Unknown Sea: Work as a Pilgrimage of Identity*. New York: Riverhead Trade, 2002.

Whyte, David. *Everything Is Waiting for You*. Langley, WA: Many Rivers Press, 2003.

Whyte, David. *The Three Marriages: Reimagining Work, Self, and Relationship*. New York: Riverhead Trade, 2010.

Whyte, David. *River Flow*. Langley, WA: Many Rivers Press, 2012.

Whyte, David. *Pilgrim*. Langley, WA: Many Rivers Press, 2012.

Yogis, Jaimal. *Saltwater Buddha: A Surfer's Quest to Find Zen on the Sea*. Boston: Wisdom, 2009.

Yogis, Jaimal. *The Fear Project: What Our Most Primal Emotion Taught Me about Survival, Success, Surfing . . . and Love*. New York: Rodale, 2013.

Young-Eisendrath, Polly. *The Self-Esteem Trap: Raising Confident Kids in an Age of Self-Importance*. New York: Little, Brown, 2009.

Zack, Devora. *Networking for People Who Hate Networking: A Field Guide for Introverts, The Overwhelmed, and the Underconnected*. San Francisco: Berrett-Koehler Publishers, 2010.

APPENDIX D

Other Introvert Websites

reddit INTROVERT

A place for introverts to gather and chat.
www.reddit.com/r/introvert/

Julia Cameron Live

Julia Cameron, author of the *Artist's Way*
www.juliacameronlive.com

Natalie Goldberg

Natalie Goldberg, author of *Writing Down the Bones*
www.nataliegoldberg.com

The Myers & Briggs Foundation

The MBTI Instrument for Life
www.myersbriggs.org

David Whyte

David Whyte, poet, author, speaker
www.davidwhyte.com

The Highly Sensitive Person

Elaine Aron, author of *The Highly Sensitive Person*
www.hsperson.com

Exquisite Mind

Arnie Kozak, author of *Wild Chickens and Petty Tyrants: 108 Metaphors for Mindfulness*, *Mindfulness A–Z: 108 Insights for Awakening Now* (forthcoming), and *The Everything Guide to Buddhism* (2nd edition).
www.exquisitemind.com

APPENDIX E

Online Videos

Susan Cain: The Power of Introverts
www.youtube.com/watch?v=c0KYU2j0TM4

Doug Hertle: Introverts and Extroverts
www.youtube.com/watch?v=BfZatw7B5_I

12 Rules for Taking Care of an Introvert
www.youtube.com/watch?v=Pmf4T1J3rhk&feature=youtu.be

Brené Brown: The Power of Vulnerability
www.youtube.com/watch?v=iCvmsMzlF7o

Brené Brown: Listening to Shame
www.youtube.com/watch?v=L0ifUM1DYKg

Polly Young-Eisendrath: Getting Free of Self-Importance Is the Key to Happiness
www.youtube.com/watch?v=dmX6Deiyyvk

Index

A

B

C

P

Q

R

S

Y

Z

We Have
EVERYTHING®
on Anything!

With more than 19 million **copies sold, the Everything® series** has become one of America's favorite resources for solving problems, learning new skills, and organizing lives. Our brand is not only recognizable—it's also welcomed.

The series is a hand-in-hand partner for people who are ready to tackle new subjects—like you!

For more information on the Everything® series, please visit *www.adamsmedia.com*

The Everything® list spans a wide range of subjects, with more than 500 titles covering 25 different categories:

Business	History	Reference
Careers	Home Improvement	Religion
Children's Storybooks	Everything Kids	Self-Help
Computers	Languages	Sports & Fitness
Cooking	Music	Travel
Crafts and Hobbies	New Age	Wedding
Education/Schools	Parenting	Writing
Games and Puzzles	Personal Finance	
Health	Pets	